Pilgrimage of the Heart

Pilgrimage of the Heart

The Path of Romantic Love

JOHN R. HAULE

SHAMBHALA
BOSTON & LONDON
1992

Shambhala Publications, Inc.
Horticultural Hall
300 Massachusetts Avenue
Boston, Massachusetts 02115

Shambhala Publications, Inc.
Random Century House
20 Vauxhall Bridge Road
London SW1V 2SA

9 8 7 6 5 4 3 2 1

FIRST PAPERBACK EDITION

Printed in the United States of America on acid-free paper
⊗
Distributed in the United States by Random House, Inc., in
Canada by Random House of Canada Ltd, and the United
Kingdom by the Random Century Group

Library of Congress Cataloging-in-Publication Data

Haule, John, 1942–
    [Divine madness]
    Pilgrimage of the heart: the path of romantic love/ John R.
Haule.
        p. cm.
    Originally published under title: Divine madness.
    Includes bibliographical references and index.
    ISBN 0–87773–669–3 (paperback: acid-free paper)
    1. Love. 2. Interpersonal relations. 3. Love in literature.
I. Title.   91–50780
[PN56.L6H38   1992]   CIP
809'.93354—dc20

For Mary, Kathy, Dani, and
above all Susan,
in love and gratitude

Contents

Acknowledgments

All of my friends, relatives, teachers, students, analysts, and analysands have contributed to this book. I would like to thank especially those who have read parts of the manuscript and offered their support, criticism, and suggestions: Susan Alt, Joan Cavitch, Jack Edmonston, my brothers James and Robert, my wife Susan, Paula Klimek, Barbara Miller, Priscilla Murr, Dani Nikas, Cathy Rogge, Seth Rubin, Virginia Senders, and the trainees of the C. G. Jung Institute–Boston. In addition to these kinds of contributions, Katherine Reeder and Bobbi Coogan have done the very laborious work of securing stacks of permissions to quote material published by other authors.

1

Romantic Love and the
Love of God

If puppy love is foolishness, a mature romantic love is full-blown madness. The lover has strayed from the highways and mainstreams of our placid and well-planned common life to build a solitary hut somewhere in a wilderness of disgraceful and deranged notions. There is no convincing the love-mad of their errors and delusions; they would rather disabuse us of ours. Whether love is an insanity grandiosely claiming to be wise, or a sublime wisdom masquerading as folly, seems not to admit of calm debate. We do not persuade one another about love. We find ourselves already lined up on opposite sides: one throng facing east, eyes sharp and clear; the other facing west, eyes hooded with scales.

Although, aside from periods of famine, it is hard to imagine a time when eros did not occupy a prominent position in human culture and society, romantic love as we know it today is an outgrowth of the courtly ideal, which sprang up suddenly as a dominant theme in twelfth-century Europe. Denis de Rougemont's classic book, *Love in the Western World*, traces its beginnings to one William IX, Count of Poitier and Duke of Aquitaine, who can be called the first troubadour. He wrote ribald songs boasting about his sexual prowess and kept a notorious woman, known as La Dangereuse, in a tower of his castle. When two of his repudiated wives formed a convent to liberate women from the servitude of sex, William retaliated by forming an anticonvent of courtesans whom he praised in songs resembling monastic hymns.

This theatrical gesture turned out to be less silly than it may sound. William of Poitier and Aquitaine was a complicated man: petty, cynical, self-indulgent, insensitive and mean to his wives, but still high-minded and very much in earnest in other ways. His versifying and irreverent mockery was more than a passing whimsy for him; rather it drew him into a compelling and transformative lifelong project. His songs gradually began to shift from the lewd to the spiritual. Very likely the religious form of the monastic hymns he was satirizing exerted an influence on the imagery and ideas of his songs. For, although they retained their erotic quality, a different order of longing began to find expression in them.

In particular, William started exploring an image he referred to as "The Unknown Lady." From the day he first dreamed of her while out riding, his compositions began to voice a deeper aspiration underlying his promiscuity. The Unknown Lady assumed greater and greater importance as William came to know her better. She grew into a kind of erotic, mystical queen whom he served with his whole heart and soul. He did not know what difficulties and tasks she had in store for him, but he was burning to undergo them, so great was her worth. Obedience to her coincided with perfect fidelity to himself. "Through her alone," he sang, "shall I be saved."

The fact that within a few years hundreds of troubadours were wandering about Europe indicates that the work of this satirical libertine had far more than personal implications. The songs expressed an important unconscious yearning in European culture as a whole. De Rougemont argues that there were two roots of this movement, both religious: one came out of a dualistic understanding of Christianity and the other from Islamic mysticism.

The Christian movement was Catharism, a dualistic philosophy that held that God had created only the spiritual world, the good portion of reality, whereas Satan had created the material world intrinsically evil. The human condition, therefore, is characterized by the incarnation of a sublime spirit, and the primary task of human existence is to free that spirit from its imprisonment in an evil body. The Cathars quite logically condoned suicide and forbade sexual intercourse, which they saw as a demonic device to imprison free souls in bodies. They considered marriage an "organized vice" and favored celibacy as the best way to deal with human sexuality. Still they tolerated casual sex, especially sodomy, for these practices, while avoiding the imprisonment of souls, relieved instinctual pressures for the great majority of individuals who did not qualify to be counted among the elect.

Catharism, therefore, requires a spiritualized love that denies or, at its weakest, tolerates the body. It finds expression in the fundamental principle of courtly love, whereby the knight dedicates all his efforts to the service of a lady he may have no hope ever of marrying. He is inspired by an erotic spirituality to do great deeds that advance both his kingdom and his own honor. Such a spiritual love exists outside of convention and free from the procreative instinct. In its most characteristic form, as we see in the stories of Tristan and Isolde or Lancelot and Guinevere, the most virtuous and powerful knight of the kingdom is the queen's lover. Because they cannot be married, their love is forced into an essentially spiritual form, or else it is illicit.

Unlawful as this love may be, however, the stories agree that God surely tolerates and may even actively favor the union. For example, in the story of Tristan and Isolde, the lovers are brought together again and again by fortuitous (God-directed) natural events, such as the currents of the sea and the birds of the air. They are saved from death and punishment by gusts of wind; and Isolde at one point passes a "divine judgment" by lifting a red-hot iron bar without burning her hands. When Tristan is bringing Isolde back home to be wed to his king, they inadvertently drink a love potion, and after this no power can dissolve their union. In one of the five earliest versions of the tale, Beroul's *Romance of Tristan,* they are confronted by the Hermit Ogrin who tells them they are living in sin. They protest that it cannot be sin, as they have drunk a potion that puts it beyond the power of their wills to separate. The Hermit *accepts* the argument and takes them under his roof.

The second cultural current that contributes to the tradition of romantic love in the West is Sufism, the mystical tradition in Islam. Although Islamic mysticism embraces a multitude of divergent doctrines, practices, and attitudes, the vast majority of Sufis hold that love is the only genuine way of coming to know God. Islam itself has even been called a "love-mad" religion (Schimmel, 1982: 11–13). In the Sufi view, "Everything in the world is in some mysterious way connected with Love and expresses either the longing of the lover or sings of the beauty and glory of the eternal Beloved who hides His face behind a thousand forms" (ibid., 77f.). Love between men and women is part of *divine* love, for the human

3

experience both conceals and reveals the ultimate Lover and the ultimate Beloved. Indeed the love of God is really the only love there is. Divine love is the depth, meaning, and esoteric secret residing in profane love. The eleventh-century Sufi Ibn al-Arabi writes:

> It is God who in each loved one manifests himself to the gaze of each lover . . . for it is impossible to adore a being without imagining the divinity present in that being. . . . Thus it goes for love: a creature really loves no one but his Creator. (Corbin, 111)

The romantic love that results from Cathar and Sufi currents, therefore, is a powerful expression of the human spirit. It is an ennobling bond between two human souls who are separated by physical, moral, and social constraints—typically in opposition to the rules of matrimony and liberated from the procreative instinct. Its sublime goal is a mature and individuated love of God. Just as God is one, so are we one with God and with one another when we love.

> Those on the way are almost invisible
> to those who are not. A man or a woman
> recognizes God and starts out. The others
> say he, or she, is losing faith.
> (Rumi, 1986: 44)

We are, indeed, talking about a matter of faith—but not the kind of faith that can be written down as a set of propositions. Rather it is the faith that is rooted in our life experience. The Greeks called it *gnosis:* either you have had the experience, and know the truth about the invisible, or you have not. What is more, "gnostics," the mystic *cognoscenti, love* their madness and believe it has peeled the scales from their eyes. Their opponents say that love has blinded them. This book sides with the madmen and explores their madness sympathetically: its rapture, its pain, its wisdom, its power to lead us astray, and its fiery pillar that leads us through the night of our ignorance toward a promised land that is glorious in ways we have not dreamed—but is generally not at all the way we had always imagined it would be.

Perhaps the most articulate mad lover of all time was Jelaluddin Rumi, a thirteenth-century Muslim from Iran who fled the Mongols to Turkey, where he succeeded his father as an expert theologian and had a sizable following of orthodox believers. He scandalized them all, however, when one day a weirdly dressed mystic, or "Sufi," appeared on the edge of his audience. This man, Shamsuddin of Tabriz, fascinated Rumi, who closeted himself with the newcomer to learn a more emotional and flamboyant way of loving God. He came out of seclusion dancing, and introduced musical instruments (forbidden to orthodox Islam) and the whirling dance of the dervishes to his skeptical followers. They killed Shams in hopes of getting back their beloved teacher; but divine madness, once experienced, cannot be renounced. Rumi became Islam's greatest poet and most famous lover of God. He says,

> Let the lover be disgraceful, crazy,
> absent minded. Someone sober
> will worry about events going badly.
> Let the lover be.
>
> (1986: 7)

Leave the lover alone because he or she is onto something the rest of us have missed. We find a sense of wholeness in love that reveals the poverty of life without it. Plato expressed these sentiments in his *Symposium:* he has Aristophanes relate a legend whereby we humans were originally round hermaphrodites, spheres with four arms, four legs, and two genders, each. In this time before time, we were whole and satisfied. But later we were separated into male and female halves, each going about restlessly in search of its mate—each of us haunted by an inchoate memory of the wholeness toward which our entire being tends. When we fall in love, we slip into feelings of oneness and completeness; our aching comes to rest. And when we lose our beloved, we plunge into an emptiness and insufficiency like nothing we have ever known before. From the outside, it looks like the most pitiful derangement, to suffer so at being no more than human. But the lover seems to have found a deeper truth. There is wisdom in that suffering—and a sublime kind of joy.

> When I am with you, we stay up all night.
> When you're not here, I can't go to sleep.
>
> Praise God for these two insomnias!
> And the difference between them.
>
> (Ibid., 1984: quatrain 36)

In the one case our beloved is so near us, and our enjoyment so important, intense, and soul-satisfying, that we cannot bear the vague parting that sleep brings. In the other case we actually love the insomnia and pain we experience during a night alone, for this binds us to our beloved in a new and no less significant way. Our beloved is present, also, in his or her absence. Even this pain is a blessing because it reveals another dimension of our union. We even find we need the separation in order to appreciate, by its contrast with the bliss of togetherness, the shaft of light that binds our minds and hearts and spirits. If we have ever fallen in love, we have known the agonizing bliss of union of which Rumi sings.

Rumi and most of the other love-mad poets of Islam refer again and again to the legends of the human lovers Layla and Majnun to describe their own love affair with God. These legends were part of Middle Eastern folklore long before the coming of Islam in the seventh century. Although the stories are filled with a great number of incidents, there is no beginning, middle, or end of a single narrative. Majnun, whose name means "madman," and Layla, whose name means "night," are a pair of lovers who—like the Sufi and God—almost never see one another. She lives under the constant guard of her tribesmen, who would be dishonored if they were to let her wed such a tramp as Majnun. Meanwhile, he lives alone in the wilderness with only wild animals for companions. Love fills them both and makes them sensitive to the messages they hear in birdsongs and to the sounds of one another's sighs carried for miles on the desert breezes. Gradually they discover that they have become more a single unified being than mere bodily togetherness could ever have effected. Because they have become one in soul and substance, they find that they no longer need to see one another face to face. The Persian poet, Nizami, collected most of the lovers' legends into a single poem, which mainly follows the life of Majnun and observes how love transforms everything he is and does. He becomes, in fact, a kind of hermit troubadour:

> Love was glowing in [Majnun]. When it burst into flames it also took hold of his tongue, the words streaming unbidden from his lips, verses strung together like pearls in a necklace. Carelessly he cast them away. . . . Was he not rich? Was he not free? Had he not severed the rope which keeps men tied together? (Nizami, 1966: 126)

Their oneness transforms them, painfully but gloriously; it also separates them from their fellow humans and makes them outcasts: "Once I was Layla . . . now I am madder . . . than a thousand Majnuns" (ibid., 145).

According to the Sufi, this state is just as true of God-intoxication as it is of human love. It is a madness to be desired, because the Majnuns of the world are tuned in to a deeper reality than are the ordinary run of people. The true lover knows a different love and a different universe. Nizami's poem of Layla says:

> Love, if not true, is but a plaything of the senses, fading like youth. Time perishes, not true love. All may be imagination and delusion, but not love. The charcoal brazier on which it burns is eternity itself, without beginning or end. (Ibid., 35)

The Christian mystics, too, are aware of this divine madness that comes over them. It is a mad wisdom that is scorned by the uninitiated but reveals the Beloved in everything the lover encounters. An Italian Franciscan of the thirteenth century, Jacopone da Todi, filled a large volume with poems of praise to his divine Beloved. He treats madness like this:

7

I know well, O highest Wisdom
That if I am mad, it is Your doing—
This dates from the day I surrendered myself to Love,
Laid aside my old self and put on You
And was drawn—I know not how—to new life.

(262)

This book—as a series of psychological meditations on the nature of romantic love and human relationship—takes the apparently religious perspective that the love of God lies at the root of human love; *apparently* religious, because it is not at all an arbitrary doctrine that we can elect to follow, as one might change churches after a dispute with a pastor. What religion calls the love of God expresses the foundational and central activity of the human psyche, and human love is real and satisfying only insofar as it expresses this root matter. Because the human psyche has the structure that it has, human love is but a species of divine love. The mystics recognize this in seeing the love of God as the meaning of human love. And, having arrived at this insight, they have traditionally seized upon romantic love as a model to explain the love of God to their followers.

Whether our beloved is human or divine, there is no escaping love's madness or its pain. Unity belongs to the soul, but we are bodily beings, and body brings about separation, distance, and pain. Tristan, in Richard Wagner's version, curses the love potion that brought him all his pain. In this psychological reading of the legend, Tristan knows that the poisonous potion had always been stored in his own heart and not in some bottle on a shelf:

> The terrible drink,
> which made me familiar with direst anguish,
> I myself, myself,
> did brew!
> . . . . .
> Oh, terrible draught that I brewed,
> that poured into me,
> bliss I ever enjoyed

sipping—
be accursed!
Accursed be he who brewed you!

(Act 3)

The mystic knows this pain very well and has learned that there is no remedy for it, other than the pain itself (Wilson and Pourjavady, 81). The pain even has a certain pleasure in it. The Sufi poet Nasimi puts it this way:

> Old Man Love:
> "Come in, come in:
> don't loiter around
> outside!"
> Inside:
> SPLENDOR,
> cups of pain.

(Ibid., 74)

The sixteenth-century Spanish mystic John of the Cross says that the pain increases as the soul draws nearer to God, because nearness leads to a progressively "greater experience within yourself of the void of God"(*Canticle,* 13.1). God's presence, we would have to say, is simultaneously God's distance. The only solution, both for John of the Cross and for Tristan, is death: "Why, since You wounded this heart until it has become sorely wounded, did You not heal it by wholly slaying it with love?" (ibid., 9.3). Rumi says:

> First there's dying,
> then Union, like gnats inside the wind.

(1987: 51)

In the literature of romantic and courtly love, there are only two ways by which the lovers can overcome the painful distance that is proof of love's absoluteness and purity. The first is madness, a complete leaving of one's senses and of the world of consensual

9

reality. Only a madman like Majnun could believe he has become Layla. Wagner's Isolde, singing her final words beside the dead body of Tristan, has a vision of him smiling and the two of them together. Oscar Wilde's Salome achieves union with John the Baptist, when she is handed his head on a silver platter:

> Ah! I have kissed thy mouth, Jokanaan. I have kissed thy mouth. There was a bitter taste on thy lips. Was it the taste of blood? But perchance it is the taste of love. They say that love hath a bitter taste. But what of that? What of that? I have kissed thy mouth, Jokanaan. (120)

The other way to overcome the painful distance of romantic love is death. In the Tristan legend, rose bushes grow from the separate graves of the lovers and entwine as a single plant, seeming physical proof that love continues—unabated and unhindered—beyond the grave. Romeo and Juliet lie in the same grave, and Nizami predicts that "One tent will hold [Layla and Majnun] in the world above" (199). Death is the only logical fulfillment in romantic love, for soul can directly cleave to soul only in a world where separate bodies have been completely transcended. Madness and death both do away with the hindrances of body, social convention, consciousness, and even individuality.

In psychological language, whether we speak of madness or death, the goal of love appears to be nothing less than a loss of ego and fusion with the beloved. This is dangerous territory, indeed: for are not most psychopathologies characterized by a weakening and loss of ego function? Loss of boundaries between self and others has in today's argot become nearly the hallmark of serious psychological dysfunction. Similarly, Freud spoke of the illusion of religious striving, and Jungians speak of projecting animus and anima, as false images, onto our beloved so that we see only our own fanciful image of what we want our beloved to be. In all cases, there seems to be something "sick" about the love that is so highly esteemed in the literatures of romantic love and of mysticism.

In Sufism there is a concept that allows us to see this loss of ego in a favorable light. The Arabic *fana* is a verb that means to disappear, vanish or perish, pass away. It refers to "the passing away of the individual self in Universal Being" (Nicholson, 1921: 17). "The transient, evanescent side of a man must pass away in order that something or someone lasting may reign supreme in him" (Rice, 76). *Fana* is a state of ecstatic contemplation of divine beauty (Nicholson, 1963: 18). Rumi describes it often; for example, from the fifth book of his great poem, the *Mathnawi:*

One morning a beloved said to her lover to test him, "Oh so-and-so, I wonder, do you love me more, or yourself? Tell the truth, oh man of sorrows!"

He replied, "I have been so annihilated within thee that I am full of thee from head to foot.

Nothing is left of my own existence but the name. In my existence, oh sweet one, there is naught but thee.

I have been annihilated like vinegar in an ocean of honey."
(Chittick, 180)

Christian mystics, too, have had experiences, which they describe in similar language to that of the Sufis speaking of *fana*. They had the experience, but not the concept. For example, John of the Cross says:

This spiritual marriage . . . is a total transformation in the Beloved in which each surrenders the entire possession of self to the other with a certain consummation of the union of love. The soul thereby becomes divine, becomes God through participation, insofar as it is possible in this life. (*Canticle,* 22.3)

Also the German mystic, Meister Eckhart, whose life bridged the thirteenth and fourteenth centuries, was familiar with the experience:

But if I am to perceive God so, without a medium, then I must just become him, and he must become me. I say more: God must just become me, and I must just become God, so completely one

11

that this "he" and this "I" become and are one "is," and in that isness, eternally perform one work. (208)

These words indicate that the mystics were very close to the experience of William of Poitier and Aquitaine, when he said that obedience to his Unknown Lady coincided with perfect fidelity to himself.

The passing away of *fana* is always joined with the continuation in a higher, more real existence, which is called *baqa*. The Iranian psychologist and mystic Reza Arasteh, describes this pair of concepts in almost Jungian language: *"Fana* is the loss of ego and *baqa* is gain of self" (x). He distinguishes between ego and Self as Jung does. Ego is the conscious agent, while Self is the greater and eternal personality, the potential for wholeness residing within the unconscious of the human individual.

The distinction between ego and Self requires a little more attention, for *self* is a term that is used quite loosely, both in ordinary conversation and by psychologists. In the first place, we often talk of "myself" in order to indicate only the ego. Thus, what do I think of myself? Do I have confidence in myself? These questions point to my conscious self-image, though they may imply the existence of deeper, unconscious realities. The term *self* is used in another sense by Heinz Kohut and the so-called Self Psychologists to refer to a deep structure that forms the foundation of ego. They speak of the kind of support and "mirroring" that an infant needs from its parents in order to develop a "coherent self structure." In this sense, self is something built up over the course of an infancy or a lifetime and is very closely associated with consciousness and with the individual differences that obtain among people. The Kohutian self may therefore be located between the loose, everyday meaning of *self* and the more restricted Jungian *Self*.

Self will be capitalized in this book when it refers specifically to the Jungian meaning of the term; but even this has at least two senses. In its most proper sense, *Self* refers to an ontological structure of the psyche, that is, something that belongs to the fundamental makeup of the human soul. It is the archetype of order by which opposing principles are harmonized and balanced. When our life becomes too much one-sided, it is the Self that presents us with compensating images and symptoms to encourage or even to force us to bring ourselves back into balance. This is the Self *an sich* (in itself), which we do not experience directly, but only in its effects. In its other sense, Self is this principle of order *as we experience it*. It is our sense of having a "greater personality" that is far larger and wiser than the ego. We do not possess or control this greater personality, but find ourselves contained by it. It is not so abstract as the Self *an sich,* but expresses itself in each individual's unique way of seeing and experiencing. It is potentially the lived Self.

While we all have a Self in this Jungian sense, many people are unaware of it. We may live entirely in our ego unless we undergo the experience of *fana* and thereby find ourselves centered and made whole. It is a revolutionary and transformative experience that is both humbling (as regards the ego) and expansive (as regards the discovery of Self). It parallels the encounter with God, in which we are overwhelmed with our creaturehood (humbled ego) and find ourselves enlightened by an intuitive grasp of the greater context of things (gain of Self). In the human interpersonal experience of romantic love, the same kind of passing away *(fana)* leads to wholeness and centering.

In the passing away from ego and into Self of *fana,* Sufis recognize a progressive series of steps that have an important application to romantic love. They claim that the mystic can pass away into God by passing *through* another human being. There is typically a three-stage process. The individual Sufi passes away into his own spiritual guide. But the guide's authority proceeds from the fact that he has already passed away into the Prophet Muhammad. Muhammad, for his part, expressed by his very being the ultimate *fana,* the passing away into Allah. Schimmel writes:

> The perfect sheikh is he who has become annihilated in the Prophet Muhammad. United with the *haqiqa muhammadiyya* (the Muhammadan Truth), he becomes the Perfect Man and thus leads his disciples with a guidance granted directly by God. (1975: 237)

A Christian will perhaps be reminded of the words of Jesus in the Gospel of John (17:21): "That they may all be one: even as thou,

Father, art in me, and I in thee, that they may also be in us, so that the world may believe that thou hast sent me."

Rumi's experience along these lines was rather disreputable. After being seduced by Shams into giving up his position as a respectable theologian to become a dancing, singing poet, mad with the love of God, he also lost Shams through assassination. His followers, who hoped for Rumi's return to "sanity," were disappointed, for in a deeper sense he never lost Shams. He wrote lyric after lyric praising Shams and God in the same breath. In Arabic, the meaning of Shamsuddin is "Sun of the religion"; and that Sun is the Sun of the Universe, or God.

> Not alone I keep on singing
>   Shamsuddin and Shamsuddin,
> But the nightingale in gardens
>   sings, the partridge in the hills.
> Day of splendor: Shamsuddin, and
>   turning heaven: Shamsuddin!
> Mine of jewels: Shamsuddin, and
>   Shamsuddin is day and night.
>   (Schimmel, 1982: 88)

Although he sang of Shams, Rumi continually found replacements for his mentor, human beings through whom he could pass away into God. One of these, an illiterate goldsmith named Salahuddin Zarkub, was particularly repugnant to Rumi's followers. Rumi, however, defended him as the means of *fana* into God:

> He who came in a red frock in years past,
> He came this year in a brown garb.
> The Turk about whom you had heard that time
> Appeared as an Arab this year . . .
> The wine is one, only the bottles are different—
> How beautifully does this wine intoxicate us!
>   (Ibid., 91)

If human beings are bottles containing the wine of God, the significance of the "Unknown Lady" in the songs of William of

Poitier and Aquitaine becomes clear. She is more than "anima," in the sense of a false image that leads us astray and prevents us from getting to know our beloved. The Unknown Lady contains and manifests the Self for William. The same may be said for Layla and Majnun. The reason their story is such a favorite example for the Sufis is that in passing away into one another, they pass away into God. If they can do it, why not we?

Jung points the way for a psychological understanding of this possibility, saying that when the anima is no longer projected but appreciated as an inner figure within a man, her function is to mediate between ego and Self (1928/35: par. 374). Anima and animus, like Self, are structural components of the psyche. While Self is the archetype of wholeness and balance, anima and animus are the archetypes of relationship. Like Self, they belong to the "collective unconscious," our common human heritage that is as much a "given" of the human condition as two arms and two legs. All of us are born bisexual, in the sense that we all have both male and female characteristics. Owing to the distribution of genes and the influence of our environment, we tend to identify, consciously, with one sex or the other. What is not developed consciously remains in the unconscious. Consequently, a man has a feminine soul (*anima* means "soul" in Latin) and a woman's unconscious has a masculine quality (animus).

In Jungian psychology there is a good deal of theorizing and some debate over the characteristic differences between animus and anima. In this book, however, I will be dealing only with those aspects of anima and animus in which they are strictly equivalent to one another and the gender differences are of little importance. The problem created by the gender-specific language of *anima* and *animus* corresponds directly to the difficulties English has with the third-person singular pronouns *he* and *she*. I have tried to avoid gender-specific language as much as possible, for I believe what I say to be applicable equally to women and men. However, when it cannot be avoided, I shall write as a heterosexual male, calling the lover male and the beloved female. Readers may reverse one or both of the pronouns without damage to the argument.

The simplest way to understand animus and anima is to say that when we fall in love, the man unconsciously projects his anima onto the woman and the woman her animus onto the man. We thereby invest one another with a mysterious and mythological power that is so foreign to our ego that we are sure it is "objective." We wonder how we can have been favored with such good luck as to have fallen for such a goddess, or such bad luck as to be obsessed with a demon. Generally it is a god or goddess we see in one another, so that anima and animus perform the very important service of giving relationship a compelling interest for us.

Anima and animus may, however, be involved in a disservice we can do ourselves, if we fall in love with an illusion. In illusory romantic love, the lover is bewitched by his own projected anima and never comes to know the unique personality of his beloved. The same may, of course, be true of us when we believe ourselves burning with love for God. The soul may, in the words of Augustine, be "constructing an image of unreality and placing its hope and love in a lie" (223). In the extreme case, we can become so possessed by an illusory image of our beloved that we are kept out of engagement with the "real" world. This is portrayed in fairy tales when the young man falls in love with a mermaid or a fairy and allows himself to be drawn into an alien world. Eventually it becomes unsatisfying, and he asks permission to go back home. Sometimes the fairy world has been so fascinating that three or four centuries have passed before a single thought of the world of space and time ever crosses his mind.

In such cases we may say that our anima or animus has led us astray. It has not mediated between ego and Self. It has broken out of its place in the psyche and stands for disarray rather than the harmony of the Self. We become fascinated by something that is peripheral to our real life. If we have fallen in love this way, we have, indeed, "passed away." We have lost the "reality function" of the ego. But we have not gained the Self. We are alienated from ourselves and unhappy.

It would be nice if there were some kind of formula for discovering the difference between true and illusory *fana*. The Catholic church is not alone among orthodoxies that have tried to protect against heresy by inventing such formulas—usually with mixed results. In one case the great mystic Teresa of Ávila fell afoul of a well-intentioned rule that all visions must be reported to one's confessor. A rather thickheaded and inexperienced Jesuit told her to "give the fig" to her visions. "The fig" was an obscene gesture that corresponds to what today would be called "the finger." Genuine mystic that she was, she did not doubt her ability to discern visions sent by Christ from those sent by Satan. Still she could not disobey her confessor. So she sobbed and begged forgiveness when she gave "the fig" to the Christ visions. She claimed the difference between the two kinds of visions lay in the feelings associated with the images. She said the Christ visions were characterized by a "purity" of feeling that would "release her from all other loves" (Lincoln, 61).

This is characteristic of true *fana,* that it connects us with the Self and that we experience it as integrating, centering, and whole-making. Teresa's *fana* connects her with God, the ultimate Center; and the effects of this are a feeling of harmony and monumental significance. All the other loves she might have had are exposed in their insubstantiality and off-centeredness. She has found the touchstone for reality. In contrast, an illusory *fana* is an incautious submission to something peripheral and less than ultimate. We pass away into irreality.

For all its insubstantiality from the viewpoint of the Self, illusory *fana* can be awfully compelling. It may take the form of a painful fusion in which each partner seems to lose his soul. Instead of finding our way to a wholeness where we can relax into our greater being, we fall victim to a compulsive and usually aggressive striving for satisfaction in which each of us attempts to possess and control the other. Alban Berg's opera *Lulu* richly illustrates this kind of failure of *fana.* The title character uses her lovers as much as they use her. A portrait of her in the bloom of her youth dominates every scene of the drama. In the last act, Lulu and her pitifully enchained hangers-on have lost all their money in the stock market crash and are living in a London garret on the proceeds from Lulu's prostitution. One of them finds the lost portrait and Alwa, who appears to be the character Berg himself identified with, rhapsodizes over it:

ALWA:(*Suddenly with new animation.*) . . . With this picture before me, I feel my self-respect is recovered. I understand the fate which compels me. (*Somewhat elegiac.*) Who stands before those lips with their promise of pleasure, before those eyes as innocent as the eyes

17

of children, before this white and rosy-ripening body, and still feels safe within his bourgeois code of rules, let such a man cast the first stone at us! (Act 3)

The emphasis on image here is no accident. The portrait was painted many years before, when Lulu was just married to her first husband and the future looked rosy. Now, many years, marriages, love affairs, murders, and suicides later, her eros-possessed followers are still in love with the old picture. There has been no growth, either in the characters or in their expectations. They have only led themselves more and more hopelessly into their self-destructive dead-end. Lulu's lovers and admirers try to possess an anima image of her instead of seeing her for who she is. They get stuck in a tortured irreality instead of passing away *through* Lulu, as the Sufi's *fana* leads through his master into God. They have come to know neither her nor themselves. They get hung up on the image and have no concern for the truth it symbolizes and reveals. They have fallen in love with the image rather than the woman. In religious language, we would say that this pseudo-*fana,* which stops at the image rather than proceeding on to the truth it stands for, is idolatry.

When we get hung up on a particular image of our beloved, we do not allow the beloved to become what she must. In order to possess her, we freeze her within a specific image. It is an illustration of determined one-sidedness in an ego that has definitely not passed away. Whether we are whisked away from reality by our fascination with an anima or animus image or try to force our beloved into the mold of our projection, the image we cherish of our beloved operates as a *mask* to hide her from us.

But anima and animus need not always function as *masks* that hide the truth. They may act also as *lenses* that bring the truth into focus: the truth about our Self as well as the truth about our beloved. This, in fact, is the import of the Sufi notion of *fana*. Animus and anima are the psyche's organs, as it were, that allow us to see with the heart. The knowing of truth we have through *fana* is affective rather than cognitive. This is the constant theme of the mystics of the major religions. For example, the anonymous Christian author of *The Cloud of Unknowing* says: "God . . . is always incomprehensible to . . . the knowing power. But to . . . the loving power, he is entirely comprehensible in each one individually" (123). If the human soul is capable of passing away through love of the spiritual master into an affective contemplation of divine Truth, the soul must also be capable of passing through the anima or animus image to the Self of the beloved.

Ibn al-Arabi claims precisely this regarding his relationship with the beautiful Iranian girl Nizam, whom he came to know in Mecca. A reference to her in his writings is, he says, an allusion to "a sublime and divine, essential and sacrosanct *Wisdom,* which manifested itself *visibly* to the author of these poems with such sweetness as to provoke in him joy and happiness, emotion and delight" (Corbin, 139). Henry Corbin comments on these words, as follows:

We perceive how a being apprehended directly by the Imagination is transfigured into a symbol thanks to a theophanic light, that is, a light which reveals its dimension of transcendence. From the very first the figure of the young girl was apprehended by the Imagination on a visionary plane in which it was manifested as an "apparitional Figure" *(surat mithaliya)* of *Sophia aeterna.* (Ibid.)

This is an experience of anima that is transparent to the Self it mediates. Ibn al-Arabi sees through the lens of his Nizam projection all the way to the ultimate Center. The anima is not acting as a mask here, but as a lens. His affective seeing does not stop short with the image; rather he sees *in* the anima, or *through* the anima, a divine vision—Sophia. In Christian language, Sophia refers to the Holy Spirit; for it is always the Old Testament wisdom *(sophia)* literature that the churches employ to shed light on the nature of the divine indwelling Spirit. Thus Ibn al-Arabi sees God in Nizam. She is the occasion of his *fana.* He passes *through her* to the Truth. In the language of Jungian psychology we would say that that divine woman, Sophia, is an image of his anima. And the *divinity* in that woman is an intimation of the Self that she mediates to him.

Ibn al-Arabi is not afloat in a neurotic, illusory cloud. True, Sophia is just about the grandest form the anima can take; and the Persian girl, Nizam, beautiful and cultured though she may be, needs the eye of an Ibn al-Arabi to *become* Sophia. The imagination of the heart is surely involved. But on the strength of the consistent wisdom in Ibn al-Arabi's writings, I believe he was seeing Nizam through the lens of his anima. His numinous vision is true because it is anchored in the Self. This is precisely the kind of experience Jung refers to when he speaks of the anima's "higher function." When the anima becomes "depotentiated" of her demonic power, Jung tells us, and no longer controls us as an autonomous complex of the unconscious, she becomes "a psychological function of an intuitive nature, akin to what the primitives mean when they say, 'He has gone into the forest to talk with the spirits' " (1928/35: par. 374).

The demonic power of the anima or animus resides in its bewitching mask. When we can see through that to the psychological realities that it symbolizes, our intuition can "hear the spirits talk." Our ego and our Self are acting in unison, linked by our anima or animus. When we hear the spirits talk and understand what they are saying, we acquire a more profound understanding of what is before us. The spirits belong to the archetypal world of the collective unconscious. They have a broader perspective than that of our conscious ego. Whereas we tend to understand things in the context of other mundane events, they see things against the background of the largest possible reality, the All. The spirits *know* the All, and they appreciate every object, person, and event in the context of that Wholeness.

God is the name we give to the center, source, depth, and end of the All. Similarly, the *love* of God is the center, source, depth, and end of romantic love. We can appreciate this in an experiential, transformative, and enlightening manner only when we have learned to use our anima or animus as a lens. As long as they mask our beloved from us, the relationship between romantic love and the love of God remains merely theoretical.

When anima and animus act as a lens, they bring the Self and its designs into focus. This applies in two directions. On the one hand, we become centered ourselves; and on the other, the lens of anima brings the unique individuality of our beloved into focus. Subsequent chapters will develop these themes. Here it is only necessary to appreciate the metaphor of anima as lens and that it brings something wonderful into focus for both partners.

Also something *accurate* is brought into focus. The lens image suggests eyeglasses, microscopes, and telescopes; I learn to know my beloved down to her minutest detail, and I see deep into the inner space of her world. Because I see her through the intimate lens of anima, I see something that perhaps no one else has been fortunate to behold. I sometimes may see what she has never known about herself; and in my seeing, I reveal it to her—just as she discloses new vistas of my inner space. Our lenses enable us to become explorers of one another's continents and seas; and at the same time we come to know our own.

Anima and animus are not just internal organs in our psyche, somehow stuck inside our skin. They relate us to our beloved. They are the archetypes of relationship. Their function does not end by mediating to us our Self, as a purely internal event. They stand outside us, between us and our beloved. They open us to one another, connect us. They are more than the ocular metaphor of lens can convey, for our feelings sweep further than our eyes can see, into territory of quite another variety.

Furthermore, when our animus or anima has enabled this kind of connection with our beloved, we find that mere physical presence—however desirable—is no longer necessary for us to enjoy the trans-formative intermingling of our beings. Such a realization lies behind the ideal of courtly love, insofar as the errant knight is inspired by a lady who is comfortably lodged back home and whom he can barely approach even when he returns. Distance causes pain; but as the lover of God knows, distance is another form of presence. On the contrary, if our relationship has been characterized primarily by the projection of anima and animus as masks, we may not have found any satisfaction to ameliorate our distance. A genuine appreciation of our Self-Self connection is necessary if our love is to grow from the separations imposed by physical distance, quarreling, and the like.

Rumi, in all his poems, speaks of his love for God. He tells us the Sufi loves the night, when he can be alone either with God's soothing presence or torturing absence. We know what Rumi means if we have ever seen another through the lens of our anima or animus. We have known the love of God in the *fana* by which we have passed through our beloved into an extraordinary clarity. Such a night is the center around which our life revolves:

> Night comes so people can sleep like fish
> in black water. Then day.
>
> Some people pick up their tools.
> Others become the making itself.
>
> (1986: 38)

The black water he speaks of may also be called the black tresses of Layla, who personifies the night. Water and ocean in Rumi's symbolic language always refer to God or the life *in* God that we enter through our *fana*. Rumi also tells us that these moments of union in which we "sleep like fish" transform the rest of life. If we have really passed away, we no longer "pick up our tools" and work at things from the outside. We become our work; and our daytime life, too, is suffused with love.

In a similar vein, Jung says that analysis does not work unless the analysand fulfills his "duty to life" (1917/43: par. 113). Psychological transformation does not happen only—or even primarily—in the consulting room. Rather, God willing, patients gain a certain understanding in the therapeutic dialogue that sends them back out into life. When we fall in love, we find ourselves caught in a flow of psychic energy that takes us passionately into life; and this is by no means limited to erotic pursuits. In my practice as an analyst, I have seen repeatedly that a man's professional life and his life in relationship are connected. When he loses contact with his anima, he loses interest in both spheres; and when he regains it in one, he regains it in the other. Hillman says as much in his book on anima: "Loss of anima means both the loss of internal animation and external animism" (1985: 109). Anima and animus are not something to be conquered. They must be lived. That is to say, we must live the life into which they draw us. For they open to us the course of our individuation when they mediate the Self and bring our beloved into focus. Most people experience this draw of destiny in an unmistakable manner only through relationship. How to follow such a fascination, and not get led astray, is not easy. This is why Jung says, "If the encounter with the shadow is the 'apprentice-piece' in the individual's development, then that with the anima is the 'master-piece' " (1934/54: par. 61).

Anima and animus lead us on a path of recreating ourselves. This book describes the psychological and spiritual dimensions of that path. It is both archetypal and personal. We all have a great deal in common as we pursue this course, but it is in each case an individual journey. The guidelines are found within, in our development through anima and animus of a confident relationship with Self.

2

The Naked Sword: Opportunity for Love's Transformation

In the Middle Ages, one way of indicating that two people had fallen irretrievably in love was to say they had drunk a love potion. This meant that they were no longer in control of themselves. Their entire beings were bound to one another in a mystical and magical way, to be sure, but also in a physical way. As lead into gold, they were transformed by the alchemical draught they had imbibed so that they were no longer two. They were now entirely of one single substance, bound in such a way that even God could not separate them without abrogating the laws of Nature. They were changed so profoundly that the ordinary laws of society and church no longer quite applied to them. True enough, God prevents Lancelot, on account of his sinful liaison with Arthur's queen, from as full an experience of the Holy Grail as that enjoyed by the virginal Galahad. But God does favor him with two semiconscious views of the Grail and twenty-four days of Grail-inspired visions. Tristan, too, is actively favored by God's benevolence and the allegiance of the people. In the whole of heaven and earth, only the grasping barons are against the liaison of Tristan with his uncle's queen. Only scoundrels could possibly be against a love so powerful and pure.

Still, scoundrels there always are: clever, powerful schemers who appeal self-righteously to the rules of the social order and of the church to bring down shame upon the heads of the lovers. Obstacles always abound to keep the lovers apart. Commonly the biggest obstacle to their union is moral or social: for Lancelot and Tristan it is that their beloved is already married, indeed, to the king to whom they have sworn fealty. The obstacles to romantic love may take the form of any substantial barrier such as physical distance, class difference, the death or captivity of one of the parties, or political hostility between their respective peoples. But most significant of these obstacles is one that is freely chosen by the lovers themselves, and the prototype of this is the naked sword, which they sometimes place between themselves when they sleep in the same bed. Romantic love is by no means always chaste, but distance between the lovers is not just accidental. It is a necessary dimension of a transforming, ennobling love.

Our examination of the tension between the mystic potion that binds the lovers inescapably and the enigmatic sword that keeps them apart begins with a story from *The Lais of Marie de France.* The writer is a late twelfth-century poet of Brittany. The story is titled simply with the name of its hero, "a knight worthy and courtly, brave and fierce: Eliduc" (111).

The Story of Eliduc

As the story opens, Eliduc is the beloved and highly trusted right-hand man of his king. Envious, less fortunate knights slander him, with the result that he is "banished from the court without formal accusation." He leaves behind a beautiful, wise, and high-born wife, with whom he has enjoyed many years of mutual love and loyalty, and goes wandering as a mercenary. It is not long before he finds a besieged king to serve and acquits himself very well, reversing the fortunes of the war and making himself as indispensable to the second king as to the first. Guilliadun, the beautiful daughter of this second king, gives herself unreservedly to Eliduc, whose heart is "trapped" by her although he has not forgotten his promise to remain faithful to his wife.

Eventually Eliduc's first lord gets into trouble and urgently requires the services of the man who was always the best and most loyal of his knights. As a result Eliduc becomes indispensable to two kings and the lover of two women. He finds, however, that he is no longer satisfied

with his wife and therefore sets sail with his beloved
Guilliadun. Although he has made sure to select the smallest and most loyal group of assistants he could assemble,
on encountering a fearsome storm, one of the sailors cries
out:

> "What are we doing? Lord, you have with you the
> woman who will cause us to perish. We shall never make
> land! You have a loyal wife and now with this other
> woman you offend God and his law, righteousness and
> the faith. Let us cast her into the sea and we shall soon
> arrive safely." (Ibid., 121)

Out of fear of the storm and her despair at learning of
Eliduc's wife, Guilliadun falls into a deathly swoon. Eliduc
intends to bury her at a hermitage in the woods but
cannot bring himself to do so as long as the color remains
in her cheeks. His wife becomes suspicious of his frequent
visits to the hermitage and finds the maiden. Chancing
just at this moment to observe a weasel revive its companion with a certain herb, Eliduc's wife places the same
flower in the maiden's mouth so that she returns to her
senses.

The two women identify themselves to one another,
and Eliduc's wife promises to restore Guilliadun to Eliduc
and step out of the way herself by taking the veil. Once
she does so, Eliduc and Guilliadun marry and live in
perfect love and happiness for many years "until such time
as they themselves turn to God." At this point, Eliduc
builds a monastery, which he enters "with his own men
and other pious persons," and Guilliadun enters the
convent of the first wife.

> [The women] prayed that God might show their be-
> loved His sweet mercy and Eliduc in turn prayed for
> them, sending his messengers to see how they fared and
> how their spirits were. Each one strove to love God in
> good faith and they came to a good end thanks to God,
> the true divine. (Ibid., 126)

Literally, there are no naked swords in anybody's bed in this tale,
but the meaning of the sword of separation is unmistakable. Sepa-

ration in love cannot be avoided. Every relationship, however shallow or deep, however long- or short-lived, suffers its partings and its failures to join. Indeed, loneliness lies at the very heart of love. It is there at the very first moment when we feel ourselves being drawn by the person who is not quite yet our beloved, for she is calling us out of our aloneness. We may not have adverted to this loneliness or become aware of our isolation, but it is there as the context that makes her very being into a call for us. Second, we find ourselves alone in a whole new way during our beloved's inadvertent or deliberate absences. If we had been unaware of our loneliness before she appeared, we are now more intensely alone than we had ever imagined it possible to be.

The naked sword between the lovers symbolizes this aloneness acknowledged, taken up, and lived. In our present cultural situation, we have very little in the way of models or precedents by which we could begin to understand the symbolism of the sword. Why should anyone deliberately place a sword—let alone monastic walls—between himself and his beloved? Even the famous monastic lovers, Abelard and Heloise, did not *choose* their seclusion from one another. To our everyday consciousness, it sounds like some kind of perversion—masochism is what most people seem to think it is; but the sword of separation can be a blessing in disguise.

Denis de Rougemont sees the symbol of the sword exclusively in terms of its effect of setting the lovers aflame, and he identifies this as pathological. He says:

> Tristan loves the awareness that he is loving far more than he loves Iseult the Fair. And Iseult does nothing to hold Tristan. All she needs is her passionate dream. Their need of one another is in order to be aflame, and they do not need one another as they are. What they need is not one another's presence, but one another's absence. (41f.)

De Rougemont is not wrong to see their choosing the sword of separation as inflaming. But he is wrong in believing that there is nothing more to the sword's significance than that. A great deal more than heating up can be accomplished through separation. Jung adverted to this in his 1928 dream seminar, when he said:

The strongest thing in man is *participation mystique*, "just you and your dog in the dark"; that is stronger than the need for individuality. . . . This identity, this clinging together, is a great hindrance to individual relationship. . . . Relationship is only possible when there is separateness. (1938/84: 63)

The English novelist Thomas Hardy was also very much aware of the opportunity that distance provides in a romantic love relationship. This is to be seen in all of his novels, but particularly in the plot of *Far from the Madding Crowd*. There, between the time Bathsheba Everdene loses Gabriel Oak and finds him again, she struggles through relationships with two lesser men: the sanctimonious manipulator Boldwood, whose heart she tries very hard not to break, and the callous heartthrob Sergeant Troy. When Bathsheba and Farmer Oak are finally united at the end, Hardy sums up the theme of the novel, as follows:

Theirs was that substantial affection which arises (if any arises at all) when the two who are thrown together begin first by knowing the rougher sides of each other's character, and not the best till further on, the romance growing up in the interstices of a mass of hard prosaic reality. This good fellowship . . . is seldom superadded to love between the sexes, because men and women associate, not in their labours, but in their pleasures merely. Where, however, happy circumstance permits its development, the compounded feeling proves itself to be the only love which is strong as death— that love which many waters cannot quench, nor the floods drown, beside which the passion usually called by the name is evanescent as steam. (1984: 368)

Hardy's commentary tells us that distance, the sword, enables us to get to know our beloved better; but the plot of the book, looked at psychologically, tells us that distance makes it possible to get to know ourselves better. Hardy is right on both counts. The Bathsheba who could blunder into an entanglement with an emotionally petrified Boldwood was not yet capable of falling for the gallant flatterer, Troy. She becomes capable of recognizing her "strong-as-death" connection to Gabriel Oak only after these earlier mistakes have been understood. Thus she needs to experiment and to dare to live life actively, but above all she needs to experience her loneliness.

Clark Moustakas, a professor of social work and the author of several books, learned this lesson some thirty years ago when his five-year-old daughter died in his arms, in convulsions, and screaming at him that he was the devil. Afterwards he found himself inconsolably alone, but instead of fleeing his loneliness, as most of us are prompted to do, he entered into the experience and discovered that it transformed him and his life in ways that he could not have imagined. He discovered new capacities and resources within himself. He also found that the world took on a new liveliness, vividness, and importance. He found himself anew, and he found a new sensitivity whereby he came to be more in touch with his own existence and more deeply aware of others'.

> Being lonely involves a certain pathway, requires a total submersion of self, a letting be of all that is and belongs, a staying or remaining with the situation, until a natural realization or completion is reached; when a lonely existence completes itself, the individual becomes, grows from it, reaches out for others in a deeper, more vital sense. (1961: 8)

He appears to have learned, entirely on his own, a fundamental principle of human psychology that Jung calls the "transcendent function." When life does not allow us to go forward any further on our path, when our child dies, when our beloved abandons us, we fall into a depression. At this point, our energy no longer flows outward into our worldly activities, but backward, in and down into our unconscious where it activates dormant and long-neglected talents, capacities, images, feelings, and the like. Moustakas understands this. He says, "In loneliness man seeks his inner nature" (ibid., 54). Jung would agree, but I think he would turn the statement around: In loneliness our inner nature seeks us.

In romantic love, our inner nature has been seeking us all along. In the first instance, it appears to us embodied in the person of our beloved. We do not yet know our inner nature—our anima or animus—but find it in projected form. This is why our meeting with our beloved seems so "meant to be," as though it were "destined," "fated," or "made in heaven." Our beloved seems to complete us, by bringing us into contact with this "inner nature" of ours that has been neglected and ignored. But then, when our beloved leaves us and we fall into depression, we experience our aloneness as if for the first time. She walks away carrying with her the anima we have projected onto her. Now we know something is missing; and through our projection onto our beloved, we have developed a pretty good notion of what it is. We are prepared—even if we do not know it yet—to recognize our "inner nature" when it approaches us from within. But this does not happen without a struggle. We have to struggle with ourselves to give up the quest for what we are missing outside of ourselves. We have to give up searching and let ourselves be found.

These psychological realities are frequently expressed in myth—for example, Demeter's grieving for her daughter Persephone who has been stolen by Hades, the god of the underworld. Demeter is the goddess of grain, and she mourns every year between the harvest and the planting. For then her daughter, the very kernel of her "inner nature," lies dormant. Her loneliness and despair, therefore, bring forth the new fields of grain that sprout in the next growing season. Similarly, in the myth of Eros and Psyche, the maiden Psyche loses her god-lover, whom she has known only unconsciously and sexually. He visits her bed every night, and she is forbidden to look upon him or to ask for his name. When, out of self-doubt, she violates this rule and his visits cease, she has to suffer a quiet, helpless abandonment and loneliness for some time before she is finally given tasks and therewith the hope of winning him back. These tasks symbolize the inner work that must go on in our depression. Furthermore, they are beyond Psyche's powers to carry out. Instead, she has to allow herself to be assisted by ants, a reed, and an eagle—an indication that the important work is being done by her unconscious and not by her ego. In her isolation and loneliness, her inner self seeks her.

I do not mean to imply by this that we should merely give up and become passive. We may be well advised to get to work in an indirect manner. For example, Clark Moustakas has written at least ten books on loneliness and related issues. He had in a sense precipitated his daughter's death by deciding in favor of surgery to correct her congenital heart defect. It was a side effect of the operation that brought on her horrible, convulsive, and very, very lonely death. Her deranged fear and loathing for the father she could not recognize must have affected Moustakas deeply, for he has spent a great deal of time studying loneliness in children. In particular, he "decided to listen to the experiences of children in hospitals . . . to know the truth of the lonely process in its most basic, objective forms" (1975: 16). Later he gave workshops to nurses and physicians to teach them what he had learned and what could be done to make children's hospitalizations more pleasant and more psychologically constructive. Also, in addition to his workshops for adults on the experience of loneliness, he developed experiments in childhood education to "humanize learning" by "fostering and encouraging individuality, autonomy and self-direction" (ibid., 5). In all of this it is clear that Moustakas has placed the experience of losing his daughter at the very center of his life's work. Thus, despite her distance, she is present in his life in a remarkably intimate and transformative way.

In the twelfth-century Persian poem *The Story of Layla and Majnun,* the lovers spend nearly their entire lives apart, a situation that enables them to achieve a sublime kind of oneness. Despite their separation, however, they do not stagnantly pine for one another. Rather a great deal goes on "inside" them. A recurring image for this inner work is Majnun, the "madman" and desert-dweller, as lord of the animals:

> [E]ven a Majnun has companions. His were the animals. . . . He had crept into their caves without driving them out. . . . He possessed a strange power, unlike that of the lion, the panther or the wolf, because he did not catch and devour smaller animals. . . . [T]hey came flying, running, trotting, creeping, drawing narrowing circles around him. Among them were animals of every kind and size, but—what a miracle—they did not attack each other, and lost all fear, as long as this trusted stranger stayed in their midst. . . . It was a peaceful army that travelled with Majnun as he roamed the wilderness, his animals always at his heels. . . . Many [people]

pitied him and brought him food and drink, knowing that out of love of Layla, he had become a hermit. But Majnun accepted no more than a bite or a sip. Everything else he gave to his animals. (Nizami, 1966: 126–29)

Symbolically, this means that he made friends with his anger, pain, loneliness, and despair, so that, far from being rent to pieces and devoured by these powerful emotions and instincts, he gave them their due and they became the source of his strength. It is a process of integration and whole-making. Majnun was more than "sought" by the core of his identity; that identity was assembled and forged as he patiently plumbed the dank, reeking caves of his loneliness.

The Jungian analyst Robert Stein names this process "psychiza-tion"; more felicitously, James Hillman calls it "soul-making" (1983: 26–28). They refer to that increase in consciousness that results when the instinctual forces within us and their projected images outside us lose their "otherness" and we begin to integrate them. Generally this requires the sword of separation. When the immediate fulfillment of our needs is frustrated, the inhibited instinctual drive can "stimulate the formation of images which are mental equivalents of the desired object" (Stein, 28). The desired object, our separated beloved, is no longer an autonomous other. We begin to find that the beloved is part of us, a part that had long been unconscious. The greater the disruption or transformation she has effected in our everyday life, the more important a piece of our soul the beloved represents. In soul-making, we come to know this part of our soul for its own sake. Jung calls it "withdrawing the projection" from the person we love so that we can (1) see her for who she really is and (2) allow this piece of our soul (our anima or animus) to become a helpful, functioning part of our psyche (1928/35: par. 374).

Jung means that when we renounce our ego-bound intentions regarding our beloved, we begin to find our soul's own guide within us. This is why Nizami's Majnun can say: "The name [Majnun] is only the outer shell and I am this shell, I am the veil. The face underneath is hers" (125). This process, which Jung calls "withdraw-ing the projection," we might more picturesquely call "becoming Layla." Or "becoming Majnun," for Layla undergoes the same process and becomes "madder, more 'Majnun' than a thousand Majnuns" (Nizami, 1966: 145).

These considerations give us new access to the story of Eliduc, which ends with the three lovers building monastery walls between themselves—deliberately choosing the sword of love. If our contemporaries cannot comprehend such a story, they do not understand the work that goes on in loneliness and depression. We can hardly blame them, insofar as our extraverted culture has provided us with so few models that we scratch our heads, too, at the stories of Eros and Psyche or Layla and Majnun.

Death is the ultimate sword of separation, for there is no longer any possibility of waiting for the beloved to return. It is not a sword we freely choose; but please note that, also in the stories of Demeter and Persephone, Eros and Psyche, and Layla and Majnun, the sword is not actively chosen but rather freely accepted after tragedy has made it unavoidable. This implies that neither death nor the sword accomplishes anything by itself. What is of utmost importance is our attitude toward the obstacle that separates us from our beloved.

Consider for a moment one of the most famous death-robbed lovers in English literature, Heathcliff from Emily Brontë's *Wuthering Heights*. About thirty years ago I saw a television dramatization of the story that ended with the following words—words so impressive that they still come back to me; they seemed to hold some ultimate truth:

> Catherine Earnshaw, may you not rest as long as I am living! You said I killed you—haunt me, then! The murdered *do* haunt their murderers. I believe—I know that ghosts *have* wandered the earth. Be with me always—take any form—drive me mad! only *do* not leave me in this abyss, where I cannot find you! Oh God! it is unutterable! I *cannot* live without my life! I *cannot* live without my soul! (163f.)

After watching the television drama, I borrowed the book from the library and turned immediately to the end, where I could not find these passionate words. On reading from the beginning, I discovered that they occur at just about the midpoint of the book and that I had no interest in the eighteen chapters that followed. Apparently the author of the screenplay and I, as well as the majority of the television audience, were suffering from the same terror as Heathcliff, the fear of being abandoned in an abyss of loneliness. We could not bear eighteen more chapters describing this torment.

A few pages before the end of the book, Heathcliff says:

> I cannot look down to this floor, but her features are shaped on the flags! In every cloud, in every tree—filling the air at night, and caught by glimpses in every object, by day I am surrounded with her image! The most ordinary faces of men, and women—my own features mock me with a resemblance. The entire world is a dreadful collection of memoranda that she did exist, and that I have lost her! (Ibid., 307)

At this point, he knows his torment is coming to an end; it is an image of eighteen years of standstill:

> She has disturbed me, night and day, through eighteen years—incessantly—remorselessly—till yesternight; and yesternight I was tranquil. I dreamt I was sleeping the last sleep by that sleeper, with my heart stopped and my cheek frozen against hers. (Ibid., 274)

The horror of *Wuthering Heights* is that Heathcliff got the haunting he prayed for, and he has not changed a bit. His single-minded devotion to Cathy's memory would almost be admirable were it not so beastly and repulsive. He is at the opposite extreme from Layla and Majnun; instead of going into his loneliness and learning from it, he fends it off with his obsession. He must literally possess Cathy, even though she is dead, because he is uncertain of the strength of her love and uncertain of himself. To this end he carefully plots his financial moves so that he becomes the owner of Wuthering Heights; and he arranges with the sexton to have the sideboards removed from his and Cathy's coffins so that when he is buried his cheek can literally "freeze" against hers. He needs her to dote on in order to escape himself. He flees aloneness by refusing to "withdraw" his projection. By clinging to her image impressed on the flagstones of his kitchen floor, he prevents himself from sliding down into his inner abyss. He therefore never begins the work of loneliness. Because he never finds his anima, his inner Cathy, he never "becomes Cathy" the way Majnun "becomes Layla." He never accepts the inevitability of the naked sword. Heathcliff, we can understand.

What gives us trouble is Eliduc and his two wives in their respective monasteries. Heathcliff uses his pain to flee life rather than to embrace it. Eliduc and Majnun are madmen in our blighted view because they do not flee the abyss of loneliness. We cannot imagine how they bear it.

John of the Cross calls this pain the "dark night of the soul." It occurs only to those who have already experienced the considerable joys of divine love and favor. They have already developed a "desire to feel and taste" God in receiving communion (*Night*, 1.6.5), as well as an "intense satisfaction in the performance of spiritual exercises because God is handing the breasts of His tender love to the soul" (ibid., 1.1.2). They are possessed as well by a "solicitude" that "goads them, preoccupies them, and absorbs them to such an extent that they never notice what others do or do not accomplish" (ibid., 1.2.6). In short, these beginners in the love of God resemble us very closely when we are embarking on an affair of romantic love. At such time we delight in the slightest word, gesture, or notice from our beloved. In the early stages of infatuation we will do anything to provide for our beloved's comfort and to win her favor— so much so that we become oblivious of everything else around us. In Jungian language, we say we are "possessed" by our anima or animus. Our ego is paralyzed and obsessed by the unconscious entity that we call anima or animus. In the medieval language of courtly love, we may say that we are wholly under the influence of the love potion; we have not yet felt the keen edge of the sword.

Like Majnun and Heathcliff, the soul in love with God does not seek out the calamitous sword of separation. The dark night is always God's initiative, and it comes as a blessing in disguise: "Until a soul is placed by God in the passive purgation of that dark night . . . it cannot purify itself . . . God must take over and purge them in that fire that is dark for them" (ibid., 1.3.3). In exactly the same manner, we require the intervention of physical, moral, social, or other obstacles to our union with our beloved if our love is to be deepened and transformed.

In the experience of John of the Cross, the first move comes from the divine Lover. God attracts the soul to spirituality by providing the so-called sensual delights of enjoying one's spiritual exercises. If this were to continue, we would surely develop a fixation on God's "nurturing breasts" and remain oblivious of much more sublime states of union (ibid., 1.7.5). To prevent this arrest in our development, God withdraws these sensual delights from the soul. Left to itself, the soul would respond to this withdrawal by becoming quiet, and God would "infuse" it with contemplation. But the beginner tends to fight the soul's inclination to be quiet (ibid., 1.10.1), just as we do when our beloved leaves us. Heathcliff's prayer to be haunted the rest of his days corresponds precisely to our wish never to lose the delights we have in our beloved's presence and in our habitual fantasies about her. For John of the Cross, this would mean that we cling to first impressions and let them block the way to deeper appreciation of our beloved. He thereby points out two very powerful inclinations in the soul: a conservative and ego-centered desire rigidly to retain what we have and another, much less conscious impulse, to explore regions that are still unknown. He has, therefore, made the same distinction Jung makes between ego and Self. Ego is the center of consciousness and decision making, while Self is the principle of balance and wholeness within the greater psyche, including both conscious and unconscious.

John of the Cross observes that the only way to proceed, once God has placed the naked sword of separation between the lovers, is to be quiet and to dare to embrace the abyss of loneliness. He says:

> If those in whom this [sensual night] occurs know how to remain quiet, . . . they will soon . . . experience the interior nourishment. This refection is so delicate that usually if the soul desires or tries to experience it, it cannot. (*Night,* 1.9.7)

In our psychological language, we would say that we need to remain quiet on the ego-level of our psyche in order to allow expression from that deeper kernel of our identity, the Self. Whereas our ego can be pulled this way and that by "sensual" and "spiritual" loves, the dark night puts our several loves into "reasonable order" (ibid., 1.4.8). It does this because it silences the ego and makes room for the balancing and whole-making activity of the Self. In the mystic's words:

> My intellect . . . no longer understands by means of its natural vigor and light but by means of the divine wisdom to which it was united.

> And my will . . . no longer loves in a lowly manner with its natural strength, but with the strength and purity of the Holy Spirit. (Ibid., 2.4.2)

These words might well be a commentary on the words of Saint Paul describing his own transformation, "I have been crucified with Christ; the life I now live is not my life, but the life which Christ lives in me" (Gal. 2:20). For Jung, the experience of Paul is one of the classic examples of what he calls "enlargement of personality," an enrichment that comes from within. "The apparition of Christ came to Saint Paul not from the historical Jesus but from the depths of his own unconscious" (June 1939/50: par. 216).

It is this same enlargement of personality and this same Christ from the depths of the soul that John of the Cross describes in the *Dark Night*. And he knows whereof he speaks. He is describing his own experience and that of the monks and nuns whom he served as novice master and spiritual director. He describes the dark night as painful and terrifying, but it is also the sole means by which lover and beloved encounter one another. Faithfully undergone, it transforms a beginner into a proficient and a proficient into a mystic. It is "contemplation" (*Night*, 1.8.1) and "an inflow of God into the soul" (ibid., 2.5.1). It humbles the soul only in order to exalt it (ibid., 2.9.1).

The same is true of the sword of separation, in very much the same way and for the same reasons. Distance from our beloved provides the opportunity for love to transform us both. Because the separation brought about by the sword of love is meaningless without the drawing power of the love potion, this kind of distance is never absolute. It always implies some kind of presence of the lovers to one another. Indeed, this is the fundamental tension of romantic love: that the couple must always be both present to and distant from one another at every moment. Sometimes the distance is more apparent and sometimes the presence.

The legend of Layla and Majnun, for example, describes what I call "presence amid distance." Physically, the lovers are nearly always apart, but their story is worth telling because the abyss of their mutual absence is filled with the golden light of a very powerful spiritual and psychological presence. We can see a hint of this in Edith Wharton's novel, *The Age of Innocence*. Newland Archer and the Countess Olenska have decided to end their affair and not see one another again. Four months after their parting, we catch a view of Archer's inner world:

> Since then there had been no farther communications between them, and he had built up within himself a kind of sanctuary in which she throned among his secret thoughts and longings. Little by little it became the scene of his real life, of his only rational activities; thither he brought the books he read, the ideas and feelings which nourished him, his judgments and his visions. Outside it, in the scene of his actual life, he moved with a growing sense of unreality and unsufficiency, blundering against familiar prejudices and traditional points of view as an absent-minded man goes on bumping into the furniture of his own room. (262)

This is very ambiguous. We do not yet know whether Archer will profit from his dark night. Clearly the image of his beloved has become a center of integration in his life. I am reminded of the composer Leoš Janáček, who wrote nothing of enduring significance before the age of sixty when he fell in love with a young Jewish woman, Kamila Stoesslova, who did not reciprocate his love but who did allow him to write her love letters. Thenceforth his music became inspired. Distance between Janáček and Kamila enabled something very important to happen, a kind of integration of the composer's inner life around the anima nucleus. Clark Moustakas did something very similar with his distance from his deceased daughter: all the books and training courses nourished by that "presence amid distance." If something like this is happening to Wharton's hero Archer, then perhaps he is "becoming Countess Olenska" as Majnun "became Layla." Although it is too early for a prognosis, it is clear that the light that fills the abyss of Archer's loneliness is the irreal, silvery light of the moon and not yet the golden light of the sun, which brings out all the rough edges of things in three-dimensional relief. He has no connection with the real world. His experience, though, when we compare it to that of John of the Cross, shows that there are stages in the dark night, moving toward a realization that Jelaluddin Rumi has described very eloquently:

> Lovers don't finally meet somewhere.
> They're in each other all along.
>   (1984: quatrain 1246)

Rumi and John of the Cross can talk primarily about presence, because in their experience the sword of separation is more evident to profane eyes than is the love potion. There are cases, however, in which presence predominates over distance; and there the lovers long for the introduction of the sword and the dark night—even if not consciously. When they are "in each other" all the time, they lose their individuality, or perhaps never find it. They begin to struggle with one another, even to invent arguments in order to get free and discover themselves. Whether they know it or not, they long for the abyss of loneliness and for what it can bring about in their lives. Richard Wagner's opera *Tannhaeuser* describes this situation very well in its first act. Heinrich Tannhaeuser, a wandering troubadour, has been making love with the goddess Venus for such a timeless time that he has lost all sense of orientation. He misses the earth, the sky, the seasons, and the song of the nightingale. Without the tension created by distance in romantic love, he is beginning to languish. He does not at all denigrate the delights he has been enjoying; rather, he promises to sing the praises of Venus on earth if only she will let him go.

From now on my song will praise only you!
Your reward from me will be sung aloud!
Your sweet charms are the source of all enjoyment,
And every precious wonder stems from you.
The flame that you have struck in my heart
Will blaze brightly for you alone!
Henceforth I will be your bold and
Tireless hero, taking on the whole world—
But for this I must return to earth;
With you I can be never more than slave;
For this I require freedom;
For freedom I thirst—for freedom.
I will stand fast in any strife,
Should it lead even to my death.
But to do this I must flee your realm.
Oh Queen, Oh Goddess, let me go!

(Act 1, scene 2, my translation)

Tannhaeuser would rather devote his life to singing the praises of Venus than dally in timeless union with her. Heathcliff would never understand such a sentiment, but Eliduc and Majnun know very well what he longs for.

This concept of distance amid presence gives us a valuable tool for examining relationships. I refer, for example, to the fact that the occurrence of an extramarital affair nearly always evokes suspicion that the partners have in some way become estranged from one another—that the love potion has disappeared from their union. It may be, however, that one partner or the other—like Tannhaeuser—longs for relief from too much presence. Since in our culture we have so little that addresses this issue, it is not likely that we would be able to recognize our plight as a search for the sword of separation.

De Rougemont believes marriage is wholly incompatible with romantic love and that our contemporary romantic notions—mere fragments of the medieval ideal of courtly love—have distorted our contemporary expectations. He thinks we want to keep ourselves in the early stages of erotic involvement where our fantasies about our partner preponderate over accurate perceptions. He thinks romantic love is a kind of sickness that we have to outgrow. It appears to me that he comes to this point of view because he has barely begun to appreciate the significance of the naked sword. The sword does far more than inflame our lust; it sends us back and down into the transforming dark night of the soul whence we have far more of ourselves to bring to our partner and our partner has far more to bring to us. Marriage works as a transformer of romantic love and not just a social and economic institution of convenience when we can be simultaneously both present and distant.

3

The Love Potion:
Metaphors of Depth

In the legend of Tristan and Isolde, the love potion symbolizes the depth, the inevitability, the transcendence, and the eternality of their love. But it is not the only symbol that points in this direction. For example, God actively assists the lovers despite what appears to be their sin, and the people are unanimously behind them despite their violation of the rules of the social order. Furthermore, when Tristan is wounded the first time and no medicine in Cornwall can save him, he sets to sea in a boat without oars; and the sea carries him directly to the shores of Ireland, to Isolde the maker of the poison that threatens him and the only person in the world who can cure him. Likewise, after Tristan has been cured and returns to Cornwall, to sing of Isolde's beauty rather than pursue a relationship with her, a bird carries a strand of her golden hair across sea and land directly to King Mark, who agrees to marry only the woman to whom it belongs. Tristan is dispatched to find her. We may say, then, that the image of the love potion sums up the various forces that draw Tristan and Isolde together: God, the people, and all of nature.

A few years ago I met a professor of one of the "hard" sciences who had fallen in love with his secretary. It had been a short-lived, difficult affair that ended with her rejecting him and seeking new employment. This naturally did not end the psychological connection between them, for he remained preoccupied with her. His obsession took the form of cataloguing the "synchronistic" events that surrounded their meetings and activities. Birth dates, names, geographic locations, dreams, automobile license plates: he wove a fascinating picture of significant linkages that criss-crossed every dimension of their lives. It consoled him to list such marvels, for it seemed to prove—as in a medieval tale of courtly love—that all of nature and God, too, were behind his liaison with his beloved. True, he was overly excited about these things; but I have no doubt that the great majority of his coincidences were accurately described. Extraordinary events like this tend to cluster around a profoundly felt love affair. Another couple reports that when they first met, they communicated largely by reading one another's minds while tossing nonsense phrases back and forth. Now, twenty-five years after the end of their affair, they still regularly communicate a "psychic" request for a phone call over the thousands of miles that separate them.

Plato tells a legend in *Phaedo* that souls are granted, prior to their birth, a vision of the *eide,* the eternal, transcendent ideas or essences of things. We cannot know them with our sense organs, but only by "remembering" our prebirth vision. Romantic love is filled with such uncanny knowing. Once we have looked into the soul of our beloved through the lens of our anima or animus, we know her or him better than we thought we could ever have known anyone. We feel we have just awakened from a dull lethargy to the vibrant colors of "real life." We seem to be so familiar with our beloved's soul that we feel we have always known one another. People become convinced of the possibility of past lives when they struggle to explain these magical effects of having drunk the love potion.

In Alban Berg's opera *Lulu,* the heroine declares she can tell in the dark the man who is "made for her" because she dreamed of him during an adolescent sickness. It must have been a swirling reverie that surrounded Lulu while her body lay fevered in her bed. Very likely there was an incident of sexual awakening associated with her illness, too. In any event, this image of her animus comes from deep in her psyche. Evidently her sickness lowered the level of her consciousness from the higher frequencies we use in our daily life to lower ones that we generally overlook in our wide-awake states. She had to have been fascinated with this dream figure and believed there was some kind of destiny linking their two souls. He seems to be— and as an inner figure he *is*—the other half of her own being. She knows the resonance of that place in her psyche and that there is a type of man who vibrates in harmony with it. This is why she can recognize him in the dark. She does not need her eyes for this kind of recognition.

Hans Christian Andersen, too, in his version of the Turandot legend,[1] presents us with a picture of this kind of pre-knowing that implies different levels or "depths" of psychological involvement. The hero, Johannes, first encounters the image of his anima in a dream. Later he hears about a princess who beheads her suitors, and he declares her "horrible":

> "She should be switched, that is what she deserves. If I were the old king, I would beat her till I drew blood."
> . . . [But] when Johannes saw her, his face became as red as blood dripping from a wound and he could not utter a word. The princess looked like the girl with a golden crown that he had dreamed about the night his father died. She was so beautiful, and he already loved her so much, that he could not believe that she was an evil witch who ordered men to be beheaded or hanged, because they could not guess the answers to the questions she asked them. (49)

One part of Johannes very correctly perceives the princess as a demon-possessed, murderous, spoiled brat. This assessment stems from a part of his psyche that is well adapted to the real world. But another part, the part that in his dream has drunk the love potion, responds to an entirely different order of reality. She is, indeed, "meant" for him; he is the only man who can save her; and she is the only woman in the world who can complete him. Both parts of Johannes are right. The rational, practical, socially conscious part of him is overwhelmed by deeper and more powerful feelings from another stratum of his psyche. If he gives in to this in an uncritical fashion, he is sure to be destroyed, as have all the suitors who have preceded him. But he cannot ignore it. He is drawn by a sense of destiny that seems to him to be coming from the very center and deepest portion of his soul.

When we are pulled in this way, we are, indeed, confronted with a "fateful" challenge. It is a "call" in the sense of "vocation," because

---

1. Turandot is a fairy tale by Nizami (1959) and an opera by Puccini. It appears in many traditions, including "The Bewitched Princess" (Zaunert) and "The Travelling Companion" (Andersen).

it requires us to tangle with an issue that is central to our psyche. If we accept the challenge, we may surely perish; but if we avoid it, we are resigning ourselves to a much narrower spectrum of experience. We are reducing our expectations in such a drastic manner that we are sure to pay for it with depressions or other neurotic symptoms in the future. Johannes is at a crossroads that will determine the scope and vitality of the rest of his life. Unfortunately, however, the Andersen tale does not allow the reader to experience the tension between these alternatives. In that tension, we will be able to explore the psychic "depths" to which the love potion brings us. But for that we need a story whose drama turns on that tension between different "levels" of the psyche. Richard Wagner's opera, *Lohengrin,* provides such a tale.

Elsa is accused of murdering her brother in order to grab the throne of the Duchy of Brabant. In fine chivalric tradition, God is called upon to declare judgment *(Gottesgericht)* in the form of a duel between the accuser, Telramund, and whatever knight will champion Elsa's cause. When the call for a champion goes out and none responds, Elsa prays God to send her the glorious knight she has seen in her dreams. The knight actually appears on a barge drawn by a swan and wins the duel for Elsa. They will be married, but Elsa is never to ask his name or origin.

Before the wedding can take place, however, Ortrud, the wife of the defeated Telramund, begins to insinuate doubts into Elsa's mind—perhaps Elsa's great love is a foolish adolescent crush. Although the wedding takes place as planned, Ortrud's insinuations have effect; and as soon as they are alone in their bridal chamber, Elsa begins to question Lohengrin. She notes how sweet her own name sounds from his lips; should she not be allowed to pronounce his? Can he not make her proud through his trust in her and thereby prevent her perishing in worthlessness? In answer, Lohengrin appeals to the wonders that attended his appearance and his intimate knowledge of her dreams. These are insufficient, and Elsa finally demands to know his name, title, and land.

Lohengrin reveals that he is the son of Parsifal, the Grail King, sent to work righteousness upon the earth. If Elsa had only been able to tolerate his anonymity for a period of two years, they would have lived happily ever after. But now he must return to the

Kingdom of the Grail. As he departs, Elsa sinks slowly to earth, *entseelt*—"disensouled." Apparently Elsa's soul has departed with Lohengrin to reign with him forever in the Kingdom of the Grail.

Two themes in this story illuminate the symbol of the love potion and metaphor of love's depth: (1) the fact that Elsa was able to conjure her animus dream figure into bodily existence and (2) her subsequent struggle with doubts about Lohengrin's value—does he represent something deep, central, and divine or something shallow, peripheral, and magical?

The first of these themes may sound wholly fantastic to those who have not had much exposure to the synchronistic events that so frequently attend archetypal experiences. As an analyst I have heard quite a few such stories. In particular, I think of one man who reported that he had conjured his anima into existence one semester in graduate school when he had written several passionate papers on the female beloved in American literature. When she appeared in the flesh in the stacks of the library, he recognized only that she was important. In a few weeks he knew she was central, but it was several months before he realized that she was the one he had been writing about. They had a tumultous relationship over a period of two years, including many experiences of mind-reading, meeting one another unannounced in odd locations but with seemingly certain fore-knowledge, and the like. There were painful separations and uncertain rejoinings until the woman's fear of their emotional intensity drove her into marriage with another man. The first man accepted this as a "naked sword" that separated them physically while leaving them psychically connected. Twenty years later, as a college professor, he began to deal with the issue in analysis and was eventually inspired to put together a college course on certain aspects of romantic love in literature, explicitly with the object of coming to understand what had happened to him in his youth. No sooner had he put the final touches on it than he received a phone call from a woman of his own age, a graduate student from another college who wished to consult with him on completing her master's degree thesis. This time he knew at once that a new chapter was beginning in his own thesis. She proved to be another perfect embodiment of his anima—even better, perhaps on account of the years of maturation they had both gone through.

We also know that there is something right about the earnestness of Elsa's fidelity to the image of her animus. It is important that she does not conjure Lohengrin lightly or idly. She waits for a fateful moment, when her own life and the serenity of all Brabant are hanging in the balance and God has been called upon by the entire community. Everything points to the center; everyone is holding his breath; and the tension is underlined by long moments of silence in the orchestra. Wagner makes it unmistakable that Elsa is longing unwaveringly with her whole nature.

The college professor, however, did not know he was conjuring up his anima. Of him, we would have to say that his nature longed unwaveringly but *unconsciously* for the woman who carried the image of his soul. Ignorant as he may have been about conjuring, the professor was hardly a passive player in his own story. In the first case he had written several passionate papers describing the woman he did not know he was looking for. We must assume he had put more of himself into that work than even he had realized. He himself says that he recognized—only in retrospect—the importance of his term papers as documents describing his own soul. Without knowing it, he had been fleshing out the image of his anima, getting to know her in detail. The second time he did very much the same thing. He even realized consciously that he was working on an issue of momentous importance for his soul. But the notion of conjuring up a female Lohengrin had never entered his mind.

There is something else different about the way the college professor and Elsa expressed their longing. He longed more in the style of Andersen's Johannes than that of Wagner's Elsa. There is something boyish about it, somewhat like the experience of the twelve-year-old Jung who, for several days, fought an inner image of God defecating on the Basel cathedral. It was entirely an inward struggle. Neither the boy Jung nor the college professor had any notion that they were looking for something to appear in the outer world. Both were moved by an inner necessity, a need to set something straight inside themselves. They had no plans for conjuring. But by the very fact that they each touched something central in their psyche, they found that the *world* had changed for them, no less than their own souls. When young Carl finally allowed himself to experience the thought that terrified him, he found it wholly

changed his relationship with religion. Whereas his father, a minis-
ter, got into a crisis of faith by trying to conform his mind to the
philosophy of Kant and traditional interpretations of the bible, Jung
learned that the Holy Spirit speaks directly to one's soul. Jung
writes: "With the experience of God and the cathedral I at last had
something tangible that was part of the great secret—as if I had
always talked of stones falling from heaven and now had one in my
pocket" (1961: 41).

Clearly Elsa and the college professor are both carrying very
important "stones" about with them in their pockets. She had talked
of a knight no one believed existed. Even her devoted people feared
she was mad and a dreamer (act 1). The professor had written and
spoken about the beloved he had not yet met, in what he believed
was a theoretical manner; but the woman's appearance—twice, and
with a twenty-year interval—was as solidly real as two stones in his
pocket.

The audience of Wagner's opera has no doubt that Elsa's longing
proceeded from her "center," her Self. The dramatic conflict in the
story, however, revolves about her doubt: Does she love him from
her center or from her periphery? Is he sent from God or merely a
magician? She is inclined to believe she and Lohengrin are connected
from their centers. Her words to Ortrud reveal her fervent naivete:
"sweet bliss of purest trust . . . you'll never know how free from
doubt my heart loves." I think we have to believe she was unaware
of any doubt at all about Lohengrin's centrality. But she has not yet
looked into Lohengrin's soul through her anima lens. Lohengrin
remains for her a projection from her dreamy unconscious and may
be an animus mask. Her naive and virginal trust knows nothing of
the autonomous otherhood of a partner, another human being with
plans and dreams of his own.

Elsa has had a very powerful inner vision of her animus. It has
been so convincing that it has pulled her out of the world of space
and time into a romantic, adolescent dreamscape. Perhaps she has
been in shock since the abduction of her brother. In any event, she
seems to be in the kind of reverie Lulu describes—where she met
the animus figure she can recognize in the dark. This "altered state
of consciousness" is not restricted to inexperienced adolescent girls.
It can easily be had by successful men in their fifties, for we are all

relatively inexperienced when it comes to dealing with a *living* animus or anima figure—living, because it is surprising and has a wiley mind of its own. When the anima or animus has this much vitality, it regularly "blindsides" us. Its astonishing and tricky power comes from its unconsciousness. The man or woman we can recognize in the dark or conjure out of thin air has lived a long time, shut away from everyday life. As an inner figure, our "shadow," it has been locked in the closet of our unlived life and is attended by all the urges and longings we have repressed out of the fear they will turn our life upside down.

Ortrud knows exactly what she is doing in questioning Elsa's certainty. She knows that Lohengrin is too pure and ethereal to be complete. There has to be a swarm of less worthy motives somewhere just out of sight. A figure this powerful that admits of conjuring—even if he comes from the center—must arouse unfamiliar realms of the psyche. Ortrud is an expert in this field of experience, for she is a magician. She worships the old pagan gods who stand discredited by the biblical God occupying the center of the medieval cosmos. She relates, therefore, not to the psyche's center, but to the unintegrated and unharmonized instincts. Ortrud is able to tap their power to work her own will. She represents an ego-centered longing. She conjures from the conscious "periphery" of the psyche rather than from its unconscious center.

Elsa wants to know if Lohengrin is a figment of her imagination or a stone in her pocket. She is so inexperienced, she does not know the difference. She does not have a "feel" for this kind of thing. She could profit from an interview with Catherine Earnshaw from Emily Brontë's *Wuthering Heights*. Cathy knew very well with which level of her psyche she loved. Indeed, she had a lover for each of them. She tells Nelly, the narrator:

My love for Linton is like the foliage in the woods: time will change it, I'm well aware, as winter changes the trees. My love for Heathcliff resembles the eternal rocks beneath—a source of little visible delight, but necessary. Nelly, I *am* Heathcliff! He's always, always in my mind—not as a pleasure, any more than I am always a pleasure to myself, but as my own being. (84)

This passage tells us the nature of Cathy's tragic mistake in *Wuthering Heights*. She loves Heathcliff from the eternal rocklike depths of her psyche. But, knowing their love is timeless, she takes it for granted and marries Linton because he can supply the smooth aristocratic style she longs for. She wants both loves and believes they can hardly conflict with one another, since they are so different. Her love for Linton is shallow, because she cannot connect with him through her Self. She uses him to insure her social standing, respectability, and wealth. This may be a "good enough" reason for marriage, insofar as that institution is a social, legal, and financial sort of companionship. It is the kind of marriage that was "arranged" in former times and which may be sought by pragmatic individuals who have never known the divine madness of love—or who *have* known it and decided it was too painful. But Cathy is not someone like that. She knows love's depths and has no intention of losing Heathcliff. If Elsa had had a more trivial love (like Cathy's Linton), she would have known by the contrast that her connection with Lohengrin belonged unmistakably to her center, to the "eternal rocks" of her psyche.

When we speak of "levels" or degrees of "depth" in the psyche— between seasonal trees and eternal rocks, what is central and what is peripheral, and so on—we reflect the theoretical division Jung began to articulate in the second decade of this century. He distinguished "personal" and "collective" levels. The personal psyche includes ego consciousness and the "personal unconscious." The latter is comprised of the forgotten, overlooked, and repressed material that has accumulated over the course of our own personal biography. It is characterized by personal idiosyncrasies and knows something of time—insofar as, say, a dream image can be identified as belonging to one's sixth or sixteenth year and is saturated with the joys and traumas of that period of life. There is an ordinary, "everyday" character to it, whereas the "collective psyche" is characterized by a kind of impersonality, transpersonality, and timelessness—very frequently with an extraordinarily impressive, even uncanny, feeling tone. The collective psyche includes those dimensions of our psychic life that all of us as human beings have in common, regardless of our biographical differences. It is the realm of what Jung calls the archetypes. Jung's language can be somewhat confusing on the nature of the archetypes; one reviewer (Hobson, 1980) counted more than thirty meanings of *archetype* in one volume of the *Collected Works*. I find it useful to distinguish three levels within the collective unconscious: the level of mythic images, the Self level, and the level of instincts or "inborn releasing mechanisms" (see the accompanying diagram.[2]

Personal Psyche	{	ego consciousness
		personal unconscious
Collective Psyche	{	mythic images
		Self
		instincts (inborn releasing mechanisms)

Lovers who have drunk the love potion relate to one another from the level of Self. This means that each feels complete and united within; they feel united with one another; and they feel one with the whole world. Thus Bedier says of Tristan and Isolde, when they are living together in the forest, that they were lords of the woods (73) and that Tristan could call the birds so that they would fly into their hut and sing for them (ibid., 72). Tristan and Isolde could speak to one another in birdsong (ibid., 97) just as Layla and Majnun were kept in touch by birds during their separation. Such

---

2. This differentiation of the collective unconscious is inspired by the later writings of Pierre Janet, where he develops a model of the psyche with nine levels, three of which cover the ground Jung includes in the term *archetype*. A careful reading of Jung (cf. Haule, 1984) will reveal his indebtedness to Janet's psychology to be about equally as great as to Freud's. However, he appears not to have read beyond Janet (1903), where the doctrine of mental levels is first introduced. It is my belief that developments in Janet's psychology between the late 1920s and the end of his life can contribute valuably to Jung's thought while remaining within the spirit and conceptual framework of Jung's writings. Consult Haule (1983) for an exposition of these categories in language closer to that of Janet and applied to Jungian clinical practice. There is not much available in English on the psychology of Janet, but Ellenberger (386-94) presents an extensive summary of the nine mental levels Janet describes in his writings after 1920. For the English-speaking reader not ready to tackle Janet's straightforward declarative French, the two volumes of *Psychological Healing* (1919) are an excellent place to begin, although these were written before the "grand synthesis" of nine mental levels had been developed.

unity, such mystical participation,[3] frequently is attended by the so-called "psi" phenomena of mind reading and synchronicity.

Essentially we have two means of access to the world and other people. One is the usual way, through the activities of ego consciousness. This includes the use of the sense organs, directed thinking, feeling, and the like. The other way is through the Self level of the psyche. Our mental level can be lowered by erotic involvement to a mystical participation with our beloved in which we understand one another wordlessly, glimpse one another's souls through the lens of anima or animus, and find ourselves immersed in a common emotion. But such phenomena are not limited to the experience of lovers. Any experience that involves the activation of an archetype brings about such a drop in the level of consciousness as to give us access to other individuals through the Self. The best documented material of this type is to be found in the literature on shamanism—the study and practice of ritual healing methods in preliterate societies.

The world over, wherever shamanism is found, there are individuals with a special talent for deliberately passing into an ecstatic trance in order to gain access to a very similar state of unity with nature and with their patient that lovers know with one another. In Eliade's words, "The shaman is the great specialist in the human soul; he alone 'sees' it, for he knows its 'form' and its destiny" (1951/64: 8). The shaman's calling, talents, and training provide access to virtually all human souls, while the lover has access primarily only to the soul of the beloved. In both cases the access is achieved through the Self-level of the psyche. The shaman has learned to gain this access, this lowering of the mental level, deliberately and on conscious demand, whereas the lover does so passively as a result of

3. Jung generally uses the French phrase *participation mystique*, which he borrowed from anthropologist Lucien Levy-Bruhl (1857-1939). Levy-Bruhl argued that "primitive mentality" was characterized by, among other things, a lack of individual autonomy. Egohood was diminished to the advantage of social cohesion. There was no urge to automomy, as the member gained primary satisfaction from mystically participating in the group. Jung applies the term *participation mystique* to describe any occurrence of this ecstatic relinquishment of consciousness between individuals. It need by no means be a pleasurable experience, for any overwhelming emotion between two or more people is capable of becoming an instance of *participation mystique*. "Mob psychology" would be a particularly abhorrent example.

the experience of falling *deeply* in love. For it is not all lovers who have this access, only those whose love has attained such depth that we can truly say of them that they have drunk the potion.

The shaman sees the condition of the patient's soul to diagnose illness and particularly perceives its absence in truly life-threatening diseases, often of psychological origin. For example, Marjorie Shostak (291f.) tells the story of the shamanic healing of a young !Kung woman near death in her struggle with malaria. The dangerous element in her condition appeared to be psychological, namely the recent death of her father. The shaman went into trance, and his soul made an exploratory journey to the world of the dead, where he found the spirit of the sick woman tenderly enfolded in the arms of her father who was rocking her and singing to her. The shaman addressed the father, asking why the daughter was in the land of the dead instead of with the living, where she belonged. The father said he had been desolate without her, whereupon the shaman argued passionately for her return to the obligations of life, saying that she would rejoin her father after she had experienced what life had to offer and had grown old. In the end, the dead man's soul agreed to these terms, the shaman brought the woman's soul back to her body, and she recovered.

Unlike most of the cultures Eliade reviews in his classic book on shamanism, the !Kung do not reserve shamanic powers to a small elite of practitioners. They believe—and it is evidently the case—that every man and woman possesses and has access to the shamanic healing force they call *n/um*. Some, of course, are more skilled than others in using it. *N/um* is usually dormant and must be activated by deliberately lowering the mental level through music, and especially through a strenuous trance dance, which may go on for hours. This is their way of reaching the psychic level of Self that lovers attain erotically.

This connection, which the !Kung point to with the notion of *n/um* and I describe with the psychological metaphor of Self-level, Jung (1952/55) sometimes calls "unconscious *a priori* knowledge" or "absolute knowledge." The shaman somehow "knows" the nature of the patient's illness and what to do about it, but it is not like the knowledge we attain with thought. We might say he "knows with his body," the expression Carlos Castaneda attributes to the Yaqui

Indian shaman he calls don Juan Matus. The lover "knows" the beloved in much the same way. In *Anna Karenina,* Tolstoy says of Kitty and Levin, "Through her love she knew his whole soul" (433). It is not a knowledge that can be reduced to words or images. Indeed, it might as well be called a "being" as a "knowing." That is why Cathy Earnshaw says, "I *am* Heathcliff," and Majnun calls himself the veil that hides the face of Layla (Nizami, 1966: 125). Very likely it is similar to what the evangelist means when he has Jesus say, "I and the Father are one" (John 10:30).

The shamanic and love-potion connection between people can also be expressed by the metaphor of seeing. Lovers say they "see" into one another's hearts or souls. The shaman "looks for" the patient's soul when it is "lost"; he "sees" the condition of the soul's strength and health. In similar manner, I like to speak of the anima or animus serving as a "lens" whereby the lover brings into focus the soul or Self of the beloved, as well as his or her own. This "seeing" bears as little resemblance to sight as *n/um* "knowing" to a bachelor's degree. For Castaneda, "seeing" is the primary metaphor for shamanic activity; and as one reads through the eight autobiographical volumes chronicling his apprenticeship, one finds the connotations of the word *seeing* gradually but steadily reduced and simplified. As Castaneda begins to experience for himself what don Juan has been trying to describe for him, he drops some of his more fanciful expectations and presumptions. The activity of "seeing" transcendent, nonbodily realities becomes less a fancied, radiant goal and more a tool of everyday living.

The metaphor of "seeing" is particularly compelling because *images* are so closely related to an interpersonal connection at the level of Self. The !Kung shaman, for example, actually enters a kind of dreamscape when he goes in search of the woman's lost soul. It is not a private dream of exclusively personal significance for the shaman. Rather it has an "objective" quality about it. It is a dream about the Self-level connectedness of shaman and patient. He obtains a true (because effective) insight into the psychological condition of the woman. She no longer wants to go on living; she would rather be with her father in the land of the dead. But she does not experience this as an attitude of her own. For her, it is the "pull" her absent father exerts that draws her out of life and dissolves her interest in the affairs of the living.

Upon activating his *n/um,* the shaman first experiences these facts in a direct, imageless intuition. This is connection at the psychic level of Self. At this point he has a nonspecific grasp of the serious- ness of the woman's condition, which he expresses by saying that her soul is "lost." He does not know quite "where" it is or what is "detaining" it. In order to describe her condition more specifically, he needs imagery and therefore sends his own soul on a "journey" into dreamscape. Having lowered his mental level to that of the Self in order to obtain an effective mystical participation with his patient, he now needs to *rise to the level of mythic image* where those deep, unarticulated interpersonal facts can be represented in a useful manner. The shaman's role in primitive societies is precisely this, to be able to control the level of his or her psyche's functioning so as to (1) access the soul/Self of the patient and (2) articulate the condition of that soul in imagery that is redolent of transcendent cultural meanings and social consensus. Thus Lévi-Strauss says of another shamanic cure, "The shaman provides the sick woman with a *language* by means of which unexpressed and otherwise unexpres- sible psychic states can be immediately expressed" (193).

Elsa's dream of Lohengrin is a manifestation of this same mythic level of the psyche, as was the initial dream of an analysand of mine in which an angelic man bathed in a golden light protected her and gave her the task of raising a baby, which was herself. She dreamt it the night before first meeting with me and told me that she knew I was the analyst she should work with because the man in the dream was me. This phenomenon manifested itself somewhat differently, however, in the case of the college professor who twice seemed to conjure his anima into bodily existence. He did not have a dream image of the woman. Instead he pasted together, as it were, a montage of his anima, culled from literary sources. The mythic image-level of his psyche expressed itself implicitly in the academic work that he believed was wholly conscious.

Insofar as anima and animus images at the mythic level adequately reflect realities at the "deeper," imageless level of Self, they are inherently true. They "feel" true, also, because they imaginatively represent central aspects of our psyche. Even when we have not yet made the acquaintance of these facets of our Self, they speak with the self-evident conviction of Plato's anamnesis, as though we are remembering essential matters from a prebirth vision. As an image for the other half of the round being we originally were before time began, a vision of our anima or animus presents us with a hitherto unknown part of our Self.

Such is surely the case with Elsa. Her vision of Lohengrin proceeds from her Self. It is true and in harmony with God's will. Lohengrin's defeat of Telramund in the *Gottesgericht* duel is merely secondary evidence for the centrality of Lohengrin in her psyche. Still she doubts, and it is important that she do so. She is a naive, dreamy young girl who can easily be led astray by peripheral concerns that only *seem* central. In fearing that Lohengrin may be a magician rather than an emissary of God, Elsa entertains the possibility that the image of Lohengrin may have come from some shallower level of her psyche.

That would be the level characterized by personal imagery, by the memories and repressed material from her own life history. The level of the personal unconscious is above all the "space" in the psyche where "outer" and "inner" issues mingle. Here, mythic images emerging from below are "clothed," as it were, in personal associations and take on an appearance peculiarly suited to each individual's past experience and future hopes. Here, too, we encounter imagery consciously and subliminally gathered from our environs. It is the reason fragments from televised beer commercials and science fiction movies find their way into our otherwise quite sober-seeming dreams.

Elsa's doubt emerges from her awareness that she is lonely for companionship and understanding. She would love to have a knight-champion more angelically intimate and militarily powerful than any other. He would satisfy her deepest needs and justify her in the eyes of Brabant. Perhaps she has conjured him out of ego-centered desires. A magician or witch (like Ortrud) works by precisely such means (cf. Gray, Bonewits, or Crowley): one determines the exact effects one wishes to bring about and then gathers intrapsychic emotional and image associations, amplifying them with mythic imagery and environmental effects. Having thus "mapped out one's own being" (Crowley, 12), one lowers the mental level with a powerful and focused emotion and "fires it" at the goal (Bonewits, 159). In short, the magician exploits the readily available imagery and desires of the personal level of the psyche to imitate the action of the archetype.

Elsa's solution to her dilemma is to violate the rules by which she can maintain an unconscious relationship with Lohengrin. She tells him that a relationship in which she cannot call him by name is not sufficient for her. She wants to have it out with him. She unquestionably does the right thing, even though it brings her sorrow; for relationship cannot survive if we leave our feelings undifferentiated. The complexity of the interchange in the opera is expressed primarily in Wagner's music, which, I am afraid, exceeds my ability to describe in words. However, we can investigate the problem of distinguishing feelings coming from the center from those coming from the periphery if we turn our attention from Elsa to Turandot.

All the several versions of the Turandot legend turn on this problem of center versus periphery or deep versus shallow. The hero Johannes in the Andersen version, cited above, has no doubts about himself or the princess, once he has seen that she is the very woman he dreamed about. Nizami's (1959) hero is a bit more complex. The beautiful Princess Turandot has mastered all the ordinary arts and sciences and the occult arts as well. She builds a castle of iron and steel atop a mountain and has magic swords guard the single path that connects her with the rest of the world. She paints her likeness, life-sized, on a silk banner and hangs it from the gate of her father's city with the promise to marry any man who can disarm the swords, find his way into her castle with its hidden door, and answer a battery of riddles. The hero of this tale knows he has "lost his head" as soon as he sees Turandot's likeness. Unlike the others who suffered physical decapitation, however, he does not proceed immediately to the challenge. He deliberately *chooses* the sword of separation. He spends several years studying with the world's greatest spiritual teachers. This means that he familiarizes himself with his center. On this basis he succeeds.

Turandot, herself, does not dare choose a husband, because she cannot trust her feeling or intuition to distinguish the center from the periphery. In Nizami's version of the tale, she has already fallen in love with the hero as soon as he enters her castle. But she does not reveal her emotion to him. Rather she coldly insists on the ordeal of the riddles. As I view the riddles, they are explicitly an attempt to test feelings—to see if the feeling of being in love comes from the center or the periphery. Have they really drunk the love potion, or do they just wish they have?

In her first test, Turandot breaks an earring in two and gives the prince its two identical pearls. In answer, he adds three pearls of the same weight and gives the five to her. Her first gesture seems to say, "Our two souls are such a matched pair of jewels as these." She even believes this message, though it is tainted with her doubt. If he accepts it uncritically, she can throw handfuls of such pearls in his face and order his decapitation. The message is true but also a trick, as the pearls are anything but unique. She desperately wants to believe in love and the destiny of their two souls, but is afraid of falling for foolish romantic drivel. The first move in the game is to determine whether he is as softheaded as she fears she is herself. None of this is lost on the prince, who keeps his wits, restrains his feelings, and shows he understands by adding three identical pearls of his own.

In her second test, Turandot grinds the five pearls to powder and mixes in sugar. He responds by pouring the mixture into a glass of milk. She drinks the sweetened milk and recovers the exact weight of pearl dust. In grinding pearls she reveals the aggressive desperation of her situation. She is nearly paralyzed by the fear of opening herself to a man who may not deserve her intimacy. She sugars the results of her violence. She is still testing whether he can discern the difference between sweet romance and hard reality. From the prince's side the message is slightly different; for in crushing both her own contribution and his, she threatens the five, the "quintessence" of their relationship, the give and take, the spirit of mutual trust without which communication and exploration become impossible. Unlike nuggets of gold, pearls cannot be reconstituted from dust; they have their value in the irreplaceable beauty of the whole. The sugaring of the dust suggests the threat of "sweet unconsciousness" that would result if he were to allow her to crush his individuality. In dissolving the sugar in milk, he invites her to *enjoy* the sweetness of their love. This answer is typical of his centered, Self-level replies. He accepts what she gives him for precisely what it is (two matching, valuable, but not unique pearls; a mixture of pearl-dust and sugar; and so on), but he transforms the meaning of the contributions. She tenders them in a fierce spirit of cynical mistrust. His careful acceptance widens the horizons of her suspicious world.

As a third test, Turandot gives her suitor a ring. He puts it on his finger and gives her a "wonderful" pearl. The ring, by implication a wedding ring, continues her obsessive self-distrusting queries: What will he do if I finally give myself to him? His answer, the truly "wonderful" pearl, symbolizes himself, the most valuable and unique gift he has.

In their final exchange, Turandot finds a pearl identical to the one the prince has just given her and ties it to his with a thread. He, unable to distinguish one from the other and not having a third, ties a glass marble to them. She puts the marble around her wrist, hangs the pearls from her ears, and directs the wedding to be prepared. Superficially, this appears to be a repetition of the first test, but this time the pearls are really unique. The offer is genuine. It is typical of her self-deprecation that she disguise her offer of herself by first making several feints, as if to say, "Do you really value me? Do you know what I'm giving you? Are you ready to take me seriously?" She demands his total attention; she must be the center of his interests. She wants to remain eternally the darling princess and is terrified at the prospect of going on with her life, of becoming wife, queen, and mother. Her question also means, "Can you love me as I have never been able to love myself?"

His answer of the glass bead shows his recognition that she has finally admitted her love, her belief that their two souls are unique, matching pearls. The bead seems to say: Alongside these pearls, which are ourselves, all else is trash; there is no third. But it says more than this, for in giving her a worthless bauble, he also tells her he has seen her mean, petty, self-doubting side and accepts it, too. Her final gesture, hanging the bead from her wrist, amounts to an acceptance of that in herself, an identification with the lowly piece of glass. This sentiment is repeated in the image, at once sexual and violent, with which she sums up the meaning of the riddles: "the falcon is enthroned on the breast of the pheasant."

Both Turandot and Elsa have "stones in their pockets," but neither can quite trust her miraculous good fortune. Each attempts to solve the dilemma by examining her incarnated animus image. In a certain sense Elsa is more admirable in this, as she takes the risk of loss on her own head in demanding that Lohengrin identify himself. Turandot is much more cunning, desperate, and dangerous, but she accomplishes more. The two heroines are alike in that they have determined that their erotic bond with their lovers proceeds from the depth of Self. The difference is that Elsa has built no foundation for an earthly life. She has, as it were, granted reality exclusively to the realm of the archetypes. This explains the ending of the opera, her sinking disensouled to the earth, presumably to live bodilessly in the airy Kingdom of the Grail. In contrast, Turandot is brought down from her eagle's nest and will spend her life with her prince on the earthly, temporal plane.

Elsa's solution, the denial of the personal and temporal in favor of the archetypal and eternal, may be met with quite frequently in an analytic practice. It is the man or woman who avoids all personal involvement by living in a dream world with the ghostly image of an anima or animus. It is also the individual who sleeps with several different partners a week, frequently not even learning their names. These people use the physiology of sex to lower their mental level to a deep mystical participation and never integrate this experience with the personal level of the psyche.

The personal level poses more of a challenge to the love-potion experience than the shallow distraction that Elsa and Turandot so desperately fear. It demands integration. This level of the psyche, which Jung calls the personal unconscious, is the bridge between ego consciousness and the deep unconscious. In our personal-image dreams and fantasies, a *life-world* is created. We imagine how our life might and might not be lived in the light of the mythic images arising from below and the environmental demands intruding from without. At this level mythic, generically human, issues are personalized, reduced to size, rendered in a form that we can recognize as our own. The myth becomes individualized and livable. Simultaneously, our personal perspective is broadened and becomes rooted in the deep psychic matrix that has seen thousands of generations dealing with the same set of problems. Our life becomes connected with the divine images that inform it with transcendent meaning. Turandot's loss to the guru-apprentice prince turns out to be a twofold gain: she learns to trust her feeling connection with the deep Self level of the psyche, and she lays the groundwork for integrating this with everyday life.

Giacomo Puccini recognized the necessity of integrating objective and personal levels in his operatic version of the Turandot legend. He has the prince demand a task of *her,* namely to discover his name. In contrast to Wagner's Lohengrin, who tries to hide behind the numinous aura of his animus origins, Puccini's Calaf asks Turandot herself to penetrate the glow of transcendence. In his directions to his librettist, he says his intention in the love duet in act 2, scene 1, is to show how Turandot and Calaf are made human and brought into the real world through their love, and that the expression of that love through music and words must fill the opera house.

This integration is the master stroke in romantic love. It is no small matter to have a distinct vision of the anima or animus. It is genuinely marvelous when this angelic image can be conjured into bodily existence and related to. One may not ever *expect* to have "stones in the pocket." But to *build something* with those stones, that is what truly transforms a person. It is also the only act of the drama in which consciousness plays a major role. To *have* the image and even to conjure it into bodily existence, is an "act of grace," an unmerited boon from God. But to make it one's own, to find a way to *live* it, requires deliberate choice, resolution, judgment, and will.

Integrating the levels of personal image, mythic image, and Self in an episode of romantic love is a metaphor closely related to three others that have already been discussed: withdrawing the projection, using anima as a lens, and becoming Layla. In withdrawing the projection, we relinquish our clinging to our external beloved and recognize his or her image within us. Through this inner image, as through a lens, we bring into a kind of preimage focus of feeling or intuition or "body knowledge" the deeper Self whence the anima or animus image has emerged. And because we do not merely gaze at this image but integrate it into a way of life, we become the veil before the face of our true being—our Layla.

4

Love's Wound:
Locus of Agony
and Rapture

The previous chapter explored the experience of oneness—even of fusion. In order to understand this from a psychological perspective, it has been necessary to articulate a view of the human psyche. Because we are universally inclined to speak of the "depth" of our love or the "depths" of ourselves that have been touched by our beloved, I have emphasized a model of the psyche based on five "levels" or degrees of depth. At the lowest, "instinctual," level— which has been left out of consideration until now—we may imagine a collection of pretty much unrelated giants, powerful and crude. Each possesses awe-inspiring strength, but little sense of direction or ability to cooperate with the others. Jung speaks of a chaotic bundle of instincts:

> The bundle of instincts of man, his chaotic ensemble of instincts is not integrated at all. Instincts are most contradictory, and man is torn by them. They are like animals in a zoo, they do not love each other at all, they bite each other and try to run away. (1938/84: 108)

Jung cites insect mating rituals to illustrate how the instinct/ archetypes work. He mentions the yucca moth and the leaf-cutter ant (1919/48, 1946/54), both of which must perform an extremely complicated series of activities to complete a reproductive episode. As the species makes no provision for an older generation to teach younger individuals, an insect must be born with the capability of "recognizing" appropriate weather and plant conditions and then "knowing" what to do with them. Jung calls this inborn capacity for recognizing and performing typical patterns an archetype. It is not a mythic image; and—unlike the Self—it has no appreciation for wholeness. It is less organized than that. "Archetype," in this sense, refers to a blind propensity to repeat the same behavior over and over again.

These behavior-regulating patterns have also been called inborn releasing mechanisms (IRMs), because it is clear that the individual has no way of *learning* the very well-defined conditions that "release" rigid response patterns (cf. Eibl-Eibesfeld, 20-25). For example a newborn chick can "recognize" the shadow of a chicken hawk passing over the barnyard and "knows" enough to run under a wagon for protection. Experiments with artificial chicken hawks have shown that there are very definite limits within which the hawk shape can be varied in order to obtain the desired IRM behavior from the chicks. This blind kind of knowing, which snaps shut like a steel trap, is also the way our human psyche operates when our level of consciousness is lowered to that of the instinct/archetypes.

As we proceed up the psychic levels toward consciousness, the raw force behind the behavior decreases and its flexibility and refinment increase until we reach the conscious ego, with its ability to make its own decisions and combine old notions into new and creative ideas.

The ego is an extremely important element in holding together a coherent and flexible psychic unity in the face of day-to-day events. But it rests on a deeper foundation, the Self, which is the source of all unity and balance within the psyche and between psyche and the outer world and other individuals. Externally, the Self unites us with our beloved and with the cosmos in an undifferentiated oneness. Internally, it unites the several instinct/archetypes into a harmonious whole. This wholeness is more primitive than what might be accomplished through imagery, for mythic images arise only at the next higher level of the psyche. There, fragments of what seems to be a comprehensive narrative arise in our dreams and waking fantasies and seem to imply a deeper unconscious knowing in the Self from which they appear to emerge. Jung describes this emerging and fragmentary narrative as a "personal myth," which we are living whether we know it or not:

Myth, says a Church Father, is "what is believed always, everywhere, by everybody"; hence the man who thinks he can live without myth, or outside it, is an exception. He is like one uprooted, having no true link either with the past, or with the ancestral life which continues within him, or yet with contemporary human society. . . . The psyche is not of today; its ancestry goes back many millions of years. Individual consciousness is only the flower and the fruit of a season, sprung from the perennial rhizome beneath the earth; and it would find itself in better accord with the truth if it took the existence of the rhizome into its calculations. For the root matter is the mother of all things. (1912/52: xxiv)

A rhizome is a rootlike plant stem that grows under the earth, roughly parallel to the surface of the ground, and sends out at intervals along its length roots reaching downward and vertical stems with leaves and flowers that extend above the earth, as in the iris. The rhizome that connects individuals with one another and with the earth lies as a de facto source of unity prior to all image and representation. It is the Self-level of the psyche, the origin of mythic image and a partial source of personal image within the psyche. It provides us an intuitive or unconscious knowledge of the unity and balance within ourselves and within the macrocosm.

The greatest possible contrast obtains between the premythic unity of the Self and the snarling tiger pit of the instinct/archetypes or inborn releasing mechanisms. Every individual feels the tension between these levels of the deep psyche as a kind of uncertainty or precariousness in Self's synthesis. In the language of Buddhism, the flaw in human nature resides in our untamable desire, also a reference to the IRMs. In biblical language it is "original sin," the flaw in human nature brought about by the fall of Adam and Eve from a state of paradisal unity into a world whose very ground is cursed and where we have to earn our bread by the sweat of our brow (Gen. 3:19).

We all experience ourselves as wounded. But as lovers, we experience the tension between Self and instincts more acutely. Romantic love is experienced as a tension between the love potion and the naked sword, between the bliss of union and the abyss of separation. Pain and delight are always closely allied for the lover. The foremost image for this is love's wound, which is praised and bemoaned by both romantic lovers and mystics. Majnun's condition is in no way unusual; he appears to have fallen victim to the snarling instincts:

> On my way through a mountain gorge I met a creature writhing on the stones like a goat, like a madman in pain, like a lonely demon; his body was so wasted that every bone was visible.
> . . . now talking to himself in verse, now moaning and sighing. He wept, stood up and collapsed again, he crawled and stumbled, a living image of his own fate. He swooned and was hardly conscious, so that at first he did not recognize his own father. (Nizami, 1966:42f.)

Majnun's father tries to get him to pray to God to be saved "from this vain ecstasy." But Majnun prays quite differently:

> I ask thee, my God, I beseech thee, in all the godliness of thy divine nature and all the perfection of thy kingdom: let my love grow stronger, let it endure, even if I perish. Let me drink from this well, let my eye never miss its light. If I am drunk with the wine of love, let me drink even more deeply. (Ibid., 38)

For Majnun the pain is no mere torment. As the "passing away" of *fana,* it contains within itself the promise of attaining the greater Self and the greater unity of *baqa.* It is not only a torment that cannot be avoided, it is one that we implicitly long for. Gottfried von Strassburg's Tristan says, "I do not know what has come over poor Isolde and me, but we have both of us gone mad in the briefest space of time with unimaginable torment. . . ." (201). Similar imagery appears in the twentieth-century novel of Erich Maria Remarque, *Arch of Triumph.* The action takes place during the German occupation of France; and the lovers, Joan and Ravic, are meeting again in a bar. This time they are enjoying a really fine bottle of calvados. Joan says, "After this calvados I'll never drink another kind." Ravic says she will: "It will taste even better than it really is. It'll be a calvados with the longing for another calvados. That in itself makes it less ordinary" (169).

The notion of the wound resides in that unrequitable longing for the one and only object that can satisfy by bringing us into unity. We find this sentiment among the mystics no less often than among romantic lovers. For example, Jacopone da Todi says:

> Oh, that my heart would not stumble and sag!
> That I were able to love more intensely,
> That I had more than myself to give
> To that measureless light,
> That sweet splendor.
> I have given all that I have
> To possess the Lover who constantly renews me,
> That ancient Beauty forever new!
>
> (259)

In his *Spiritual Canticle,* John of the Cross enumerates three traits of a soul sick with love of God. First, such a soul is always longing for health and therefore has her heart fixed on her divine beloved. Second, she has lost her taste for all things. And third, she finds all of her dealings with others to be burdensome and annoying (*Canticle,* 10.1). These three traits are equally applicable to romantic love. John of the Cross goes farther than this, for he recognizes that the pain of the wound is an important manifestation of the mystical participation that unifies the lovers: "Among lovers, the wound of one is a wound for both, and the two have but one feeling" (ibid., 13.9).

One of the lais of Marie de France provides a rather complete picture of love's wound. Guigemar is a young knight renowned for his physical beauty and his prowess in battle, "but Nature had done him such a grievous wrong that he never displayed the slightest interest in love" (44)—although women frequently made advances to him. While out hunting one day he comes upon a white hind that has antlers like a stag. His arrow hits the deer in the forehead and rebounds, passing directly through Guigemar's thigh and into his horse's flesh. In its pain, the hind speaks to the knight:

Alas! I am mortally wounded. Vassal, you who have wounded me, let this be your fate. May you never find a cure, nor may any herb, root, doctor or potion ever heal the wound you have in your thigh until you are cured by a woman who will suffer for your love more pain and anguish than any other woman has ever known, and you will suffer likewise for her, so much so that all those who are in love, who have known love or are yet to experience it, will marvel at it. Be gone from here and leave me in peace. (Ibid)

After this a marvelous ship made of ebony and silk takes him to an ancient city where a jealous old king keeps his young and beautiful wife in a green marble enclosure, accessible only via the sea. This is precisely where Guigemar lands and he and the queen fall equally into a torturous state of love. For Guigemar, it is so profound that he no longer feels the pain in his thigh. Just before they are discovered, the queen has an intuition of what is to come, and they pledge eternal fidelity by tying knots that no one else in the world can undo without the help of scissors or a knife. She ties the tail of his shirt, and he ties a belt around her loins.

After years of suffering separately, they are brought back together by the boat. But now the queen is a prisoner of a lord Meriaduc who wants to marry her. When she and Guigemar finally meet, they barely seem to recognize one another and do not trust themselves until they have untied one another's knots. Guigemar then pledges Meriaduc his own service and that of his hundred knights if he may marry the queen. Meriaduc refuses, whereupon Guigemar joins forces with Meriaduc's enemies and lays siege to his castle. He wins his beloved only after killing the lord and destroying the castle.

The image of the white hind is rather common in tales of chivalry. It generally leads the hunter on a long and mysterious chase that takes him completely out of familiar kingdoms and forests into a truly transformative adventure. The fact that this (female) hind sports antlers only adds to the transmuting power of the symbol. The Guigemar who meets her has mastered the manly arts of knighthood but knows nothing of the relationship realm of feeling, love, and the feminine. Through his love for the queen, he falls completely into that delightful realm. But, according to the story, he requires several years of distance and a formidable military challenge before he can win her completely, that is, integrate both masculine and feminine realms into his way of life. I believe he has to kill Meriaduc at the end because the cruel lord of the castle represents the masculine power principle that would take the woman by force. Guigemar, like the antlered hind, has married the feminine with his masculine. He has killed in himself the macho power principle represented by Meriaduc.

The story is *about* this transformation in Guigemar, and the symbol it hinges upon is that of the wound and its analogue the knot. We are told four things about the wound/knot. First, it is located in his thigh (as with Tristan and the Fisher King) and also pierces his horse, which would symbolize the animal/instinctual side of his knighthood. Second, its cure requires an equivalent wound in someone else: no one in the world suffers as these two, and they suffer equally. But, third, in some way the proximity of these two wounds brings about a temporary cure, which is as delightful as the pain was dreadful. The pain returns when they separate. And, fourth, they can only recognize one another again by placing their hands on the knot/wound.

As the story opens Guigemar is unconscious of his need and capacity for relationship. He is not at all in touch with his deep feelings. In recent decades psychology has begun to pay particular attention to this problematic realm. Robert Stein, writing in 1973 before the current interest in actual childhood sexual abuse, refers to it as an "incest wound." Michael Balint speaks of a "basic fault"; and Heinz Kohut has opened new discussion of a "narcissistic wound." Each of these refers to a weakness, a vulnerability, or a precariousness in the unconscious synthesis at the level of Self.

Stein (43) finds three symptoms of this kind of difficulty: (1) frequent rejection in relationships; (2) experience of confusion, loss of identity, and emotional paralysis in intimate relationships; and (3) obstruction of sexuality in all ways—except in relation to fantasies or an actual person for whom one feels neither love nor respect. Against this picture, Guigemar is a serious case indeed; for he has not allowed himself to get close enough to a woman ever to be rejected. He is so oblivious of women's advances that it appears even his sexual fantasies are completely obstructed.

Balint (18–20) enumerates five indicators that the level of the basic fault has been reached with a patient in analysis. The first[1] of these is that the patient "begins to know much too much about the analyst"; what is thus known is always highly personal and in many ways absolutely correct but may seem to the analyst to be utterly out of proportion. This is the "absolute knowledge" discussed in the previous chapter, the result of a lowering of the mental level to that of Self, a condition enjoyed as the bliss of the love potion's union or utilized as the shaman's tool. Balint singles it out as a fault or deficit insofar as the patient reveals himself incapable of maintaining boundaries between himself and others (in this case, the analyst).

Normalcy is imaged as a condition of easy distance between analyst and analysand, or between friends. People who are not hindered by their narcissistic wound are evidently able to contain themselves in the face of connectedness at the level of Self. We are able to keep our attention on the contents of the personal imagination as well as on our conscious perceptions and plans regarding our partners. We can ask directions to the post office and not be in danger of being swept away. Not so the narcissistic individual. Such a person finds himself somewhat in the condition of Gilbert in D. H. Lawrence's novel *Mr. Noon:*

> Gathering his courage in both his hands, he managed to look on the naked woman of his desire without starting to grovel. Which, if you have profound desire, isn't so easy. You either grovel or overween. Or else, groveling, you overween. To be neither more nor less than just yourself on such an occasion: well, that takes time and a sound heart. (1985[a]: 245)

For the narcissistic individual, the Self-level of reality is so much more important that it overwhelms the seemingly more manageable and everyday kinds of issues. As in the case of Lawrence's Gilbert, it is as though the higher levels of the psyche are partially paralyzed by the riveting stare and raw desire of one of the instinctual giants

---

1. For purposes of clarity in my exposition, I have changed the order of Balint's presentation of these symptoms. This in no way affects the content of his position.

snarling beneath the Self's precarious harmony. The level of consciousness having been significantly lowered, unitive phenomena preponderate: absolute knowledge, fusion, loss of identity, confusion, emotional paralysis. The analyst finds it disturbing that his or her own psyche seems to be an open book for the analysand. In romantic love it may not be so disturbing, for we may delight in reading one another's soul. Sometimes we want to be open to one another and have the boundaries between us dissolved, while at other times we want to limit our openness. Sometimes we are able to control our openness and sometimes not. Some individuals appear to be almost always incapable of limiting their openness. These are the ones Balint and Kohut are describing. The essence of the wound, therefore, seems to consist in an involuntary, inappropriate, and uncomfortable loss of boundaries and higher functions.

Second, according to Balint, the level of the basic fault has been reached when the analyst is constantly "in danger of subjective emotional involvement" with the patient. Although every successful analysis includes some degree of emotional involvement, Balint refers, here, to an attraction that feels dangerously compulsive and perhaps beyond one's ability to control. We may say that the analyst has been "infected" with the patient's unbounded woundedness and has lost use of some of the higher psychic functions. The analyst is no longer able to maintain an easy distance. In the story of Guigemar this is described as the painful wounds the lovers have in common and their potential to be a source of bliss when brought into proximity with one another. Guigemar was aware only of a flesh wound before he encountered the queen destiny had selected for him. In her presence for the first time, he became aware of the much greater wound in his soul. Balint implies that this experience is not uncommon for the analyst who encounters a patient badly wounded at the level of the basic fault. Stein (3ff.) verifies this in his own experience; mine has been similar; and I have profited greatly from reading Harold Searles's confessions along these lines.

Balint's three other indicators flow from the first two. The patient relies on his sense of oneness or fusion with the analyst so that: (3) it is taken for granted when the analyst provides what is needed; (4) the analyst's failure to meet the patient's expectations causes powerful feelings of emptiness and anxiety; and (5) interpretations are experienced as inappropriately attacking or gratifying. In all these instances, the patient's intense desire to have his wound soothed or healed through union with the analyst is decisive. All the hopes, disappointments, rages, misunderstandings, and pleadings revolve about the wound, its pain, and its promise of bliss.

As Heinz Kohut looks at this clinical picture, he sees a lack in the "cohesive self" required for stable day-by-day living. Without such a "self," the individual is swept this way and that by strong emotional winds. Indeed, the goal of successful treatment is to foster "an accretion of drive-controlling and drive-channeling structures" (Goldberg, 8). These are what I have called the higher-level activities of the psyche (those associated with the ego) that are lost or weakened when the mental level is lowered.

Our "woundedness" may be seen as inversely corresponding to the degree of coherence, balance, and consistency we sense in our rhizome. For the schizophrenic patient, there is very little of it: "[He] has the same complexes, the same insights and needs [as the normal or neurotic,], but not the same certainty with respect to his foundations" (Jung, 1958: par. 559). Even the normal individual's certainty regarding "his foundations" is far from absolute. We may be able to go for years without having to confront our woundedness, but it lies there always as a kind of shakiness in our foundations or an unknowability of the rhizome. The myth, as a symbolic narrative, is always inadequate to the wholeness of the rhizome—which is another name for the Self-level of the psyche. There is always something illusory about it. In his *Myths and Symbols in Indian Art and Civilization,* Heinrich Zimmer tells a very instructive tale about this illusion, or Maya, as it is called in Sanskrit.

It seems there was once a devotee of Vishnu, the god of Maya (or Illusion), who had so distinguished himself that the god appeared to the man as he meditated and told him that he would grant him any request. The devotee replied without hesitation that he wished to know the secret of Maya. Vishnu protested that this was impossible, that the man had no idea what he was asking for. But the devotee persisted; and Vishnu had, after all, promised. So eventually the god gave in and said, "All right, I'll teach you the secret of my Maya; but first, I want you to go over to that farmhouse over there and get me a cup of water."

The man took a cup and knocked at the door. It was opened by a beautiful woman he seemed to know. And she surely knew him. She invited him into the house and it seemed that her whole family was no stranger to him. Eventually he married her and took over the running of the farm. He and his wife had several children and the farm became more and more successful until our hero was the envy of the whole region. Then one year a series of monsoons threatened to wipe out everything. The nearby river overflowed its banks, and the whole family was forced to flee. Unfortunately, they were not quick enough. One child after another was swept out of its parent's arms. The last thing our devotee saw before he himself was swept away was his wife's head disappearing beneath the roiling surface of the river. He came to his senses miles downstream, washed up on a mud flat. The first thing he heard were the words of Vishnu: "Where's that cup of water? You've been gone half an hour already" (Zimmer, 32f.).

To know the secret of Vishnu's Maya may be a profound mystical insight, but it is also quite horrifying. One's farm and family, indeed one's whole life, becomes insubstantial. What is to prevent us from rattling around from one life-style or profession of faith to another? They are all attractive and promising, but ultimately not one of them can have any substance. Our woundedness is a kind of inchoate grasp of the secret of Vishnu's Maya. Every philosophy, every faith, every standpoint, every lifeworld becomes ephemeral.

Nothing is more obvious to the unreflective farmer than the density, opacity, and rock-solid reality of the ground he plows. For the individual aware of the wound, however, that ground periodically thins out, rarefies into transparency, so that what one stands on is no longer solid. It becomes as wispy and elusive as a rainbow or a bridge of fog arching over an abyss. It is a terrifying vision that saps—at least momentarily, but all too frequently—every possibility of hope and trust.

Such a wound takes its greatest toll in the realm of human relationship, where it is experienced as a kind of mystical pain, an eternal longing to return to an original state of oneness: oneness within oneself, oneness with the cosmos, and above all oneness with one's beloved. It is a most exquisitely personal pain, a sense of being marred, deformed, cast out by everyone: a sense of absolute isolation. On the other hand, it is an undefended openness, a raw, bleeding exposure of psychic nerve ends so that there is nothing in the way of immediate, intense, and very deep intimacy.

We all have a wound of this type. Those of us who are more-or-less normal have learned to protect, defend, and close the wound, whereas the narcissistic personality and the borderline individual suffer the wound very intensely. They have not learned to close it, and their defenses are rigid, brittle, stereotyped, and inadequate. The tremendous aggression associated with the borderline condition is a slashing, hysterical defense of a wound whose pain can be overwhelming.

As experienced in romantic love, the wound is a kind of sweet agony. One has been brought to the shaky ground of one's being by another who also suffers the wound. And our suffering is transformed to bliss as our wounds are brought together. It is as though the wounds fit together like a key in a lock. Remarque makes this clear in Ravic's observation of Joan in *Arch of Triumph:*

> She leaned her head back and drank. Her hair fell over her shoulders and in this moment she seemed to be nothing but drinking. Ravic had noticed this before. She gave herself completely to whatever she did. It occurred to him vaguely that therein lay not only fascination, but also danger. Such women were nothing but drinking when they drank; nothing but love when they loved; nothing but desperation when they were desperate; and nothing but forgetfulness when they forgot. (119f.)

She gives herself completely because there is nothing between her momentary consciousness and the gap of the wound. She keeps nothing in reserve; she acts directly, without reflective mediation. But still, there is something unnerving about the way she acts. There is a "nothing but" quality, a sense that only one act is performed where several might be expected. If she loves from her wound, how can she forget? How do things fall apart so readily? How does the meaning fall away? The balanced, coherent synthesis, which is the Self, threatens to give way. The instinct/archetypes, whose harnessing into a coherent myth is the job of the Self, come unglued. The mental level drops another notch to the *instinctual level* of the psyche.

Romantic love is experienced and enacted at the level of Self, where coherence, consistency, balance, wholeness, and meaning are created. The shakiness of this synthesis is the wound. When the wound rips open, when the center cannot hold, its several instinctual components become autonomous. Should consciousness drop to the instinctual level, the individual is no longer truly a lover. Ravic's Joan is capable of forgetting. Our contemporaries become addicted to sex or to seduction or the chase—or, perhaps, cuddling or conquests or basking in praise or being humiliated. In all these cases, a single archetype has separated from the Self-synthesis and dominates consciousness.

Remarque's heroine, Joan, shows the fragility of the Self-synthesis at every turn. Her wound shows even in her gait: "She always walked as if she were walking against a light wind and as if she had no goal" (205). It is an endearing image. We know why Ravic is taken with her. She promises something deep, an intimate absorption of which Ravic is incapable on his own. It is as though her wound opens and we can see the powerful forces that give her personality its mysterious, magnetic powers. Ravic cannot stop meditating on it. "He was looking at her face, which was enchanted and absorbed in the music. How easy that was for her, and how he had loved her for this easiness which he did not possess" (ibid., 271).

Joan reveals the wound as promising. Something deep and untapped is there latently, visible in a wound that is not badly infected. The Self-level synthesis is tentative but not wholly lost. In contrast, Hardy's Bathsheba, in *Far from the Madding Crowd,* shows a deliberately self-inflicted wound, an abandonment of her mythic rhizome. She is consequently demoralized and her habitual composure severely distorted during her infatuation with the faithless manipulator, Sergeant Troy:

> Bathsheba loved Troy in the way that only self-reliant women love when they abandon their self-reliance. When a strong woman recklessly throws away her strength she is worse than a weak woman who has never had any strength to throw away.
> . . . Had her utmost thoughts in this direction been distinctly worded (and by herself they never were), they would only have amounted to such a matter as that she felt her impulses to be

pleasanter guides than her discretion. Her love was entire as a child's, and though warm as summer it was fresh as spring. Her culpability lay in her making no attempt to control feeling by subtle and careful inquiry into consequences. (1984: 179f.)

Bathsheba is demoralized because she has given up her own foundations and tried to supplant them with an unjustified dependence on Troy. She has relinquished her integrity for a kind of frantic clinging. This is quite different from traversing the bridge of fog because it is the only bridge there is. She is not working with the shaky synthesis that is the woundedness of the human condition. She has gone farther than this, out onto a fragile limb that soon breaks off.

In time, after the pain of Troy's faithlessness, Bathsheba is able to restore herself, for her mythic rhizome is coherent and resilient. Such is not quite the case with Joji, the hero of Junichiro Tanizaki's early novel, *Naomi*. Joji is a petty clerk, afraid of women, when he "adopts" the fifteen-year-old Naomi with the plan of educating her and providing what her poor family cannot afford. He hopes to make of her an ideal wife, but she turns the tables on him completely. Four years later, Joji describes her as follows:

The truth is that I still didn't trust her at all, but the animal in me forced me to submit blindly to her; it led me to abandon everything and surrender. Naomi wasn't a priceless treasure or a cherished idol any more; she'd become a harlot. . . . I was being dragged along by her physical attractions. This degraded me at the same time it degraded Naomi, because it meant that I'd abandoned my integrity, fastidiousness, and sincerity as a man, flung away my pride, and bent down before a whore, and I no longer felt any shame for doing so. Indeed, there were times when I worshiped the figure of this despicable slut as though I were revering a goddess. (Ibid., 163f.)

Joji is wholly in the grip of an archetype; he has lost all sense of a myth, even one like a bridge of fog. His mental level has fallen completely beneath the Self to autonomous instinct. He has lost his freedom.

Guigemar and his lady never sink so low. In their bliss they ride the rainbow bridge, but even in their despondency they have not lost all sense of balance and harmony. They maintain consciousness at the level of Self and therefore entertain a certain awareness of the unity and coherence of things. The shakiness of this awareness (the wound) may be rather like the visual effect we have on viewing a line drawing of a rectangular box: first one side leaps out of the page at us and then, just as quickly, an opposite side flips forward so that for a moment we cannot remember how the box used to look. When we look at our wound, order and chaos oscillate in a similar manner.

What we experience in our wound is closely analogous to what Rudolf Otto describes, in his classic *The Idea of the Holy,* as a "mystery which fascinates us and makes us tremble."

> We are dealing with something for which there is only one appropriate expression, *"mysterium tremendum."* The feeling of it may at times come sweeping like a gentle tide, pervading the mind with a tranquil mood of deepest worship. It may pass into a set and lasting attitude of the soul, continuing, as it were, thrillingly vibrant and resonant, until at last it dies away and the soul resumes its "profane," non-religious mood of everyday experience. It may burst in sudden eruption up from the depths of the soul with spasms and convulsions, or lead to the strangest excitements, to intoxicated frenzy, to transport, and to ecstasy. It has its wild and demonic forms and can sink to an almost grisly horror and shuddering. It has its crude, barbaric antecedents and early manifestations, and again it may be developed into something beautiful and pure and glorious. (12f.)

This passage reveals it to be no accident that Jung's descriptions of the Self rely on images of the Absolute from the various world religions: Christ, *atman,* Tao, emptiness, and the like. Images of the irascible, jealous Yahweh of the Hebrew scriptures and the bloodthirsty Kali of Hinduism are set side by side with the Good Shepherd, the Lamb of God, and the playful Krishna. The divine is the absolutely powerful factor in the universe and within the psyche.

In Jung's language, that is Self. Insofar as it is the source of all life and harmony and unity, it may be called the mythic rhizome out of which flowers transcendent meaning with its capacity to make life secure and soul-satisfying. Insofar as its synthesis is tenuous, doubtful, fragmentary, a bridge of fog, it may be called the wound.

The fact that we encounter our woundedness most frequently in two contexts, religion and relationship, goes a long way toward explaining the close parallels between romantic love and the love of God. It also suggests the reason for our ambivalence regarding intimacy, for to become intimate means to expose our wound. It means to be seen—and to see ourselves—in terms of the flawed unity that is our shaky foundation. Tolstoy hints at this when he describes the disturbing effect that Anna Karenina has had upon Vronsky's ordered worldview:

> Vronsky's life was particularly happy in that he had a code of principles, which defined with unfailing certitude what should and what should not be done. This code of principles covered only a very small circle of categories, but in return the principles were never obscure, and Vronsky, as he never went outside that circle, had never had a moment's hesitation about doing what he ought to do. This code categorically ordained that gambling debts must be paid, the tailor need not be; that one must not lie to a man but might to a woman; . . . Only quite lately, in regard to his relations with Anna, Vronsky had begun to feel that his code did not quite meet all circumstances and that the future presented doubts and difficulties for which he could find no guiding thread. (327)

Vronsky's code is a far cry from his mythic rhizome, a reality that lies much deeper than his adventures in Tolstoy's novel ever lead him. Still the disruption of that code, its falling into doubt, is very much akin to discovering one's wound. In the story of Guigemar, for example, the naive knight at the beginning of the story had no need for any realities outside his duties of honor and military service. Women had no effect upon him. He was blissfully unaware of his wound until an arrow caromed off the head of an antlered white hind and sank into his thigh. Even then he believed his wound was only fleshly, although he gave up the hunt immediately and began to look for succor.

We frequently discover our wounds in similar indirect fashion—for example through a dream, even when it seems abstract or incomprehensible. I recall a young monk who dreamed, just about a month before he was scheduled to pronounce his vows of poverty, chastity, and obedience, that he had inadvertently cut off his own penis. His concern in the dream was that his self-mutilation would render him ineligible for vows, so he decided to hide it from his superiors. But then he discovered that, lacking a penis, he could no longer speak and this would mean that he could not pronounce the vow formula. He knew the dream meant that he should not take vows, but it was the only indication he had had. He loved his monastic life and was aware of no dissatisfactions. As he knew nothing of psychology, he decided to ignore the dream and go ahead with his vows. Approximately a year later he met a woman who opened his wound and revealed to him the narrowness of his former view of himself and of the world. He found his certainties replaced by doubts, but he also found his interests broadened and energy increased. What impressed him most was that his prayer life improved. He lost no enthusiasm for the monastery, and it took him another two years before he became convinced that his larger personality was unduly confined within the cloister walls.

Such is often the case: as romantic love brings one's consciousness down to the level of Self, one is impressed with the comprehensiveness and balance of the mythic synthesis. Objections do not occur or cannot be taken seriously. Thus Guigemar and his lady enjoy one another for a year and a half before the realities of the outer world intrude upon them. For Tristan and Isolde, there are at least two such periods: the voyage to Cornwall, during which they drink the potion, and their three years living together in the forest.

Ultimately, though, it seems to be the flaw in the synthesis and the pain of the wound that draws the lovers together. Their experience is that they know one another through their wounds: each understands the pain of the other, and each feels uniquely understood and appreciated by his or her partner. Our woundedness "fits" and is the glue that binds us. This is symbolized in the story of

Guigemar by the knots the lovers tie in one another's clothing. It implies that the wound is a kind of organ of intimacy.

We know instinctively that other people are accessible through their vulnerabilities. By this means narcissistic patients get "under the skin" of their analysts. By their own wounds, they recognize those of others. I recall a badly wounded patient, a woman of forty, who recounted one anecdote after another of her failures to establish lasting relationships with men. She would recognize their potential by catching sight of a major vulnerability, which she would zero in on and want to talk about. The man invariably fled in the face of her intensity and neediness. She did not have the stability, emotional control, or "distance" to relate effectively, but she had recognized the utility of her wound, that it could be used as a kind of magic key to unlock other people's capacity for intimacy.

Although intimacy itself is not mentioned, the notion that the wound can be an effective tool or organ is suggested by don Juan Matus, Carlos Castaneda's mentor. He says that when the shaman (or sorcerer) "sees" a human being with shamanic eyes, he sees a bundle of luminous fibers in the shape of an egg. In the abdominal area there is a dark spot, or gap in the egg. The shaman's "will" emerges through this gap to accomplish the extraordinary acts of shamanism. This language is quite compatible with ours, the notion of a flaw at the level of Self that is both our greatest vulnerability and the organ of love's accomplishment.

Don Juan goes on to say (Castaneda, 1971: 239f.) that death enters us through that gap in our integrity. The gap is simultaneously the most powerful and most vulnerable part of a person. A "warrior," a disciplined individual who orients his or her life by a well-differentiated attitude that is familiar with the All, can control the openness of that gap. Don Juan calls the controlling power "will"; but he does not mean the will of the ego. He refers to the more elusive but powerful will of the Self. One becomes a shaman by "tuning his will," by allowing death to slip into his gap and overtake him in a partial manner. He feels himself beginning to dissolve into atoms and expand into a fog, as he allows his wound to open. But then, as decisively as slamming down a window sash, the shaman can close his gap, reassemble the fog, and so reconstitute himself.

Don Juan says the shaman "assembles" himself by means of his will and that carelessness or exhaustion can leave our gap so open and undefended that we can die. We say it is the Self that assembles our myth and that the wound in that synthesis presents us with the specter of meaninglessness, chaos, the abyss. It is the point at which the death of meaning enters our life. It is here that the naive knight of military honors (Guigemar and Tristan) dies and the incomprehensible greater is born, the one who has come to know confusion, pain, loneliness, and the deepest uncertainties.

With this imagery of death and the abyss, is there any wonder people are afraid of intimacy? Guigemar appears wholly ignorant of intimacy at the beginning of his story. His ignorance may be a fear of intimacy that is so well-defended that Guigemar can maintain a blissful naivete about it. To some extent, this kind of ignorance is nearly always the case before one has been forceably exposed to the wound through falling in love. For in each case the fall in mental level[2] is surprisingly abrupt, and one's prior ignorance of the anima or animus will be found to be rather abysmal. But what I see quite frequently in my practice is people who have just enough intimation of their woundedness to be ready to flee involvement at a moment's notice. These are generally people who have never explored their wounds, but they are scared to death of "getting hurt" in relationship. What "getting hurt" might mean is never clearly known. They speak of a fear of being abandoned and seem to want some kind of assurance that this cannot happen before allowing themselves to enter more deeply into a relationship. They find themselves in a "catch-22" situation, where they know enough to desire intimacy and fear enough to flee it. Refusing to admit the patent truth that there is no relationship without substantial risk and certain pain, they remain stuck between the alternatives.

The fundamental need of the soul in any relationship is union with another person. This cannot take place unless we open our

---

2. Jung uses Janet's French expression, *abaissement du niveau mental* (lowering of the mental level), to refer to a loss of conscious control over our psychological life. We may drop from ego consciousness to any of the unconscious levels of the psyche. For example, we may fall into the dreaminess of the mythic images, as Elsa did, or to the unity of the Self level, or all the way to the snarling tiger pit of the inborn releasing mechanisms.

wounds to one another. When we protect ourselves too much, we cannot make deep contact and our needs are frustrated. We may try to compensate for this by cultivating many relatively superficial friends or by opening ourselves sexually as a substitute. But these solutions are never successful. We may also project our fear of intimacy onto our partner and escalate our demands so as not to have to confront our own woundedness. Generally the best solution is to take the risk of exposing our own wound, for the magnetism of that is nearly irresistible. To do so, we need to be confident that we can trust our partner; and if we cannot do that, we implicitly question the wisdom of sleeping with him or her. We also need to know that we will not fall apart when we expose our wound; that is to say, we need to know ourselves. Finally, we need to know that the risk is worth it. Tristan and Guigemar would have no trouble assuring us of that.

Our existential woundedness poses us the central questions not only in romantic love but in life. This situation is symbolized by Hexagram 51 of the *I Ching,* "Chen/The Arousing." It is comprised of the trigram for thunder, repeated twice. The text reads as follows:

> The hexagram Chen represents the eldest son, who seizes rule with energy and power. . . . This movement is so violent that it arouses terror. It is symbolized by thunder, which bursts forth from the earth and by its shock causes fear and trembling. . . . The shock that comes from the manifestation of God within the depths of the earth makes man afraid, but this fear of God is good, for joy and merriment can follow upon it. (197)

The young monk described above dreamt and daydreamed repeatedly of a black horse whose hooves struck thunder and lightning from stones and which he could ride through the air. His painting of the horse bespoke terror, but he was consciously unaware of that emotion. He knew his love affair was right because it expanded his awareness and because, as he repeatedly explained with great wonderment, his prayer life had markedly improved. He suffered torment he had not previously known but never doubted it was worth it. His wound, it seemed, had begun to function like a lens. It is like the thunder that strikes fear but also brings joy.

5

The Demon Lover: Obsession's Heart

In the first four chapters of this book, we have developed a language to talk about love and about the human psyche. Chapter 1 demonstrated that every love is implicitly the love of God, insofar as we pass away *(fana)* from what is lesser and limiting to what is greater. This implied that projection need not always take the form of "masking" our partner but that our anima or animus can function as a lens. In chapter 2 we considered the painful consequences of losing love's unity, and our need to lose a naive, sensual, and literal possession of our beloved in order to come into a transcendently deeper love of her. Chapter 3 returned to the topic of love's unity to consider the Self on the model of shamanism, as a functioning organ of the psyche that organizes, unifies, and balances our inner life and, no less significantly, unifies us with our beloved and with the cosmos. In chapter 4 we considered our joint woundedness as the flaw in the Self's premythic synthesis undergirded by a chaotic jumble of unintegrated instinct/archetypes. It is the basis of an existential anxiety, which has been discussed in recent psychological literature as a "narcissistic wound."

Now we employ the images and concepts developed in previous chapters to appreciate typical situations that arise between lovers. The language we have been using enables us to take a sympathetic stance toward such entanglements. As always, we wish to come to grips with the psychological roots and spiritual possibilities of love's vicissitudes. In this chapter and the next, we consider the "demon lover," a beloved who occasions a very obsessive kind of erotic bond. What distinguishes the demon lover from the beloved through whom we love God is the degree of wholeness experienced. In genuine *fana,* we are connected with our beloved through our Self and our anima or animus acts as a lens to bring her or his being into focus. In relationship with a demon lover, however, the connection turns on our respective wounds in such a way that we lose a sense of wholeness while at the same time retaining a sense of holiness. This seemingly paradoxical state of affairs is expressed very powerfully in Coleridge's famous unfinished poem, "Kubla Khan":

> But oh! that deep romantic chasm which slanted
> Down the green hill athwart a cedarn cover!
> A savage place! as holy and enchanted
> As e'er beneath a waning moon was haunted
> By woman wailing for her demon-lover!
> (Coleridge, 103)

This is the fascinating scene that may unfold when we look through the wound in the Self to the powerful chaos of the instinct/ archetypes beneath. It is as though a traveller on the bridge of fog should stop and look down, thereby daring to face his most panicky fears. Instead of a black abyss, a disjointed world of uncanny beauty calls out with the irresistible pull of the sirens' song. The very next lines of Coleridge's poem present the frightening destructiveness and mysterious promise of this "sunless" realm:

> And from this chasm, with ceaseless turmoil seething,
> As if this earth in fast thick pants were breathing
> A mighty fountain momently was forced:
> Amid whose swift half-intermittent burst
> Huge fragments vaulted like rebounding hail,
> Or chaffy grain beneath the thresher's flail:
> And 'mid these dancing rocks at once and ever
> It flung up momently the sacred river.
> (Ibid.)

Here the very earth is roused to a high pitch of blind, instinctual panting—suggesting both the rapturous dilations and ejaculations of sexuality and the agonizing gripe and expulsions of the dysentery from which Coleridge was suffering at the time he dreamt the poem.

The dancing boulders present the prospect of almost certain death to any who would venture into the romantic chasm, but the sacred river is something else.

Alph, the sacred river, runs "Through caverns measureless to man / Down to a sunless sea." It is the source of our deepest unconscious longings and images. When it is "flung up momently" to the surface, consciousness becomes flooded with its primordial darkness—but also with the long-hidden mysterious promise of that underworld of the psyche. In his final lines, the poet describes himself as enchanted by the magic of this river whereby he has had visions and heard marvelous symphonies and songs. But his intoxication with the transformation he has undergone makes him a danger to any he might encounter:

> And all should cry, Beware! Beware!—
> His flashing eyes, his floating hair!
> Weave a circle round him thrice,
> And close your eyes with holy dread,
> For he on honey-dew hath fed,
> And drunk the milk of Paradise.
>
> (Ibid., 102f.)

He is entirely beside himself. By his eyes and hair, he seems to present a kind of weird Moses—although the power that surrounds him is hardly a nimbus of glory, and he has nothing so solid to show for his experience as a tablet of stone. Having drunk the milk of Paradise, he himself has become the demon lover. The holy beverage that fills him is what makes him demonic. In the same way, the abyss beneath the bridge of fog and the horrible wound in the Self are dangerous on account of the "holy." Instead of purifying and uplifting, as we might expect, the holy has here been enlisted in a tendency toward sullying and lowering. Indeed, the danger and the promise of the demonic in romantic love resides precisely in this uncanny attraction to the holy sparks that we may find in the darkness of the abyss.

This chapter explores the twofold nature of the demonic, the uncanny holiness that is its substance and the distortions, limitations, and fragmentations that render it destructive. We have already seen some indications of the demonic in foregoing chapters. Turandot's murderous obsession, for example, is equally as demonic as her lovers' eager self-immolation. The very idea of a love potion suggests something dark and uncontrollable, for which reason King Mark's love for his nephew and his wife appears all the more admirable: "Neither poison nor sorcery, only the tender nobility of his heart, moved him to love" (Bedier, 37). Emily Brontë's Heathcliff appears a good deal less than noble on the day before his death, when he says: "I repent of nothing—I'm too happy, and yet I'm not happy enough. My soul's bliss kills my body, but doesn't satisfy itself" (316). Even the mystics speak of a nearly unendurable thirst. John of the Cross says, "Its vehemence is not continual but only experienced from time to time; although usually some thirst is felt" (*Night,* 1.11.1).

A few literary examples may help to describe what it means to lose the wholeness of the Self, to fall through the wound, as it were, and find oneself in a vale of obsessive striving. In Lawrence's novel *Sons and Lovers,* Paul and Clara get a taste of their woundedness and of the demonic as soon as they have known "the immensity of their passion":

> They felt small, half afraid, childish and wondering, like Adam and Eve when they lost their innocence and realized the magnificence of the power which drove them out of Paradise and across the great night and the great day of humanity. . . . They could let themselves be carried by life, and they felt a sort of peace each in the other. Nothing could nullify it, nothing could take it away; it was almost their belief in life.
>
> But Clara was not satisfied. Something great was there, . . . enveloped her. But it did not keep her. They had *known,* but she could not keep the moment. She wanted it again; she wanted something permanent. (1985[b]: 343)

Paul and Clara are right on the brink of the demonic. Their love has brought them to an awareness of the wholeness of the Self level of the psyche ("almost their belief in life"), of their woundedness (the sense of impermanence), as well as of the powerful obsessive pull to experience the moment again and again in the vain hope that it can somehow become permanent.

In *Women in Love,* the same author gives us a more disturbing picture of a demon lover, when the insecure bohemian, Halliday, betrays his fear of the sexually experienced young woman known as "the Pussum." Halliday "gave Gerald the impression that he was terrified of [the Pussum], and he loved his terror. He seemed to relish his own horror and hatred of her, turn it over and extract every flavor from it, in real panic" (1982: 121). This terror that fascinates reminds us again of Coleridge's "deep romantic chasm." The power that invests the fascination comes from the tiger pit of inborn releasing mechanisms, snarling beneath Self's synthesis. These instinct/archetypes constitute the drive and steerage lying behind all of our human activities. But in moments like this, when we can see a man relishing his own horror and hatred, we know that at least one of these IRMs has broken loose from the Self's synthesis and has taken possession of consciousness. Now everything is out of whack and Halliday strains compulsively in the direction of the instinct. We are probably justified in concluding that Halliday fears the Pussum because she dares to do what he both fears and longs for. In Jungian language, she embodies both his anima and his shadow; she lives his "unlived life." But to live this dimension of life would be for him to relinquish the rules and boundaries that maintain his sense of identity and safety. Consequently she represents for him both an imperative challenge and the threat of annihilation.

A somewhat different kind of example is presented in Gustave Flaubert's novel, *Madame Bovary,* where the callous libertine, Rodolphe, corrupts a foolishly romantic Emma Bovary, who then brings demonic obsession with her into an affair with a relatively unspoiled Leon:

> [Rodolphe] made of her something supple and corrupt. Hers was an idiotic sort of attachment, full of admiration for him, of voluptuousness for her, a beatitude that benumbed her; her soul sank into this drunkenness, shriveled up, drowned in it, like Clarence in his butt of Malmsey. (208)

[Leon] did not know what recreation of her whole being drove her more and more to plunge into the pleasures of life. She was becoming irritable, greedy, voluptuous; and she walked about the streets with him carrying her head high, without fear, so she said, of compromising herself. At times, however, Emma shuddered at the sudden thought of meeting Rodolphe, for it seemed to her that, although they were separated forever, she was not completely free from her subjugation to him. (Ibid., 301f.)

Mme. Bovary's career suggests a fairly common characteristic of the demon lover, namely his (or her) tendency to draw us further and further away from sanity and decency. The more villainous the individual, the more ghastly the demon must be to bring about such imbalance. This is portrayed by Dostoyevsky in his early novel, *The Insulted and Injured*, where Prince Volkovsky, as thorough a villain as may be found in literature, tells a shocking story of a beautiful woman, a model of propriety, who leads a secret life of extreme sensuality: "In the very heat of voluptuousness she would suddenly laugh like one possessed, and I understood it thoroughly, I understood that laughter and laughed too" (237).

Volkovsky delights in the fact that her majestic forbidding manner is nothing but a very well-cultivated and finely tuned veneer. The real woman behind the veneer is "the devil incarnate." When you meet that devil, you know you are meeting something ghastly but true and without pretense. Her laugh comes from her enjoyment of the ironic conflict between her highly respectable facade and her diabolic sensuality. She *is* possessed—by one of the inborn releasing mechanisms; she has brought the considerable forces of her well-developed ego into the service of that sexual instinct run amok. We hear in her laugh the painful conflict between the Self and the tiger pit. She has sided with the tigers. For that reason, she is a particularly grotesque example of the demon lover.

But let us now see what happens to the more-or-less naive lover who falls victim to such a demon. I shall again turn to a fairy tale, because the simplicity of these narratives makes them particularly useful for drawing psychological conclusions. Generally such tales turn the psyche inside out, as it were, taking the several inner psychic roles (subpersonalities), which in real life would be found in a single individual, and doling them out to separate characters (humans, animals, spirits, and the like). By its naivete, such traditional story telling achieves a compelling psychological accuracy.

In the following story, which comes from Mesopotamia, the demonic element is presented in the traditional Arabic form of the jinn (singular: jinni; often represented in English as *genie*). Nicholson (1921: 190, n. 3) describes the jinn as "ethereal creatures, endowed with speech, transparent (so that they are usually invisible), and capable of assuming various shapes." H. A. R. Gibb's description is a bit more folkloric:

> The *jinn* are, like men, created, but of fire instead of earth; there are believers and infidels amongst them, and the unbelievers will be judged with men and condemned to Hell. The rebellious *jinn* are called *shaitans* [cf. Satan]; they lead men astray, oppose the Prophets, and try to overhear what is discussed in Heaven but are driven off by shooting stars. They teach men sorcery, and were made subject to Solomon, for whom they dived and built. (57)

The distinguished modern interpreter, Seyyed Hossein Nasr, calls the jinn simply "psychic forces" (65).

The Story of Abdul

> To escape from his hopelessness and poverty, Abdul followed a bejewelled stranger to a cave in the middle of the desert, where he expected to find the key to the world's wealth and wisdom. After much horror and hesitation along the way, the stranger pointed out the entrance to the cave and disappeared. Imagining jinn huge and bloodthirsty enough to tear a man limb from limb, Abdul felt his way down a long set of stone steps and found himself in front of a metal door bearing the words: "Let the seeker kiss this door if he wishes to enter. He will receive more treasure than he can count and more knowledge than he can speak of." Abdul touched the door with his lips, and it opened upon a cave flooded with an

unearthly light that glanced off gold, silver, and jewels in every beautiful form imaginable. His eyes were pulled away from these riches by a feminine voice of indescribable beauty and compelling force commanding him to approach. He looked up to see a woman of entrancing beauty, seated on a pile of jewels. She promised him all the wealth and wisdom in the world if only he would take her in his arms and kiss her.

Abdul was only too happy to do so, and was delighted to find the tip of her tongue between his lips. As he responded with his own, she drew it further and further into her mouth, at first gently and seductively and then roughly and insistently, as though moved by a passion that exceeded Abdul's wildest dreams. Finally, she ripped his tongue out by its roots with a terrific, superhuman yank. Then she pressed her own tongue into the wound, where it implanted itself. At this point the demonic beauty fell lifeless from Abdul's arms and melted into a pool of slime.

As Abdul took to his heels in horror, a strange voice issuing from his own throat brought him to a halt. It announced that from that moment on Abdul would do its bidding or suffer severe punishment. Abdul tried to utter a prayer to banish this evil, but his lips and throat moved spasmodically without making a sound. Then he tried to scream but produced instead a hideous, ringing laugh. The tongue directed Abdul across the burning desert, where he found water enough—although it had no taste. Also a meal fit for a king could not be tasted, though the tongue praised the flavors extravagantly.

Back home, the tongue caused murderous fights to break out, divorced Abdul from his wife, and scared his son into falling down a well. Abdul then sought out mosques and holy places to have the evil exorcised; but the tongue would always curl back and strangle him before he was able to reach the sacred precincts. One night, however, he succeeded in obtaining exorcism from a holy man, walking beside the Euphrates. The saint's words drove the demon tongue from his mouth in the form of an eel. But Abdul, too, fell into the river where four huge fish devoured his limbs.

When he had recovered his health, the limbless, voice-
less Abdul was placed in a corner of the town market
where, surrounded by the riches of the earth, he wordlessly begged for whatever crumbs and sips people would
place in his mouth and whatever coins they cared to toss
on the ground before him. On learning his story, the
Caliph ordered a plaque erected on the wall above Abdul's
head to warn people that this is what happens to a man
to whom the jinn promise, and give, more knowledge
than he can speak and more riches than he can count.
(Time-Life[b], 106–20)

The bitter tone at the end of this tale nearly obscures its ambiguity. We will never know whether (1) Abdul is sadder but wiser and,
in an "inner" or spiritual sense, has really attained unspeakable
wisdom and uncountable riches, or (2) whether his knowledge only
concerns the horrendous reality of the jinn, which is unspeakable
because he is tongueless and his coins uncountable because he is
limbless. The latter alternative—literal, accusatory, and bitter—is
perhaps what the Caliph, as representative of worldly order and
doctrinal orthodoxy, intended. Sufis might be expected to favor the
first alternative. For example, Ibnu'l-Farid (d. 1235) speaks of a
cataleptic woman who is able to foretell future events and speak in a
language she never learned. He takes this as evidence that she is
under control of the jinn and argues that if such a relationship is
possible between bodily and spiritual beings, how much the more a
relationship between creature and Creator (Nicholson, 1921: 220,
n. 225). Jili (d. 1412) has a similarly complex view of relations
between mystics and the jinn who believe in God:

Their night is our day, and their day our night. After the sun sets
in our earth, they appear on it and fall in love with the children of
men. Most of these spirits envy the disciples of the Mystic Way,
and taking them unawares bring them to ruin. (Ibid., 124)

It appears from this that these jinn want to love and serve God,
insofar as they fall in love with and envy the Sufis. But, like the

"elementals" of western occult literature, they are partial beings, one-sided, incapable of maintaining a vision of the whole. They have "one-track minds" so that their best intentions are perverted and distorted. The psychological picture that emerges from this is that of the instinctual level of the psyche, where the instinct/archetypes have lost the harmonious whole-making perspective of the Self and fall apart into autonomous elements, each striving blindly for its own ends.

Although the jinn are unique to the Arabic and Islamic cultural world, the role they play is given other names in other traditions. Buddhist cosmology speaks of "hungry ghosts," which occupy the second lowest of twenty-seven ranks of beings, just two ranks below humans (Rinpoche: 24f.). To be possessed by hungry ghosts is to be in "the mental state in which a host of desires arises in our minds . . . [such that] we do not know how to be satisfied even when we attain our desire of the moment" (Niwano, 8). Chögyam Trungpa describes it much more graphically:

> Now [the individual] experiences great hunger for more pleasura-
> ble, spacious conditions and fantasizes numerous ways to satisfy
> his hunger. . . . Each time he seems about to achieve pleasure, he
> is rudely awakened from his idyllic dream; but his hunger is so
> demanding that he is not daunted and so continues to churn out
> fantasies of future satisfaction. The pain of disappointment involves
> [him] in a love-hate relationship with his dreams. He is fascinated
> by them, but the disappointment is so painful that he is repelled
> by them as well. (139)

In these mytho-psychological words, Trungpa describes the founda-
tional insight of Buddhism, namely that (profane) human existence is characterized by pain and that pain originates in desire. Hungry ghosts, like jinn, personify our frantic, obsessive alienation from ourselves. They have a good deal in common with the inborn releasing mechanisms of the psyche's instinctual level.

Hinduism warns its ambitious seekers after enlightenment to beware of *siddhis*, or miraculous powers (cf. Eliade, 1954: 85–90). The universal experience of accomplished yogins is that, at a certain level of spiritual achievement, one naturally acquires certain superior-seeming talents. For example, one may understand the cries of all creatures, the details of one's own previous existences, the mental states of other men, and the like. These are very much the phenomena discussed above in Chapter 3, on the love potion. They stem from achieving a conscious connection with one's own unity (the Self) and that of the universe. *Siddhis* represent psychological powers that may well be used for good ends; but they can also sidetrack the yogin into a pursuit of numinous, nonultimate matters, so that he forgets about nirvana or union with God.

In romantic love, the instinct/archetypes snarling beneath the Self's synthesis, too, are powerful psychic agents that can be used for good. But when they fall out of harmony with one another, they threaten to sidetrack our life. This is exactly the state into which Abdul has fallen. His greed is not only for gold. He was always seeking wisdom, as well; and in the beautiful woman of the cave he thought he had found sexual and emotional fulfillment also. Jinn, hungry ghosts, and obsession with *siddhis* all point to tension between a centered relationship of one's whole being on the one hand and, on the other, a distorted, unbalanced perversion of desire. The motivation symbolized by the Queen of the Jinn comes from a stratum of the psyche more primitive than that of Self. Because these psychic elements are so archaic, powerful, and alien to the ego, they are quite outside of our control. Furthermore, as they belong to a very low stratum in the psyche, they personify the considerable raw power, which we described in chapter 4 as resembling that of giants or tigers. Consequently, we experience the demon lover as gripping us with superhuman power. We find ourselves compelled to act in ways we would repudiate if only we were in our right minds. We obsess about these things, as "drunk" with our obsession as Mme. Bovary, while with another part of our mind, we find it silly and beneath our dignity. In this regard, we are exactly like Abdul, who wants to praise God but cannot prevent his tongue from pronouncing the most heinous blasphemies; who runs to his wife for comfort, only to suffer the tongue's divorcing her; who tries to reassure his son, only to give the tongue opportunity to kill the lad.

The story of Abdul derives its horror from the storyteller's device of clearly dividing the psychic agency between Abdul's ego and the autonomous will of the tongue. Although the separation of powers is more subtle in our everyday experience of the demon lover, portraying the conflict through distinct protagonists is a common literary device. I think, for example, of Octavius and Tanner in G. B. Shaw's *Man and Superman*. Tanner, who most resembles the Shaw who wrote the introduction to the play, has just described women—and Ann, in particular—as lionesses who devour their mates.

> OCTAVIUS: I do so want her to eat me that I can bear your brutalities because they give me hope.
>
> TANNER: Tavy: that's the devilish side of a woman's fascination: she makes you will your own destruction.
>
> OCTAVIUS: But it's not destruction; it's fulfillment.
>
> TANNER: Yes, of her purpose; and that purpose is neither her happiness nor yours, but Nature's. (60)

By "Nature," here, Tanner and Shaw refer to the propagation of the species. For them, woman is nothing but an embodiment of this instinct/archetype. Tanner uses his cynicism as a shield to prevent his falling for the demon lover, Ann, while Tavy cannot wait to be devoured. The one wants his independence at the price of dishonesty while the other is willing to buy illusory bliss at the cost of his individuality. They are two parts of a single person, drawn to and yet fighting off the demon lover.

Splitting and fragmentation is a central manifestation of involvement with a demon lover. The picture of a whole world and a whole Self breaks into pieces. We blind ourselves to one reality in order to believe in or enjoy another. Abdul wants one thing while his jinn-possessed tongue achieves another. In Lawrence's *Women in Love*, Birkin correctly diagnoses this fragmentation in Gerald:

> "Part of you wants the Pussum, and nothing but the Pussum, part of you wants the mines, the business, and nothing but the business—and there you are—all in bits—"
>
> "And part of me wants something else," said Gerald, in a queer, quiet, real voice. (1982: 154)

A "real" romantic love, one that pulled Gerald together at the level of the Self, would not leave such a gnawing sense of dissatisfaction. Gerald's "wound" is open. Closing it is beyond his ability, so he can only find temporary and fragmentary relief in the Pussum, in the mines, or even in Gudrun, the woman who evidently loves him—as we see about a hundred pages later when he enters her bedroom without warning in the middle of the night. "He was a perfect hard flame of passionate desire for her. Yet in the small core of the flame was an unyielding anguish for another thing" (ibid., 256).

All of this suggests why the hungry ghosts are hungry. What they long for can only be achieved through the harmony that the Self provides. But, by themselves, they know nothing of cooperation and harmony. They only know how to strive for the single, limited end that is inborn within them. Beneath the wound in the Self, therefore, are an indefinite number of autonomous and unyielding desires: sensuousness, safety, comfort, meaning, purpose, power, self-worth, self-annihilation, and many more. Each of these has the capacity, indeed the propensity, to put itself forward as the central or absolute requirement of the personality. Unless harmonized by a Self, these inborn releasing mechanisms fire again and again, blindly and compulsively, pushing us toward an illusory vanishing image of satisfaction.

If the demon lover threatens to pull us into a dark, fragmentary world reeking of death, why are we so fascinated with him or her? Abdul cannot resist the Queen of the Jinn. Mme. Bovary, being deprived of Rodolphe, spends her time and money lavishly on an affair with Leon, a man she does not really love. Gerald keeps returning to the Pussum. The demon lover is rewarding, certainly not in an ultimate sense, but rewarding enough that we cannot leave him or her alone. In a flippant moment Lord Byron had a word to say about it:

> In her first passion woman loves her lover,
> In all the others all she loves is love,
> Which grows a habit she can ne'er get over
> And fits her loosely—like an easy glove . . .
> (Canto 3, v. 3)

These facts are just as true, just as irrational, and just as inescapable for men as for women.

Indeed, a rather common scenario for a man includes a youthful period of courting and exploration in the field of erotic relationship. At this time it may seem to the man that his whole interest is taken up with the mysterious realm of otherness and transcendence that he finds in the souls and bodies of his partners. Perhaps he pursues these for stimulation or forgetfulness. But let us assume that he is serious-minded and looks for a soulmate. Even so, very few men in their twenties make the eros bond their primary concern—whatever they may believe about it themselves. The reason for this is that there are several inborn releasing mechanisms seeking sufficient scope to realize their purposes. Perhaps the most important of these is the drive to professional achievement, a steady, unrelenting force that is backed up by social pressure and even the necessities of carrying on a bourgeois relationship, such as "bringing home the bacon." Thus a young man is encouraged, both from within and without, to settle this matter of eros and companionship so that he can get on with the work of day-to-day living and his career.

If he succeeds in this, everything settles down to a daily routine in which he pursues his professional conquests by day and comes home to the lap of his family at night to dandle the babies and relax with his wife. Everything may go quite well for fifteen or twenty years until the crises of middle age, when he finds that the comfortable structures that have made his life run smoothly are now confining him. He wants freedom from the demanding, rigid, mechanical, exhausting, emotionless world he has constructed for himself. He may not even know this. But he discovers it one day when he meets a woman who challenges all his assumptions. He thought he knew himself and had his life figured out; he was unaware of his dissatisfaction until the day he is blindsided by a woman who appears as a revelation to him. Because his life has been so smoothly ordered, she may very likely be a woman whose life is in pieces.

She may have suffered a great deal with the disorganization and dissatisfactions of a life that she was never able to get on track. She has left a trail of dissatisfied lovers because she cannot commit and does not know what she wants; but she plunges into one thing after another with great energy, hope, and joy—all shot through with a bleeding sense of desperation. She is wide open, powerfully needy, and inspires him with a desire to take her under his wing, to make everything right. But his fascination goes much deeper than that, for he is entranced and uplifted by her boundless energy. He sees as a delightful quickness and sensitivity her inability to sit still with any one thing. Nothing escapes her attention; she picks up on his slightest gesture, movement, or sigh and finds significance that challenges and delights him in areas he has totally overlooked.

They have an affair that lasts perhaps a few months. It satisfies longings he never knew his heart harbored. Their sexual communication is tender and exciting beyond anything he had imagined. They have moments of revolutionary closeness, sometimes even when physically distant from one another. He likens it to two blocks of mist coming together, interpenetrating and mixing with one another so that her molecules and his are no longer distinguishable. They have become more fully one than Plato's round being, for that was only two halves sticking together at their flat sides; this is intermingling.

The demonic element appears most clearly in their struggles, for union is not constant. Indeed, she fears it intensely and pulls way with cruel words about his being married and unavailable. He cannot understand this. He is more available than any other man has ever been for her. True, he will not consider leaving his wife; but he points out that she was afraid of constancy and commitment under any circumstances. He is merely being logical, referring to his knowledge of her past. In actual fact, her withdrawal rips him open and he becomes acquainted with a wound he never knew he had: longing, neediness, depression, a desolation that seems to extend into eternity. Moments of remembered bliss come back to him, and he mourns for them from his broken heart. Her intuitions and challenges—some of them quite nasty—come back to him like arrows piercing his soul. How can he live without this other side of life, which has become more important for him than order, achievement, and bourgeois peace? He *will* not live without it. If she will not have him, he will find someone else.

He knows what he is after now, he thinks, and will not be stopped short of his goal. From our psychological perspective, we know that he is searching outside himself for what he must learn to find within.

His anima has become a mask covering this woman with all the needs harbored in his unlived life, his "shadow." He runs here and there, pursuing one chimera after another—acting possessed, as by a demon. He finds one cure after another, but they all fall flat. Indeed, every "cure" unbalances the psychic system and requires, in its turn, to be cured. Beneath it all lies an eternal longing to return to some original state of oneness.

He has seen something in this woman who is his demon lover—a promise of transcendence and light and bliss, a glimpse of life and wholeness that never occurred to him before. Although he is held by his wound and obsessed with her sexuality and intuition and fragmented multiplicity, he believes he sees something deeper and more central. She, too, is held to him by his intuition of her center and potential wholeness, for she finds herself terrifyingly fragmented. They are, indeed, each other's missing half. And although they are in torment, feel themselves ripped and bleeding from their wounds, find their obsessions loathsome and their compulsive behaviors almost irresistible, they are aware of something promisingly transcendent in one another. What gives life to the demon lover is the same divine spark that makes the love of God the source, depth, and meaning of romantic love. Let the butterfly suck nectar from the rose, let the soul suck mere sustenance from eros, the divine spark in romantic love makes the soul a moth plunging back and forth through the flame of self-transcendence.

The demon lover has long been the bugaboo of romantic love. It may at first seem strange to find the divine spark animating him, giving him life, giving him soul or "anima." The Christian theologian Paul Tillich, however, would not be surprised.

Demons in mythological vision are divine-antidivine beings. They are not simply negations of the divine but participate in a distorted way in the power and holiness of the divine. The term must be understood against this mythological background. The demonic does not resist self-transcendence as does the profane, but it distorts self-transcendence by identifying a particular bearer of holiness with the holy itself. . . . The claim of something finite to infinity or to divine greatness is the characteristic of the demonic. (3: 102)

In similar manner the demon lover represents the power and holiness of the divine, in large part because he or she represents what is lacking to our own wholeness. There is more than a hint of wholeness in the demon lover, and a very powerful promise of self-transcendence. We may even catch glimpses of a potential centeredness in her or him through the lens of our anima or animus. But still there is distortion in that one or more of the inborn releasing mechanisms has become too dominant and sets itself forward as holiness itself. There is, no doubt, a divine spark at work in our erotic bond, but the unity, balance, wholeness, and life of romantic love has been distorted. Our obsession is fueled by the IRM(s) that exceeds the limits of the Self's peaceful harmony.

We can get a sense of how this demonic compulsion arises in an individual's life if we look at Lawrence's novel about Paul Morel, *Sons and Lovers*. The story begins with Paul's mother's need for a caring partner with an interest in the life of the mind. She thought she had found that in Paul's father, but eventually came to despise him for his neglect. As he fled to drink and rage, she turned her attentions to her eldest son, William, and after his death to Paul, her second son, in order to have someone with whom she could share her inner life. As late as age twenty-three, after two significant love affairs of his own, Paul preferred living with his mother to marrying (1985[b]: 239). There can be no doubt that Paul Morel's relationship to his mother lies somewhere at the root of his demonic eros.[1] We are presented first with a picture of massive insufficiency passed on from generation to generation. In looking to his wounded, needy mother, Paul can hardly ignore the fact that he is no higher than her third choice. She wanted *his* attention, and gave him scant recognition for his efforts at becoming independent and particularly for the occupation that lay closest to his heart, his painting.

His first and more significant love was related directly to this lack of attention. Miriam, who thought herself "a princess turned into a swine-girl" (ibid., 142), found Paul quite intimidating at first. This young man like a Walter Scott hero, who could paint and speak French and commuted every day to Nottingham to work, taught her

---

1. The "mother complex" is frequently involved in issues of romantic love. I am not prepared, however, to generalize the case of Paul Morel too widely.

his own nature mysticism through observations on life in the countryside about them and through his art. He always seemed to have "painted the shimmering protoplasm in the leaves . . . and not the stiffness of the shape" (ibid., 151). He vivified things that previously had had no meaning for her. Miriam supplied what Paul's mother was unable or unwilling to give in the form of human warmth and encouragement and understanding regarding his painting. But then something stopped him. He could not abide her pouring intensity, as she bent over a flower, his work, or himself; it was too intimate. He required her attention to his ideas, but he had to trample them out brutally on her soul—just to become acquainted with them himself—as though punishing her for getting too near or in order to drive her away (ibid., 223). Paul ended their relationship because they seemed unable to express their affection physically. They were both highly ambivalent. "She wanted to run her hands down his sides. She always wanted to embrace him, so long as he did not want her" (ibid., 187). When they attempted lovemaking, he was completely put off, finding "the look at the back of her eyes, like a creature awaiting immolation" (ibid., 282). He feared being sucked dry.

What was left out in his relationship with Miriam, Paul poured into his affair with Clara, who represented the physical, instinctual dimension of relationship. He ignored her sensitivity, intelligence, and love of reading, but was very conscious of her breasts and arms and the down on her cheek. At one point they go to a play:

> A kind of eternal look about her, as if she were a wistful sphinx, made it necessary for him to kiss her. . . . He was Clara's white heavy arms, her throat, her moving bosom. That seemed to be himself. Then away somewhere the play went on, and he was identified with that also. There was no himself. The gray and black eyes of Clara, her bosom coming down on him, her arm that he held gripped between his hands, were all that existed. Then he felt himself small and helpless, her towering in her force above him. (Ibid., 321)

If Paul could blame his first failure in love on Miriam, Clara would blame him for his second. She complained that he never gave himself to her. He replied, "If I start to make love to you, I just go like a leaf down the wind." "And leave me out of count," she returned (ibid., 352). "She was afraid of the man who was not there with her, whom she could feel behind this make-believe lover; somebody sinister, that filled her with horror . . . it made her feel as if death itself had her in its grip" (ibid., 374). "There was something evanescent about Morel, she thought, something shifting and false. He would never make sure ground for a woman to stand on" (ibid., 393). Paul felt this very keenly:

> You know, mother, I think there must be something the matter with me, that I *can't* love. When she's there, as a rule, I *do* love her. Sometimes, when I see her just as the *woman*, I love her, mother; but then, when she talks and criticizes, I often don't listen to her. (Ibid., 339)

He knows the answer to his own question: no other woman can hold him so long as his mother lives. He says it himself on the next page. Unfortunately the novel ends too soon after Mrs. Morel's death for us to learn whether Paul has, indeed, been freed from the grasp of the demon lover.

It is easy to see why he is mortally afraid of being sucked dry by Miriam or of being overwhelmed by Clara. These are but shadows of the threat his mother poses for him. Because Mrs. Morel has been so needy and clinging, intimacy has, in Paul's experience, come to mean the threat of being drained and smothered. Miriam and Clara function for Paul as fragments of his mother, and they see him as undeveloped, undependable, unable to love, and unable to be loved. For all his charms and accomplishments, he is a "mama's boy" who flees intimacy.

Paul's mother lived in an inaccessible narcissistic cocoon,[2] leaving Paul feeling abandoned and unworthy of love and companionship.

---

2. By "narcissistic cocoon," I refer to the remoteness and self-referenced quality of an individual suffering from what Balint calls the "basic fault" or what Kohut calls the narcissistic personality. It is as though these people cannot be reached for genuine interpersonal communication, even though they may be sufficiently socialized as to hide this "wound" from superficial observation.

Her emotional treachery taught him that he was unworthy of real affection or high regard. He was *almost* worthy. He would do in a pinch to distract her from her grieving over the people she evidently preferred to him. Still, she gave him an illusory solidity—as long as he could tolerate her draining, smothering, and clinging behavior. Because it was such a relief from abandonment, Paul found these conditions quite agreeable, indeed a privilege. As seems often to be the case, he clung all the more tightly to a withholding mother—as though she might at any moment gratify his needs and begin supplying him stability and support. Because he remained suspended between her illusory promise and his own gaping wound, his mother's death might prove a blessing for him. It would surely end his suspension; and if he did not find another woman to depend upon, he might begin to explore his own resources.

For Paul Morel, then, the demon lover's power derives from her seeming to offer him access to the unity, balance, and foundational stability of the Self. In Tillich's language, Paul sees Clara and Miriam as bearers of the Holy Unification of Self. They do bear this, as everyone does. Paul is not wrong about their having very great significance for him. His mistake is to believe that he will achieve self-transcendence through them, by possessing them in a literal sense. In this literalism he distorts them as symbols of his own self-transcendence.

There is no wonder that our demon lovers always mirror our own psychic woundedness. They are a crystallization of everything that is unfinished, unwhole, and unbalanced in us. We fall in love with them because we rightly see in them the secret of our potential wholeness. I would like to think that our association with demon lovers can crucially assist our striving for wholeness. This is the topic of the next chapter. Abdul's grotesque experience with the demon lover may very possibly have made him not only sadder but truly wiser and truly richer. Perhaps his love affair with the Queen of the Jinn has transformed him so profoundly that he now is familiar with truths the rest of us are very unlikely to encounter and that he is rich in a way we cannot fully appreciate.

6

The Unholy Marriage: Obsession's Soul

Common sense and, I fear, the majority of psychotherapists would have us avoid the demon lover like sin. According to this view, we get involved in self-destructive patterns of behavior, and the only way to deal with them is to recognize them for what they are and exert our willpower to stop. Such a view underestimates the deeper strata of the psyche and the powerful unconscious "will" of the archetypes. These deep structural elements are stronger than the ego and, if not integrated, are sure to find some means of expressing themselves—whether in boredom and depression or in new self-destructive patterns. The common view also overlooks the divine spark in the demon lover. We are obsessed with him (or her) for a reason; he is challenging us with important psychological work, the kind of work James Hillman so felicitously calls "soul making." When we encounter someone who arouses a response of this magnitude, an obsession this insistent, we are being confronted with some essential part of our soul that hitherto has been inaccessible to us. To forget, close off, or suppress this tantalizing new dimension of our psyche is very difficult to accomplish. The cost of successful repression is to remain undeveloped, carrying around with us a certain deadness or flatness. We become like Paul Morel, unable to get on with life after his mother's death.

That we have a healthy need for the demon lover may be concluded from some of the initial symptoms of our fascination with him. Very frequently people seem to "come alive" on beginning an affair with an individual who later proves to be the focus of a powerful obsession. I have seen several cases in which a marriage seems to profit when one of the partners falls in love with a third person. The fact that immense difficulties lie in wait in the near future can hardly deny the signs of health that such an influx of new psychic energy occasions. It is a sure indication that the individual and/or the marriage has been only half alive. Flaubert describes Mme. Bovary quite flatteringly during the same period that she was sinking into her "sensual drunkenness":

> Never had Mme. Bovary been so beautiful as at this period; she had that indefinable beauty that results from joy, from enthusiasm, from success, and that is only the harmony of temperament with circumstances. . . . Charles, as when they were first married, thought her delicious and quite irresistible. (211)

Charles and Emma had married in a most unconscious manner, each expecting the other to do the work of keeping them joyful, enthusiastic, and successful; neither took any responsibility for the other or for himself. Without fundamental change in their attitudes, there is no alternative to Emma's having a chain of demon lovers. She repeats the beginning of the affair over and over, rather like an alcoholic striving for the elusive moment of peaceful well-being.

In *The Lover*, Marguerite Duras gives us a much more specific image of what the demon lover provides. In this passage, the French teenager is aware of a major contribution she makes to her Chinese lover's psyche:

> He hasn't the strength to love me in opposition to his father, to possess me, take me away. He often weeps because he can't find the strength to love beyond fear. His heroism is me, his cravenness is his father's money. (49)

If she were demon enough to rouse him to stand up to his father and embrace life on a technician's salary, and if he actually did take her away, he would begin to be a hero. He would take possession of his own soul. I doubt they would have lived "happily ever after," but he would really have begun work on the part of his soul that had been flattened and deadened by his father's money. His masculine courage would give him pride and buoyancy. His pessimism would lessen. So far from doing him harm, the demon lover stirs him to the point where he sees what is required of him. The man's pathology lies in his spinelessness, not at all in his falling in love. Life has thrown her in his path to lure him into becoming himself.

I am inclined to believe that all cases of obsession over a demon lover admit of such a diagnosis. Unfortunately, however, not all cases of obsessive love allow themselves to be delineated so crisply as Duras's narrative. Sometimes one knows one is being made more whole by one's erotic partnership even though all seems hopeless from a purely external perspective. Dostoyevsky's *The Insulted and Injured* describes just such a love affair. Vanya, the narrator, is in love with Natasha, who has fallen into a demonic obsession with Alyosha. Alyosha loves her dearly, after his inadequate fashion, but allows himself to be pressured by his father into marrying Katya (whom he also loves). Although he never positively says so, I have no doubt that Vanya feels he is benefiting in a "soul-making" fashion from his "Platonic" love affair with Natasha. He has accepted the naked sword separating them and makes little reference to his obsession. He stays as near to her as he can, participates in her life as fully as circumstances will allow, and serves her openheartedly, though not abjectly. Natasha is something of a hysterical female, tied by the conventions of nineteenth-century society in St. Petersburg, but she takes a very similar stance toward Alyosha as Vanya does toward her:

> "Yes, I love him as though I were mad," she answered, turning pale as though in bodily pain. "I never loved you like that, Vanya. . . . I don't love him in the right way. . . . Why he's sworn to love me, made all sorts of promises; but I don't trust one of his promises . . . though I knew he wasn't lying to me, and can't lie. . . . I'm glad to be his slave . . . ; to put up with anything from him, anything, so long as he is with me, so long as I can look at him! I think he might even love another woman if only I were there, if only I might be near. Isn't that abject, Vanya?" (1962: 38)

Vanya understands very well—particularly after he has himself met Alyosha:

The look in his eyes, gentle and candid, penetrated to my heart. . . .

It is true that he had some unpleasant traits, some of the bad habits characteristic of aristocratic society: frivolity, self-complacency, and polite insolence. But he was so candid and simple at heart that he was the first to blame himself for these defects. . . . Even egoism in him was rather attractive, just perhaps because it was open and not concealed. There was nothing reserved about him. He was weak, confiding, and faint-hearted; he had no will whatever. . . . Men like him are destined never to grow up. (Ibid., 40)

Alyosha's pure, gentle, childlike soul is irresistible to both of them. One can very easily imagine such a severely neurotic individual bearing the divine spark in his soul. He thereby arouses in Natasha a kind of inspiration and joy that is reward enough for all her suffering. She is not bitter about or destroyed by Alyosha's marriage with Katya. Although she sacrificed her reputation for him, there is no doubt that the hectic, short-term relationship was worth it to her. Natasha herself does not think in these terms, but it is clear to the modern reader that the affair assisted her maturation process and changed her relationship with her parents—particularly with her naive and childlike father.

The theme of the transformative potential of the demon lover occurs frequently in the novels of Dostoyevsky. My favorite is the relationship in *The Brothers Karamazov* between Dmitry Karamazov, a good-hearted but savagely impulsive soldier, and Grushenka Svetlov, a beautiful, peasant-featured, incest survivor, who has inherited money and tended it well. Both are full of self-hatred. Dmitry says he prefers women from the back streets: "There you find true adventures, . . . gold nuggets in the dirt" (1958: 124). In the frenzy of his demonic eros, he calls Grushenka a slut and says he loves and hates her at the same time (ibid., 119). He has a genuine understanding of the demon lover, saying that beauty is a terrible and mysterious thing, where "God and the devil are fighting for mastery, and the battlefield is the heart of man" (ibid., 124).

"As soon as I began visiting Grushenka, I ceased to be engaged to Katerina. I've ceased to be an honest man. I realize that alright.

. . . At first I went to beat her. For I knew . . . that she was a pitiless, cunning she-devil. I went to beat hell out of her and I stayed there. . . . That she-devil Grushenka has a kind of curve of the body which can be detected on her foot. You can see it even in the little toe of her left foot. I saw it and kissed it, but that was all—I swear! She says to me, 'I'll marry you if you like for you're a pauper. Promise not to beat me and to let me do what I like, and perhaps I'll marry you.' She laughed. And she is laughing still!" . . .

"And you really want to marry her?"

"If she wants me to, I shall marry her at once, if not, I shall stay with her just the same. I shall be the caretaker in her yard." (Ibid., 136f.)

These words, filled with self-hate, emphasize the shadow side of Grushenka. On hearing them, Dmitry's younger brother, the novice monk Alyosha, concludes that Grushenka must be a wicked woman. He goes to her, therefore, immediately after the death of his spiritual master. He says he felt drawn to her because he was mean and wicked himself. But what he found was: "a true sister. I've found a treasure—a loving soul" (ibid., 413). Again Dostoyevsky uses the device of an innocent narrator to give us a dependable perspective on things. Behind the notorious life, the cunning, and the curves is a pure soul, a divine spark.

Dmitry's impetuosity saves his soul.[1] Unlike Duras's wealthy Milquetoast and unlike Paul Morel, he dares (albeit in a frenzy) to risk a lifetime of disgrace and agony for "one hour, one minute" with Grushenka (ibid., 514). They meet, and each discovers to his surprise that the other is a bearer of a divine spark. They are gradually sobered, brought down to earth, transformed by what they have seen in the other's soul and in their own. The nature of the transformation may be surmised from the following description of Grushenka, two months after their night of love and Dmitry's arrest for the murder of his father (ironically, a crime he did not commit):

---

1. But it also results in his conviction on charges of parricide and his sentence to Siberia, whither he will probably be followed by Grushenka.

She had greatly changed, had grown thin and sallow-faced, though now for nearly two weeks she had been well enough to go out. But, in Alyosha's view, her face seemed much more attractive than before and he looked to meet her eyes when he went into her room. There seemed to be a look of firmness and greater comprehension in her eyes. There were suggestions of some spiritual change in her, of a resolution that appeared to be humble and unalterable, good and irrevocable . . . [there was] no trace of her former frivolity . . . [but she] had not lost her former youthful gaiety. . . . There was a soft light in her once proud eyes, and yet— and yet they blazed with an ominous fire at times, too, when an old anxiety stole into her heart, an anxiety that had never abated, but had even grown stronger . . . Katerina. (Ibid., 660)

Her blazing jealousy tells us that Dmitry is still a bit of a demon lover for her; but we can see how much of her wholeness she has reclaimed from behind the repressive force of her former self-hatred, frivolity, grandiosity, and cunning.

In Jungian language, the demon lover results from failure to differentiate our anima or animus from our shadow. The numinous, contrasexual other within us whose job it is to relate us to the Self (anima or animus) is contaminated with everything we wish we did not have to deal with (shadow). As a major component of the unconscious, the shadow encompasses a large quantity of psychic energy. When this is added to the energy already governed by the anima, the resulting figure can be extraordinarily powerful, fascinating, and fearsome. It is the reason the demon lover may appear so morally questionable, so immature, so bestial. Our obsessiveness on his account results from our indecisiveness. On the one horn of the dilemma, we cannot decide whether to modify, repudiate, or disengage from the values that have guided us to this point in our lives. These values have driven all contrary tendencies into the shadow. We are afraid that if we act upon this contrariety we will lose our bearings, be sent to hell, dishonor ourselves. On the other horn of the dilemma, if we hold on to the values of our past, we gain a certain security at the expense of a hollow feeling that we have betrayed ourselves by failing to meet a challenge.

Although this dilemma is apt to present itself as a momentous, once-and-for-all decision, the job of reclaiming shadow material from the unconscious proceeds in increments and requires many very ordinary decisions. A Japanese fairy tale expresses this reality through the image of transforming a shadowy, grotesque mermaid into a beautiful woman. Prince Horawi, son of the God of the Mountain, is driven by his jealous older brother out of the mountains to the sea, where he meets a man clad in seaweed and shells who takes him through a whirlpool to an undersea world of great beauty. There he meets an entrancing young woman named Toyotama, who is also a sea dragon and the daughter of the God of the Sea. They marry and live a blissful existence. Eventually Horawi feels homesick for the mountains and persuades the pregnant Toyotama to have her baby on land and to live with him there. Her agreement bears the condition that he must precede her to land and build her a hut on shore, thatched with cormorant feathers. She will appear when the baby is due, but he is not to look on her again until the baby is born.

Back on land, Horawi defeats his brother, builds the hut, and waits what seems a long, long time for Toyotama to appear. One night he hears cries of labor and peeks out to see his wife lying on the sand of the shore. She gestures in horror for him to leave. At dawn he finds the newborn child and catches sight of a sea dragon's tail as it slithers into the surf (Time-Life [a], 87–95).

Horawi's inability to stand up to his aggressive shadow, portrayed by his brother, drives him to the kingdom opposite to that of his birth. This would mean that, on account of something he cannot handle in everyday life, he undergoes a depression that takes him into depths of the unconscious where he has never been before. There he meets a monstrous demon lover in the form of a sea dragon, but he is so conscious of the divine spark she bears that he sees her as a woman of unparalleled beauty. His urgency to return to land represents his need to integrate this new unconscious material. There are three indications that he attains partial success. First, he comes back with sufficient force to stand up to his brother, indicating that a large quantity of psychic energy that had been locked away in the shadow is now available for his conscious use. Second, he finally sees the shadow side of his lover—as important for him as it was for Elsa in Lohengrin and for Psyche in the story of Eros and Psyche. Third, although the monstrous part of the shadow has slithered back into the unconscious, he is left with a baby. This would represent the newborn, undeveloped potential that his new integration has made possible. There is no blissful "happy ever after" in this story. Horawi now has to raise and enjoy his child, and probably fall in love again.

Parallels to this theme of a transforming marriage with the demon lover can be found in several traditions. The following story comes from a Siberian Goldi shaman. His marriage to the demon lover has been his schooling and the source of his personal power:

Once I was asleep on my sick-bed, when a spirit approached me. It was a very beautiful woman. Her figure was very slight, she was no more than half an arshin (71 cm.) tall. Her face and attire were quite as those of our Gold women. . . . She said: "I am the 'ayami' of your ancestors the Shamans. I taught them shamaning. Now I am going to teach you. The old shamans have died off, and there is no one to heal people. You are to become a shaman." . . .

She has been coming to me ever since, and I sleep with her as with my own wife, but we have no children. She lives quite by herself without any relatives in a hut, on a mountain, but she often changes her abode. Sometimes she comes under the aspect of an old woman, and sometimes under that of a wolf, so that she is terrible to look at. Sometimes she comes as a winged tiger. I mount it and she takes me to show me different countries. . . .

Now my "ayami" does not come to me as frequently as before. Formerly, when teaching me, she used to come every night. She has given me three assistants—[panther, bear, and tiger]. They come to me in my dreams, and appear whenever I summon them while shamaning. If one of them refuses to come, the "ayami" makes them obey, . . . When I am shamaning, the "ayami" and the assistant spirits are possessing me: whether big or small, they penetrate me as smoke or vapour would. When the "ayami" is within me, it is she who speaks through my mouth, and she does everything herself. . . . (Eliade, 1951/64: 72f.)

This shamanic initiation story is a very important model for the unholy marriage, that is, the long-term relationship with a demon lover. Even more than the tale of Horawi, it indicates the powerful transformation and integration of personality that a demon lover can effect in us. Again the demon comes from deep in the unconscious, this time occasioned by the man's sickness; in the case of Horawi, it was his defeat, expatriation, and depression that brought the demon-anima into consciousness. She is sexy or old, and dangerous as a wild animal; but over time she teaches him, gives him assistants, and shows him different countries.

This happens whenever we meet a demon lover. Since her demonic nature stems in part from the fact that she comes out of our unlived life, she has boundless realms, indeed, to show us, and scary ones, too. When we become frightened or disgusted by our tendency to obsess about her and prematurely end the relationship, we never come to learn these important things about ourselves and we never claim the psychic energy that has been locked up in the forbidden closets of our soul. Horawi returns from his marriage with the sea dragon with the power to defeat his evil brother. The Goldi shaman gains the power to heal souls and bodies.

These achievements are not easily or quickly made. In general it takes months, years, decades to learn what our demon lover has to tell us. This is why I speak of an unholy *marriage,* because it requires a substantial commitment over a good length of time. It is very frequently a daring process as well. The imagery in the shamanic experience is frightening because we cannot enter the tiger pit of our psyche to tame the wild animals without taking a sizable risk. In the Goldi story, the dangerous and beneficial power of the internal releasing mechanisms is represented by the frightening aspects under which the *ayami* can appear and especially by the three fierce animal assistants the shaman acquires and learns how to use.

Marriage with the demon lover has been a recurrent theme in Christianity. One thinks, perhaps, of Nathaniel Hawthorne's *Scarlet Letter,* Sinclair Lewis's *Elmer Gantry,* and recent scandals involving television evangelists. But the tradition goes all the way back to the New Testament (Acts 8:9–24), where a magician named Simon (Simon Magus) is described as travelling about with a certain Helena whom he claimed to have found in a brothel in Tyre and held up as the lowliest and most recent incarnation of the fallen female principle of the godhead. He believed himself a Christian, having been converted through the preaching of the Apostle Philip. The second-century Christian apologist Irenaeus portrays Simon as a gnostic and libertine dissident of true Christianity. Modern scholarship sees him as a representative of one of the multitude of competing religious trends in the late antique babel out of which Christianity eventually emerged as the spiritual standard-bearer of western culture. In Simon's mythological thinking, Thought broke away from her father, Silence, resulting in an alienation and deterioration of divine elements, which she dragged down from highest heaven into the material cosmos. The cosmos was filled with confusion and darkness, being governed by a large number of angels, each striving wickedly like jinn or hungry ghosts for mastery of the whole. Simon Magus believed he was reestablishing the order of both cosmos and *pleroma* (the heavenly "fullness" of divine light) by setting himself and Helena before his followers as incarnations of Silence and Thought, the dual object of enlightened belief.

There can be little doubt that what Simon found in the brothel was a woman on whom he could project both his anima and his shadow. She was, for him, a demon lover and probably contributed immensely to the inflation by which he identified himself and Helena, jointly, as divine. Probably, too, Simon was able to recognize the divine spark in Helena. Two factors set him outside the commonplace in Christian tradition: he marries—or at least pursues an ongoing relationship with—the demon lover, and he publicizes this. The Elmer Gantrys see their erotic pursuits as sins to be hidden and remain blind to the divine spark that inspires their obsessions. The desert saints of early Christianity became famous for their victorious bouts with sexual temptation, thereby succeeding in repressing the shadow—like Thomas Aquinas driving the harlot from his prison cell with a red-hot poker.

Like Dmitry Karamazov and the Goldi shaman cited above, Simon Magus chose a bold and dangerous course. Its justification resides in the divine spark, the confidence that one has seen the other through the lens of the anima or animus—a higher truth than that touted officially or understood by the masses. Although we know nothing of Simon's continuing career, it is evident that his path is not an easy one to follow. I have seen a number of dramatic failures.

A Catholic laborer in his late twenties, for example, although quite obsessive in his prudish ideas regarding sex, married a stripper who worked a three-city circuit and was therefore out of town more than half the time. When she was home, he was both proud and afraid of her. When she was away, he was tormented by thoughts of her unfaithfulness and the certainty of divine condemnation. Eventually the tension broke him. He fell into a psychosis and was committed to a state hospital, where he came to believe he was Michael the Archangel who drove the fallen angels out of heaven. He began preaching, writing letters, and telephoning from the hospital everyone he could think of with a message of divine love and brimstone.

A born-again Christian, also in his late twenties, a driven and highly successful salesman, one day met a neighbor who earned her living as a nude go-go dancer. He courted her earnestly with an amorous message of Christian fundamentalism. Inwardly, he struggled sincerely with his own moral principles, while outwardly he offended his coreligionists by his compromising presence in her apartment in the evenings and again early in the morning for breakfast. Finally, his firm was forced to demote him, having received a number of calls from clients complaining about the "bimbo" he brought with him on his business calls.

Clearly physical and affectionate nearness with the demon lover is not sufficient to constitute a transformative "marriage" with her or him. Something akin to the learning and redeeming experiences of Prince Horawi and the Goldi shaman is essential. Indian culture provides us some hints in this direction. Indeed, probably the first record of a Simon Magus–type figure is to be found in the *Atharva Veda* (ca. 900 B.C.), one of the four original sacred books of India. There appears a description of a *"vratya,* a non-Vedic priest, who travelled from place to place in a cart with a woman whom he prostituted and a musician who performed for him at his rites." Later the term *vratya* came to mean one who had fallen from the true practices of the Aryan religion; but the original *vratyas* may have constituted one of the sources of asceticism in Hinduism (Basham, 243). Dating from almost two millennia *earlier* than the *Atharva Veda* is a small seal from the city of Mohenjo Daro that shows a kind of animal-headed Shiva figure, sitting cross-legged as if in meditation (Shiva being the Lord of Yoga), with an erect penis (ibid., plate 9, c). Then, around A.D. 1000, one finds advocated by certain Tantrists "daily intercourse in out of the way places with twelve-year-old girls of the Candala [untouchable] caste" (Conze: 195). Eliade makes sense of this as follows:

> Every naked woman incarnates *prakriti* . . . [the] limitless capacity to create. . . . If, in the presence of the naked woman, one does not find in one's inmost being the same terrifying emotion that one feels before the revelation of the cosmic mystery, there is no rite, there is only a secular act. . . . (1954/69: 259)

Evidently he is trying to describe something very closely related to what I have called the Self, the divine spark, the unification and balance of psychic wholeness, or unity with the cosmos. The following may be taken as an indication of what he means by a "rite":

> [In] the profound mystical movement known as Sahajiya, . . . sexual union is understood as a means of obtaining "supreme bliss' *(mahasukha)*, and it must never end in seminal emission. *Maithuna* [ritual sexual union] makes its appearance as the consummation of a long and difficult apprenticeship. The neophyte must acquire perfect control of his senses, and, to this end, he must approach the "devout woman" *(nayika)* by stages and transform her into a goddess through an interiorized iconographic dramaturgy. Thus, for the first four months, he should wait upon her like a servant, sleep in the same room with her, then at her feet. During the next four months, while continuing to wait on her as before, he sleeps in the same bed, on the left side. During a third four months, he will sleep on the right side, then they will sleep embracing, etc. (Ibid., 266)

What Eliade here calls the effort to "acquire perfect control of his senses" is a part of what I have described as the larger work of integrating and redeeming shadow material. The unholy marriage with the demon lover—be she an urban American "bimbo," one of Dmitry's golden nuggets from the back streets of St. Petersburg, or an untouchable from Calcutta—transforms us only when we begin to do the very difficult and humdrum work of acquainting ourselves with our own inner demon.

If we have learned anything from this study, it is that the demonic element has at least as much to do with us as with the demon lover. If our shadow side were not so inexperienced and unacknowledged, we would not be so fascinated by the shadow we think we see in him or her. The Tantrists know that; it is the reason the male practitioner devotes a full twelve months to approaching ritually the devout woman, the *nayika*. One could hardly wish for a more detailed description of the naked sword, the deliberately accepted separation between us and our beloved. It is meant to interrupt the automatic drop in consciousness experienced in profane (as opposed to sacred) sexuality. Instead of a union in which they lose themselves, the Tantrists are striving for a union in which they become themselves more fully. For this they need the sword of their ritual to place distance between themselves and their *nayika* so that they can acquaint themselves with their lust, their longing for the bliss of unconscious rocking, their ego-centeredness, and many more shadowy motivations. All these get in their way of coming to know the Self and their partner.

I do not know the end of the salesman's story. Perhaps the demotion shocked him into catching a glimpse of his demon lover's dragon-tail. In any event, it appears that his efforts to marry his demon were very sincerely connected with his fundamentalist faith. The theological and social pressures brought to bear on him through his religion actually resulted in his accepting the naked sword. He was visiting with her in the evenings and breakfasting with her in the mornings but spending the nights in his own apartment. If he stays with the challenge she offers him and soberly deals with the difficulties—professional, social, theological, and psychological—he will begin to acquaint himself with his shadow. Simultaneously, he will become acquainted with the real woman whom he has been seeing as his demon lover.

The naked sword *enables* transformation. It gives us the distance to see what has to be done. We still have to do the work ourselves— or at least actively cooperate with an integrating process that seems to emerge from the level of Self. Very frequently, especially in the beginning of a relationship, the work consists above all in recognizing and acknowledging our shadow. An excellent example of a failure along these lines appears in Hardy's novel, *Tess of the D'Urbervilles*. It is several years after Tess's tragic deflowering. She has met a young, theologically rebellious, overly earnest, fresh-faced clergyman with the improbably appropriate name of Angel Clare. Her tragedy makes her much more conscious and capable of love than he:

> Clare knew that she loved him—every curve of her form showed that—but he did not know at that time the full depth of her devotion, its single-mindedness, its meekness; what long suffering it guaranteed, what honesty, what endurance, what good faith. (1964: 231)

He does not know these things in her because he has not become conscious of them in himself. He is inflated with his theological ideas of how things *should* be and has not taken a good look at himself. When, shortly after their wedding, Tess confesses her sin to him, he says, "The woman I've been loving is not you" (ibid., 246). It could hardly be better said. He has been loving his fanciful image of what Tess "should" be rather than the woman she is. He has been covering her with the mask of his projection: "I thought . . . that by giving up all ambition to win a wife with social standing . . . I should secure rustic innocence as surely as I should secure pink cheeks" (ibid., 255).

There is something he cannot bear to see in her. He wanted a girl with pink cheeks to match his own, and he succeeded better than he could have guessed. In fact she is still a good deal fresher-cheeked than he, in that his "forty-eight hour dissipation" with a woman appears quite tawdry in comparison with her integrity. He appears not to know how he felt about that woman, or even how he feels now as he stands facing this disappointing new Tess. Not able to bear living with the tainted, real Tess, he leaves for South America. He runs halfway around the world to avoid acknowledging the shadow of ecclesiastically and socially unsanctified love. He will not be able to understand Tess's integrity until he acquaints himself with exactly what did happen during that "dissipation" and in the relationship that made it possible.

His leaving implies that he values the security of his old beliefs, his old self-image, above the dangerous, new, wider perspective she offers him. If he can leave with so little struggle, he could hardly have seen her divine spark—at least not knowingly. He is apparently not able to see it because it is also the spark in the center of the shadow that he refuses to acknowledge. When we *can* see the divine spark, then the "asceticism" of the unholy marriage, the work of acquainting ourselves with our own shadow, becomes a good deal easier. The spark holds us. It is a light at the end of our tunnel. If Angel Clare cannot see it, there is less to wonder about his departure for South America.

The notion of a spark of divinity, reality, or truth being hidden within dark, evil, deceptive, or profane appearances is very widespread in the history of religions. The Hindu Upanishads, for example, have as their central theme the reality of transcendent, invisible *brahman* beneath worldly, material form. The goal of Hinduism is to come to realize that "Thou art that [*brahman*]" (*Tat tvam asi*). In Islamic mysticism, as in Jewish, even the words of Scripture are taken as outer form, concealing a deeper, esoteric truth. But the actual image of sparks of divine life being hidden in profane reality and awaiting the work of right-seeing human beings to set them free is most clearly to be found in the Western gnostic[2] tradition, which has given rise to important mystical movements within Christianity, Judaism, and Islam. Some of the earliest and best-documented texts come from contemporaries of Simon Magus and their descendants. Their elaborate cosmologies envisioned a pure, formless Light (the ineffable godhead) emanating a series of divine manifestations, each less purely light and more formed than the last. Finally one, usually feminine, divine manifestation breaks away from the *pleroma* (heavenly "fullness" of divine light) and falls into the cosmos, where her light is tragically scattered and mixed with matter. After this tragedy, both God and the universe are unhappy until the sparks of divine light can be restored to oneness.

---

2. The words *gnostic* and *gnosticism* are derived from the Greek word *gnosis*, meaning experiential, mystical knowledge. Christians have traditionally understood Gnosticism to be a heresy against which the second-century church struggled. Broader historical studies, however, have demonstrated that well-developed gnostic tendencies were already flourishing before the birth of Christ, and in Jewish and pagan circles as well as Christian communities.

In the Jewish mystical tradition, Kabbalah, Rabbi Isaac Luria of the town of Safed in Palestine (1534–1572) developed one of the most influential mystical theologies based on the mythic image of hidden divine sparks. In his view, the divine light emanating from the Shekhinah (literally, the divine "indwelling," the female principle within the godhead) had to be collected in bowls or vessels, lest it revert directly back to the divinity. Without "garbs" or vessels, the light could not be made manifest. Unfortunately, however, the vessels were not strong enough. When they broke, the divine light was scattered into every part of the material world. All this took place before the beginning of time. Two historical events, however, have repeated the scattering of the light: Adam's sin and the Diaspora (*galut*) of the Jews.

> Whenever we fall into sin we cause a repetition of . . . the confusion of the holy with the unclean, the "fall" of Shekhinah and her exile. "Sparks of Shekhinah" are scattered in all worlds and "there is no sphere of existence including organic and inorganic nature, that is not full of holy sparks which are mixed up with the Kelipoth ["shells" which hide the sparks] and need to be separated from them and lifted up." (Scholem 1941: 280)

However regrettable this cosmic disaster may be, it is a blessing in disguise; for it means that the whole world and all of us in it are shot through with the divine fire. It also means that we human beings who are aware of this situation, who have real experiential knowledge (gnosis) of the sparks and shells—we have an obligation and a very lofty calling. We are called to become participants with God in carrying out the divine will of manifesting the Light. We can help effect the restoration of divine unity: "The restoration of the ideal order is also the secret purpose of existence. Salvation means actually nothing but restitution, reintegration of the original whole, or *Tikkun*" (ibid., 268). In practical terms this means that when food is grown, prepared, or eaten by Jews who are aware of the sparks hidden within the shells of the fields, the grain stalks, the flour, and the bread, the sparks are freed from these material objects and returned to their Source. The same may be said for any of the activities of everyday life. For the one who has *gnosis* for the real nature of the world, every act is a sacred contribution to the divine drama of *tikkun*. "The Children of Israel 'lift up the sparks' not only from the places trodden by their feet in their Galut [diaspora], but also, by their deeds, from the cosmos itself" (Scholem, 1971: 46).

Nearly two centuries after Luria, the mystical theology of the shells and sparks was popularized and personalized by Israel ben Eliezer (1700–1760), known as the Baal Shem Tov ("Master of the Good Name") and the founder of Hasidism. He was the first to speak of each individual living in a world of his own sparks, so that each action of his life is an opportunity to lift his sparks (ibid., 190). When a Hasid (pious one) is in communion with God *(devekut)*, every act performed contributes to *tikkun*. Thus Rabbi Dov Baer, the Maggid of Mezritch, one of the Baal Shem's most important followers, says:

> Even by eating and drinking in purity and holiness, it is possible to hasten the coming of redemption, because through the *kavanot,* the intentions of eating, it is possible to remove the precious from the worthless, thus emptying the "Other Side" of the holy sparks that have remained in it. (Buber 1960: 208)

The words of the Baal Shem himself, as recorded by Buber, have a much more rough, lively, and mythic ring to them:

> It is known that each spark that dwells in a stone or plant or another creature . . . is in prison, cannot stretch out its hands and feet and cannot speak, but its head lies on its knees. And who with the good strength of his spirit is able to raise the holy spark from stone to plant, and from plant to animal, from animal to speaking being, he leads it into freedom, and no setting free of captives is greater than this. It is as when a king's son is rescued from captivity and brought to his father. (Buber 1958: 187f.)

Even sin is not without its divine spark and its implicit holiness, according to the Baal Shem:

In all that is in the world dwell holy sparks, no thing is empty of them. In the actions of men also, indeed even in the sins that a man does, dwell holy sparks of the glory of God. And what is it that the sparks await that dwell in the sins? It is the turning. In the hour where you turn on account of sin, you raise to the higher world the sparks that were in it. (Ibid., 189)

At the beginning of Dostoyevsky's novel, Dmitry Karamazov and Grushenka are seeing much more of the shells of one another than of the sparks. Even assuming some dim awareness of the sparks, they are too taken with one another in a profane manner. Dmitry is taken with Grushenka's physical beauty, her curves, her imperious air, her girlish impetuosity and mocking laughter. Grushenka is awakened by Dmitry's reckless gallantry, given a pleasant sense of hope by his optimism, and charmed by his rugged, emotional honesty. To all external appearances, they are both quite formidable and challenging individuals. No mistake there. But, within their souls, at the very center of their beings, crouch their sparks—heads upon their knees. This expression from the Baal Shem catches exactly the gloomy depression and self-loathing in the pit of Dostoyevsky's protagonists.

Their hectic, embattled *Liebesnacht* (the "night of love" in *Tristan und Isolde*) changes this. Their captive sparks have been set free. In that new sense of depth and sobriety, seriousness of purpose and humble patience in their commitment to one another, the sparks in their souls have been "raised" at least a full life-stage (as from stone to plant or animal to speaking being). There is no doubt they still have to go a long way. They have by no means overcome their self-loathing, as the following words of Grushenka make clear:

"If we are to love one another, then let's love properly! I shall be your slave now, your slave for the rest of my life. It is sweet to be a slave! Kiss me! Beat me, torture me, do what you want with me. . . . Oh, I deserve to be tortured. . . . Stop! Wait, later, I don't want to now," she pushed him away suddenly. "Go away, Mitya, I'll go and have some wine now. I want to get drunk, I'm going to get drunk and dance. Yes I will!" (Dostoyevsky, 1958: 516)

Subsequent events prove that Grushenka's submission, here, is genuine—even to the point of faithfulness to a Dmitry falsely convicted of parricide. Without relinquishing her sense of shame and unworthiness, she drops her obsession over reconciling herself with the social order (becoming an honorable woman in the eyes of the town). She finds, as we can judge by the spiritual transformation Alyosha sees in her two months later, an inner faithfulness to a spark of truth in Dmitry's soul. Shortly after his arrest, when Dmitry vows to her that he is not guilty of his father's murder, she blesses herself before an icon on the wall and turns to the examining magistrate and tells him, "He'll never deceive anyone. He'll always tell the truth, you can believe it" (ibid., 594). There can be no doubt that this comes from her heart. It is a picture of Grushenka's soul intermediate between the *Liebesnacht* and Alyosha's view two months later.

Thus what Dostoyevsky shows us of Grushenka is a pair of quite disparate views and a complicated transition between them. The "outer" view of a cunning, money-hungry, loose woman is not wholly false; but it is the "shell" that hides her spark. When Dmitry is enthralled by her outward appearance, she is thoroughly a demon lover for him. He is seeing primarily his projection onto her, as a mask that hides the deeper significance and even holiness of her personhood. At this point he does not yet know that it is the spark that holds him. All he knows is that the shell or mask has a kind of fascinating glow about it. We readers know the more profound reality through Alyosha's eyes, which are accustomed to look deeper than the shell. What happens in the *Liebesnacht* is that Dmitry and Grushenka see through to the sparks for the first time. At this point their projections are no longer acting as masks but as lenses. Having seen through to the reality of the Self, they are able to commit themselves seriously to one another; and each is able to be more tolerant with himself. Having caught a glimpse of the Self within, they can begin to let go of their desperation and get on with their lives in a much more confident manner.

It is clear from these considerations that the Hasidic metaphor of freeing the sparks from their shells and the psychological metaphor of relinquishing projection's mask in favor of its lens are very closely related. The parallel goes further. The Kabbalists say that the freed sparks return to the divine oneness, while we have said that to make use of projection's lens is to see the soul or Self level of the psyche. This means to relinquish the fragmentary and peripheral for what is whole and central. It means to come to know the divine spark within the beloved as well as in ourselves. Furthermore, to overcome the "demonism" of the demon lover means (in Tillich's language) to relinquish the "idolatry" of taking the symbol for the thing symbolized. It means to find the depth, source, center, and end of romantic love—the love of God.

The lives of the mystics provide us with many examples of an unholy marriage with a demon lover, which becomes transformed by the saint's faithfulness to the sparks concealed within the shells. I think of such major figures in the Catholic tradition as Saint Ignatius of Loyola and Saint Teresa of Ávila.

Ignatius (1491–1556) began his career as a soldier, fighting according to the romantic knightly ideal for the honor of a lady. He writes his autobiography in the third person:

> He imagined what he would do in the service of a certain lady, the means he would take so he could go to the country where she lived, the verses, the words he would say to her, the deeds of arms he would do in her service. He became so conceited with this that he did not consider how impossible it would be because the lady was not of the lower nobility nor a countess nor a duchess, but her station was higher than any of these. (23)

While recovering from a battle wound—his leg was shattered by a cannonball—he had nothing to read but a Bible and a *Lives of the Saints*. In seeking escape from his boredom and pain in these improbable volumes, Ignatius deepened his romantic love and discovered the divine spark that animated it. It introduced him to a new campaign of spiritual discovery, which led to his founding the Society of Jesus, the Jesuit Order of priests and lay brothers, under a banner reading, "For the Greater Glory of God and the Honor of the Blessed Virgin Mary." In the language of the Hasidim, we might say that the love of that earthly woman was but a shell concealing a spark of divine love, so that through his faithfulness to a single woman he discovered the One.

The story of Teresa of Ávila (1515–1582), as told by Victoria Lincoln, is not so different. The reformer, with John of the Cross, of the Carmelite Order of nuns and monks began her religious career in great spiritual ignorance—though she was hardly more ignorant than the great majority of her colleagues. She was very attractive to men, both laymen and monks, for her physical beauty and sparkling intelligence. At twenty-three she began to teach herself to pray, using de Osuna's *Spiritual Alphabet*. But it was not until the age of forty that she renounced a "lovemaking [with her confessors] that was both passionate and technically chaste" and which left her "torn between guilt and desire" (Lincoln, 37). The agent of the change was her discovery of Augustine's *Confessions,* just recently translated into Spanish. It introduced her to a love of God that transcended and deepened the love she had already known with men in holy orders.

On the basis of Teresa's sincerity and my own acquaintance with romantic love between celibate members of religious orders and their partners, I believe that those lesser loves, which she eventually repudiated, were also highly spiritual. I have no doubt that they derived their fascination for her in no small part from the divine sparks that dwelt within them and which she, with her spiritual gifts, was able to see quite clearly. Insofar as they claimed themselves to be the transcendental love she was searching for, they were demonic. For, as long as she clung to the individual men who enclosed the divine sparks like shells, she was unable to find the Source, Depth, End, and Center for which she was searching. However, through simultaneously pursuing both her relationships with her confessors and her quest to find and understand the love of God, she succeeded in freeing the divine spark from her demonic lovers. No less than this is the goal of the unholy marriage.

7

Seduction and Fidelity: Intimacy's Chambers

There is no love without some kind of drawing in or leading on—some kind of seduction. We perhaps tend to think that to seduce is to lead astray, to draw another person into sin—that seduction is the province of the demon lover. I am inclined to think, however, that we do not risk the liabilities of intimacy unless we are *enticed* into letting go our hold on the secure and familiar.

Originally, to seduce meant to lead *aside*—whether to safety or to ruin was not implied. The demon lover always leads us aside from our habitual purposes. We experience him (or her) as demonic because he leads us into dealings with our shadow that we have made it our business to avoid. He challenges our way of life and customary assumptions. When we are wedded to our old values, we inevitably fear his challenges and very possibly wonder about their morality. Then seduction seems to be a leading astray. When, however, we do not arrest the demon lover's challenge before having come to understand it, when we are led into discovering the mystery of our beloved's unique personhood—the divine spark—then we may say that we have been seduced into discovering our own Self as well as our beloved. Rumi knows the ambiguity of seduction very well, even with reference to the love of God:

You don't have "bad" days and "good" days.
You don't sometimes feel brilliant and sometimes dumb.
There's no studying, no scholarly thinking having to do with love,
but there's a great deal of plotting, and secret touching,
and nights you can't remember at all.
(Rumi, 1984: quatrain 674)

For Rumi and for me, the only love worthy of the name is that which centers and unites us—the love so transparent we can glimpse its foundation in the love of God.

Seduction's plotting, however, comes in many styles and with quite varying sets of implications. My first two examples come from Ingmar Bergman's comic treatment of the Don Juan legend, *The Devil's Eye*. When we first see the world's greatest seducer, he is in hell; and a beautiful woman is approaching him with a knife in her hand and a glint in her eye. She is evidently a victim of his villainies. he engages her boldly:

> You give me a thrill of delight. My breast will open as gladly to your dagger as your thighs opened to the sharp blade of my love. Give us the final ecstasy, the only one our bodies have not yet tasted.

Seconds later he is striving to "cool" her off by removing her clothes as he simultaneously fans the flames of her ardor with his intemperate words. There is no question the woman has been "turned aside" from her initial intention, but it is equally clear that Don Juan has led her to a deeper sentiment that underlay her rage.

In the same film, a rather different seduction is effected by Don Juan's valet, Pablo, on the matronly wife of a foolish country parson. Pablo begins by encouraging her to resist his advances on the grounds that it will heighten their pleasure. He then claims to read her character in her eyes, naming her prudence, affectionateness, and frail health, all of which forbid her to abandon herself to passion. He sees, as well, a dark, sensuous spot in her nature, which is able to express itself only in her dreams. Reminding her to resist, he says, "In your dreams you wallow in voluptuousness, to the very limit of pain and shame." She runs out of the room. But later he follows up with an appeal to her sympathy. He has suffered three hundred years of torment in hell for the ill luck of having died in the arms of his chambermaid. And now, when he has been sent to earth for twenty-four hours, he chances to meet the loveliest woman he has ever seen. He appeals to her maternal instincts. In yielding, she says: "You've done a rare thing—touched my heart—given me an experience. It entitles you to a reward."

Again, a bold display of seductive technique is based on a genuine reading of the woman's heart. The same is evidently true of Dostoyevsky's disreputable old Karamazov, father of Dmitry, Ivan, and Alyosha. General opinion holds him for a crass, sleazy libertine who succeeds in his self-centered ambitions only because he is so wealthy. He apparently even believes this himself, as he waits timidly for Grushenka to agree to become his mistress. He is believed to keep under his pillow an envelope addressed to her, his "chicken," containing three thousand rubles. But some of his words belie this portrait of a hopelessly insensitive man:

> According to my rule, you can find in every woman something— damn it!—something extraordinarily interesting, something you won't find in any other woman. Only you must know how to find it—that's the point! That requires talent! For me ugly women do not exist . . . the first thing to do with barefooted girls and ugly women is to take them by surprise. . . . They must be surprised till they're enraptured, till they're transfixed, till they're ashamed that such a gentleman should have fallen in love with such a swarthy creature. (1958: 159)

There is a simplicity and genuineness in old Karamazov that awakens our sympathy. Still his sentiments are not so different from those of Casanova or several of the literary Don Juans. I think in particular of the valet Leporello's famous aria (no. 4) in Mozart's *Don Giovanni*, cataloguing his master's conquests: "In Italy 640 . . . in Spain already 1003 . . . in winter he prefers them plump, in summer thin. . . ." He likes them young and old, fat and thin, rich and poor, so long as they wear skirts. But there is a cynicism here that we do not find in old Karamazov. It has to do with the Don's inconstancy. Molière's Don Juan hits the nail on the head:

> We savor an infinite sweetness in overcoming a young beauty's heart by a thousand acts of homage, in seeing day by day the little steps by which we progress, in combating by our transports, tears,

and sighs, the innocent modesty of a soul loath to surrender its arms, in forcing step by step, the little obstacles with which she resists, in conquering the scruples in which she takes honor, and bringing her gently to the point where we want to bring her. But once we are the master, there's nothing more to say and nothing more to wish for; all the beauty of the passion is finished, and in the tranquillity of such a love we fall asleep, unless some new object comes to awaken our desires and offer our heart the alluring charms of a conquest to be made. (322)

It is not love he is after, but conquest, an exercise of power. The marvelous mystery of the woman's soul is for him only a series of obstacles. He needs to know that soul, and to convince the woman that he knows it very well, indeed. But—here is where treachery enters the picture—in his own mind her uniqueness is but the lever he turns to accomplish his own paltry purposes.

One final example reveals another kind of seduction—perhaps a woman's style. We know from earlier discussion of Lawrence's *Women in Love* that Gerald's attachment to the Pussum leads only to partial satisfactions, diversions from life's burdens. But it, too, is based upon a deliberate and bold, yet subtle, penetration of the soul of the seduced:

> The Pussum sat near to Gerald, and she seemed to become soft, subtly to infuse herself into his bones, as if she were passing into him in a black electric flow. Her being suffused his veins like a magnetic darkness, and concentrated at the base of his spine like a fearful source of power. Meanwhile her voice sounded out reedy and nonchalant. . . . Then she found his hand, and grasped it in her own firm, small clasp. It was so utterly dark, and yet such a naked statement, that rapid vibrations ran through his blood and over his brain, he was no longer responsible. Still her voice rang on like a bell, tinged with a tone of mockery. And as she swung her head, her fine mane of hair just swept his face, and all his nerves were on fire, as with a subtle friction of electricity. But the great center of his force held steady, a magnificent pride to him, at the base of his spine. (1982: 126)

That steady force at the base of Gerald's spine, in which he takes so much pride, is what he would have to yield if he were to "pass away" through the Pussum. This scene suggests that *fana* might really be a possibility, were Gerald not so wedded to his habitual strengths and so defended against his unconscious weaknesses. He will not be able to love until he can be seduced away from those defenses.

The Pussum has insinuated herself into Gerald's soul no less subtly than the legendary Don Juan into his thousands, but she does it in such a different way. She is no less capable than he, even of manipulation. But, whereas he works under the surgical glare of directed thought beamed down from above, she proceeds up from below—feeling her way through the thick, wet darkness of throbbing arteries. While the Spanish Don is coolly analytical, she obliterates the distinctions between herself and Gerald in a warm mystical participation. There is a good deal of the love potion in her approach.

Before proceeding to draw conclusions from these quite specific examples, let us consider a story that comes from the mythic level of human imagination. It is the Grimm fairy tale entitled "Allerlei-rauh"—which means a hodgepodge of "raw" things. In this case the raw things are pelts of animals that a princess named Allerleirauh wears, sewn together into a coat.

The Story of Allerleirauh

Once upon a time there was a king who had a beautiful wife with golden hair, who, on her deathbed, made him promise not to remarry unless he could find a woman equally as beautiful and as golden of hair as she. After her death the king sent his ambassadors far and wide to find such a woman, but they were unsuccessful. As only the king's own daughter fit the description, he decided to ask her for her hand. Afraid to refuse her father, the princess set some preliminary demands: a dress as golden as the sun, one as silvery as the moon, and one as bright as the stars, and a coat made from the skin of every animal in the realm.

Upon receiving these gifts, the princess packed the dresses in a nutshell, donned the coat of sundry furs, blackened her hands and face with soot, and set out for the forest. She also took with her three golden trinkets: a ring, a spinning wheel, and a reel. When she had travelled as far as her legs could carry her, she fell asleep in a hollow tree, warmly wrapped in her furs.

Meanwhile the king to whom this part of the forest belonged was out hunting, and one of his men discovered what seemed to be a strange furry animal in a hollow tree. The king commanded that it be captured alive. On discovering that it was a maid, he put her to work in his kitchen and gave her a place to sleep under the stairs where the daylight never shone.

At the first ball held in the castle, Allerleirauh washed herself and for a short time appeared in her golden dress and danced with the king. The king was enchanted with her and asked his watchmen where she had come from, but they had not seen her arrive or leave. As soon as the music stopped, she ran under the stairs where she changed back into her fur and blackened her face and hands. Then, in the kitchen, she placed her golden ring in the king's soup bowl. The king noticed the change in the taste of the soup and called the cook, who admitted Allerleirauh had made it. The black and furry maid, however, denied all knowledge of the ring.

The same events transpired at the next two balls, where she, respectively, wore her silvery dress and placed the spinning wheel in the king's soup, and wore her star-sparkling dress and placed the reel in the soup. On the third occasion, however, the king contrived to place the ring on her finger while they were dancing and to extend the time of the dance so that Allerleirauh had not sufficient opportunity to change. She threw on her fur skins over the starry dress and failed to notice that one finger had escaped the blackening with soot. When she appeared with the soup, the king recognized the ring, espied the white finger, and caught a glimpse of starry glitter under her furs. He had her unmasked and married her. They lived happily ever after.

When a fairy tale says they were married and lived happily ever after, I take that to mean that they discovered their oneness at the level of Self. They drank the love potion, and knew they did so. They recognized the importance of their erotic bond sufficiently to want to make it a fundamental condition in their lives. Its reality becomes their touchstone in evaluating the significance of anything else. It does not necessarily mean that they decided to live together and have children. Such plans belong to the more personal levels of the psyche. Here we are at the level of mythic imagery.

Although not a predictor of marital success, "married happily ever after" is a necessary condition of genuine relationship. In the story of Allerleirauh, we can see why. The poor girl is an incest victim. Her father's offers of love are heavily freighted with demands that perhaps no daughter is strong enough to refuse outright. Fortunately she has learned to be devious enough to put him off and to reject his offer while seeming to accept it. This evidently saves her from a wedding with her father, which would have meant psychological death for her. Nevertheless, her father's attempted violation leaves her with a wound somewhat like Paul Morel's. She has been drawn into an unhealthy dependency on her father in which her legitimate expectations for support, stability, nurturing, encouragement, and the like are replaced by a demand that she fulfill *his* needs. He wants her to stop up the gap in his Self. If she gives in to this, she will never develop a sense of her own Self.

Paul Morel failed to develop a reliable relationship to his Self because he depended too much on his mother to provide him that sense of oneness, balance, and integration that makes one whole. Allerleirauh's father is offering her the same illusory security that wounded Paul.

Still, her relationship with her father has provided her with something very precious—symbolized by the three dresses. Because no seducer is more powerful than the one we trust implicitly, a parent, Allerleirauh had virtually no defense against her father's penetration to the most secret recesses of her soul. His seduction opened her to the silvery shimmer of the anima, the golden radiance of the Self, and the brilliance of the instinct/archetypes twinkling in the abyss beneath the wound.

On the one hand, she knew she needed these gifts if she was ever to establish a satisfyingly deep relationship in the future. But on the other hand, she was condemned to *wear* them. I take this as almost a defining characteristic of the narcissistically wounded individual: to live with the deepest beauties of one's soul exposed and to be unable to close the gap through which they glitter. Allerleirauh needs the coat of sundry furs and the lampblack to cover over the wound. In doing so, she hides the light of her divine spark behind the beastly shadow of the inborn releasing mechanisms (the sundry furs).

A fierce animality from the instinct/archetypes very frequently characterizes the emotional life of narcissistic and borderline individuals. Because they cannot close their gap, they have to drive us away with primal displays of aggression. They feel their vulnerability so acutely that they are glad to find sunless holes in which to hide, like Allerleirauh's bedroom under the stairs.

But at the same time, they cannot forget their extraordinary gifts. This is what the psychological literature refers to as their "grandiosity." For Allerleirauh, her giftedness is symbolized both by the dresses and by the three golden trinkets she places in the king's soup. She deals successfully with her woundedness by maintaining her sundry-fur disguise so that the king will not be inadvertently seduced by what she cannot conceal of her soul. Instead, she parcels out hints of her soul's beauty, symbolized by the quality of her soup and the valuable surprises she hides in it. By gradually revealing her soul, she deliberately seduces the king. Through the great effort and patience of this work, she builds her ego and knits together the Self, which were both so badly wounded by her father's intrusions.

If we conclude from the fairy tale and literary instances cited above that seduction always requires some kind of exposure of soul, I think we do not go far wrong. Don Juan and old Karamazov seduce by accurately reading the souls of women and reflecting back to them what they have seen. The Pussum seduces by insinuating herself into Gerald's soul and stimulating it to new life. Allerleirauh seduces by parceling out intimations of mysterious inner riches. These realities lie behind even the cynicism of Shaw's *Man and Superman,* where the Don Juan figure, Tanner, reiterates the sentiments Shaw expressed in the introductory essay:

> The true artist will let his wife starve, his children go barefoot, his mother drudge for his living at seventy, sooner than work at

anything but his art. To women he is half vivisector, half vampire. He gets into intimate relations with them to study them, to strip the mask of convention from them, to surprise their inmost secrets, knowing that they have the power to rouse his deepest creative energies, to rescue him from his cold reason, to make him see visions and dream dreams, to inspire him, as he calls it. He persuades women that they may do this for their own purpose whilst he really means them to do it for his. (61)

For Shaw and Tanner, only the artist is strong enough to stand up to woman's seduction. By *seduction* they mean a process of persuading others to do our will under the guise of seeming to do their own. What a contrast with William of Poitier and Aquitaine's regard for his Unknown Lady: obedience to her coincided with perfect fidelity to himself!

The false seducer succeeds because he imitates the behavior of real love. Even the deceiver must come to know his victim's soul. The seducer who, like Molière's Don Juan or Casanova or old Karamazov, pursues his prey out of a true appreciation of the beauties of her soul, may even win a bit of our sympathy. He honestly admires and reflects some of the deeper realities of her psyche and may even thereby enhance her life. But we know there is something wrong when he loses interest shortly after making the conquest.

It has been said that a woman seduced by Casanova feels ennobled, while one seduced by Don Juan feels demeaned. There is a grain of truth in this saying, although it is very much oversimplified. It is certainly not true of Byron's or Bergman's Don Juan that they demean. Mozart's and Molière's Don Juans badly mistreat their women. Shaw's is primarily afraid of women, and Byron's is more frequently seduced than seducing. Furthermore, Casanova is quite calculating and never sees women as of equal value with men. Casanova, however, does conquer women in order to be able to dally with them, while some Don Juan figures dally in order to conquer.

It is clearly not easy to draw the line between honorable and dishonorable seductions, but the principle is to be found in how faithfully the seducer behaves vis-à-vis the soul of the seduced. There is quite a range between the seducer who discovers the divine spark in his partner and "passes away" through her to a centering divine love and the one who discovers only enough of her soul to conquer and possess her. When Shaw's Tanner claims art as a higher principle than love, we need to know what place love has in his view. His idealized artist mistreats mother, wife, and children to such an extent that we believe his dedication to art may well be an excuse rather than a higher principle. Since he leaves no hint that art may deal with the All, we fear rootless self-expression may have eclipsed a search for Truth. Still, in all cases, even those lacking fidelity to the partner's soul, a seducer cannot succeed unless he knows or seems to know the soul of his woman.

The same is true of that arch villain among seducers, the Vicomte de Valmont in Choderlos de Laclos's brilliant scandal-causing eighteenth-century novel, *Les liaisons dangereuses*. The story concerns the efforts of a pair of "libertines," (as they call themselves), Valmont and the Marquise de Merteuil, to avenge themselves on a man who had offended them both. The revenge is to be the seduction of a fifteen-year-old girl to whom the man is betrothed. Insofar as they are manipulating hearts, Valmont and Mme. de Merteuil seem to be dealing in love. But all their actions serve their striving for power and honor. For them, love is a weakness, regrettable in oneself but useful when observed in someone else.

Despite his proud profession of faith in the power principle, Valmont finds he has an unsettlingly powerful interest in a beautiful, prudish woman who seems beyond all seductive ploys, Mme. de Tourvel. Preeminent among the devices he employs to win her heart is the disclosure or seeming disclosure of his own soul. For example, he sets up an elaborate set of circumstances to make Mme. de Tourvel believe that he is a generous benefactor to the poor (Laclos, 56ff.). Also, in order to discredit what others may tell her of him in warning, he himself recounts some of his sexual exploits in such a way that she hears it as "rare candour": "He confides freely in me, and I lecture him with utmost severity" (ibid., 36). The seduction works because she believes he is sharing his soul with her. Even faithless seductions are based on disclosures and discoveries of soul.

There is another characteristic of seduction evident in these examples. Like Allerleirauh, who hides in her under-stairs closet and behind her animal skins while deliberately parceling out glimpses of her soul, Valmont requires distance from his involvement with a woman in order to observe her reactions accurately and plan his moves:

> I looked down her from head to foot and then up again. . . . My love, that sweet gaze was fixed upon me! It was immediately lowered, but so as to encourage its return I looked away. Thus was established between us that tacit agreement, the first treaty ratified by timid lovers, which, to satisfy a mutual need of seeing and being seen, allows glances to succeed each other until the moment when they can safely meet. . . . To this end I first took one or two of her glances by surprise; but with as much reserve as could give modesty no alarm; and to put the bashful creature more at her ease I pretended to be as embarrassed as she was. By degrees her eyes, growing accustomed to meeting, met for longer, and at last looked away no more; and I saw in hers that languid softness which is the happy sign of love and desire. (Ibid., 164)

Laclos lets us right inside the head of a Don Juan figure. Byron, Molière, Shaw, and Bergman are not so obliging; Mozart only hints with his music; and even Casanova's confessions are undependable— since he is lying to himself as much as to us.

One aspect of Valmont's achievement is nearly admirable—his ability to take active part in a situation while remaining a cool, detached observer. He appears to hold this balance by denying his feelings for Mme. de Tourvel. When our consciousness sinks to the Self level of unity with another person, we enter a kind of mystical participation or unconscious identity. It is in this love-potion space that we read the other's soul. But if we have lost contact with the higher levels of the psyche, we have lost most of our ego—our autonomous subjectivity. We cease to be an individual facing another individual. If we no longer know where we leave off and our beloved begins, we have not the wits to seduce. Seduction requires at least that the seducer be free enough of the unconscious oneness in romantic love to be able to see the other as she really is.

Elsa had to ask the questions Lohengrin forbade in order to achieve any dependable accuracy in her perception of him. She drove him away by asserting her own needs, by establishing her autonomy. Blissful, unconscious oneness was the primary threat she faced. The demon lover frequently presents us with a different problem. He holds us in a kind of stalemate between two ways of life, two sets of values. Instead of driving him away, we require a fairly extended "marriage" with him before we can see the divine spark in his soul and the shadow in our own. Only then do we understand what had held us and acquire the strength to accept it or let it go.

Progress in relationship requires such distance from the beloved that each partner is free to become his or her own unique Self and each is able to observe the partner's individuality accurately. The naked sword of freely accepted distance from our beloved enables us to know both ourself and her or him. It confers a personal power on each of us. Valmont's partner in crime, the Marquise de Merteuil, is very much aware of this fact. She expresses it, here, as she wonders whether she will be able to turn Cécile, the fifteen-year-old girl she is seducing, into a powerfully aware colleague:

> She has a stupid ingenuousness . . . a weakness of character which is nearly always incurable, and is an impediment to everything; so that, while attempting to fit the girl for a life of intrigue, we should only be turning out a woman of easy virtue. (Laclos, 254)

We see here that the Marquise, though she lived two centuries ago, has a lot in common with modern feminists. She wants to develop in the girl sufficient ego and sufficient social awareness so that she can handle herself as an equal with men. She worries that the girl may be incapable of duplicity. She says there are two kinds of women in the world: those who depend on youth and beauty and those who depend on their wits (ibid., 271). She, herself, lives by her wits and finds herself superior in personal power and social achievement to most men and nearly all women. This is what she would like to be able to pass on to Cécile. We may well despise the manipulative uses to which she puts her considerable power, but we can hardly deny her achievement—particularly as she lived in an age when society forbade women all overt exercise of power.

If the Marquise redeems herself a bit in our eyes by her sympathetic tutelage of the young girl, Valmont does also in that his heart comes near to overruling his faithless conquest of Mme. de Tourvel.

Despite his protestations, she means more to him than a notch in his belt. He tells us that he is learning the delights of seductions' disclosures and discoveries:

> If our first loves . . . make much slower progress, it is not, as is generally thought, because of delicacy or modesty, but because the heart, surprised by a new feeling, pauses, so to speak, at each step in order to enjoy the delight it feels. . . . This is so true that even when a libertine falls in love, if a libertine ever does, he becomes from that moment less anxious to enjoy his mistress. (Ibid., 126)

Valmont is the libertine who—despite his best intentions—has fallen in love. For him it is a humiliation to think "that I might in any way have been dependent on the very slave I subjected to my will" (ibid., 297). Further proof of love's ascendancy over the power principle in Valmont is his desire for her to retain her independence of will. He insists on a high level of consciousness and deliberation on her part:

> It is not enough for me to possess her; I want her to give herself up. . . . But the better I know what has to be done, the more difficult I find it to do; and even if you are going to laugh at me again, I must admit that my embarrassment increases the more I think about it. (Ibid., 264)

His embarrassment belongs to the quest for power that he is on, in the context of which his tender feelings appear to be nothing but weakness. He wants her to give herself freely, to disclose her soul without reserve; and he knows that to accomplish this he has to disclose or at least seem to disclose aspects of his own soul. He thirsts for a soul-to-soul bond with her, but seems unable to allow himself. He has no notion of *fana*. In his mind, there is no "passing away" but only possession. Still, his heart protests and knows inchoately that there is an alternative to calculations based on the drive for power and conquest. Mme. de Tourvel responds to this "other side":

I love him to idolatry and yet much less than he deserves. . . . Who can know true love as he does? What more can I say? His feelings are equal to the feelings he inspires. . . . Since he has been able to give himself up without constraint to the impulses of his heart, he seems to divine all the wishes of my own. . . . What other woman could make him happier than I do? And I know from my own experience, the happiness one gives is the strongest bond, the only one that really holds. (Ibid., 316)

She is right about everything except his fidelity. But even where she is wrong, it is instructive to see what she thinks she has in Valmont. She thinks she knows his "heart" and that "his feelings are equal" to hers, that he has relinquished all that "constrains" his emotional response to her. Valmont's seduction has worked because he has made her believe that the two of them have attained a heart-to-heart connection.

We have learned that seduction—be it honest or not—requires at least two things: the seducer must disclose aspects of his own soul and/or he must discover the soul of his partner. Seduction, we might say, is an imitation and encouragement of an individual's natural inclination toward intimacy. The great seducers and libertines know this very well. Byron (who ought to know) says of Don Juan:

> His manner was perhaps the more seductive,
>   Because he ne'er seem'd anxious to seduce;
> . . . .
>   . . . with women he was what
>   They pleased to make or take him for; and their
>   Imagination's quite enough for that. . . .
>   (Canto 15, vv. 12, 16)

His naturalness and passivity allows the women he seduces to believe him too innocent and genuine to deceive them. Casanova, too, is a master of giving people what they want. He describes his successes this way: "I was not handsome, but I had something better than beauty—a striking expression which almost compelled a kind interest in my favor, and I felt myself ready for anything" (vol. 1, 53).

Can we believe that these great seducers are just acting naturally? Perhaps Byron and Casanova would like to believe that of themselves, as evidently they have cultivated a naive persona, which they find a very effective tool. But we know Casanova and Don Juan as seducers because of the faithlessness concealed behind their imitation of candor. Casanova describes himself more believably when he tells us why he considers himself ready to seek his fortune in Rome:

> The man who intends to make his fortune in this ancient capital of the world must be a chameleon susceptible of reflecting all the colours of the atmosphere that surrounds him—a Proteus apt to assume every form, every shape. He must be supple, flexible, insinuating, close, inscrutable, often base, sometimes sincere, sometimes perfidious, always concealing a part of his knowledge, indulging but in one tone of voice, patient, a perfect master of his own countenance, as cold as ice when any other man would be all fire; and if unfortunately he is not religious at heart . . . he must be religious in his mind . . . he must suffer quietly, if he is an honest man, the necessity of knowing himself as an arrant hypocrite. . . . Of all those qualities I possessed but one—namely flexibility; for the rest I was only an interesting, heedless young fellow, a pretty good blood horse, but not broken, or rather, badly broken; and that is much worse. (Ibid., 54)

The "perfidy" in his seductions is that Casanova gets a woman to give him her heart while he withholds his. To do so, he has to be "supple, flexible, insinuating," and so on, convincing her that he is ready to submit to her. Surrender is hard to avoid when one's beloved has already passed away in *fana*. The perfidious seducer convinces us of a fidelity he does not have.

In some of the most convincing literary examples, however, the villainous seducer is himself seduced by the beauty of the soul disclosed to him. He all but submits. We readers may sometimes even hope that he undergoes a permanent transformation of character. When his naive victim recognizes his vulnerability to her, her susceptibility is substantially increased. Thus the most interesting and convincing perfidious seducers walk a fine line between eros and power. For example, Flaubert's Rodolphe, the rogue who set Mme. Bovary on her downward path:

> But she was so pretty. He had possessed so few women of such ingenuousness. This love without debauchery was a new experience for him, and, drawing him out of his lazy habits, caressed at once his pride and sensuality. Emma's enthusiasm, which his bourgeois good sense disdained, seemed to him in his heart of hearts charming, since it was lavished on him. (184)

He is not awakened out of his selfishness, and his awareness of the transcending realm of eros is barely dawning—nothing like what Valmont discovered through Mme. de Tourvel. But his bourgeois quest for power and position has been called into question for the first time. His partner in dalliance has for the first time appeared as someone unique and other. She cannot be reduced to the image he had of her.

Contrast, for example, these dawning discoveries of Valmont and Rodolphe with the phony chivalry of Newland Archer in Wharton's *Age of Innocence*:

> The case of the Countess Olenska had stirred up old settled convictions and set them drifting dangerously through his mind. His own exclamation: "Women should be free—as free as we are," struck to the root of a problem that it was agreed in his world to regard as non-existent. "Nice" women, however wronged, would never claim the kind of freedom he meant, and generous-minded men like himself were therefore—in the heat of argument—the more chivalrously ready to concede it to them. (43f.)

We know from the broader discussion of Archer's affair in chapter 2 that he was in some ways more greatly shaken in his habitual worldview than the above quotation would suggest. Nevertheless, the Countess Olenska always remains for him a demon lover. The two of them do not undergo the transformation of an unholy marriage, and the psychological process that their falling in love began was never completed. Even more truncated is the adventure between Tess of the d'Urbervilles and her romantic theologian, Angel Clare. When he finds hint of Tess's demonhood in the story of her earlier seduction, he runs away to South America "and hardly knew that he loved her still" (Hardy, 1964: 272). Hardy describes Clare's psychology as follows:

> Within the remote depths of his constitution, so gentle and affectionate as he was in general, there lay hidden a hard, logical deposit, like a vein of metal in a soft loam, which turned the edge of everything that attempted to traverse it. It had blocked his acceptance of the Church; it blocked his acceptance of Tess. (Ibid., 258)

That hard vein in Angel Clare is a defense and a compensation. Its hardness compensates for his loamy soft, undifferentiated feelings that leave him so childish in the ways of love. At the same time it defends his self-centered plans and fantasies, keeping him inside his narcissistic cocoon and impervious to Tess's unique otherness. Having no distance from her and no flexibility in his defenses, he cannot see her for who she is.

Thus we have a progressive series of lovers, beginning with Clare, who cannot tolerate Tess's uniqueness, and proceeding through Archer, who is able to see the Countess Olenska's individuality when it does not clash too severely with his own habitual views. Rodolphe knows that he has found something new and wholly different in Mme. Bovary, but it is not compelling enough to halt his self-aggrandizing career. Valmont, finally, is stopped in his tracks by his genuine love for Mme. de Tourvel.

We can summarize what we have seen of seduction in three principles. First, there is no seduction without the discovery and disclosure of soul. Second, fidelity in romantic love consists in the seducer's remaining faithful to what he has discovered in the soul of his partner as well as to the disclosures he has made of his own soul. Third, while discovery and disclosure presume and develop a oneness between the partners, seduction requires a certain distance whereby the lovers retain their individuality and appreciate one another's uniqueness. There is a fourth principle: when seduction proceeds with fidelity, the seducer is as much seduced as seducing.

Most of literature's great seducers have discovered this fourth principle. Casanova says, "In trying to win over the girl I had won over myself" (vol. 2, 320). Valmont describes his success with Mme. de Tourvel this way:

> Intoxication was complete and reciprocal and, for the first time with me, outlasted pleasure. I left her arms only to fall at her feet and swear eternal love; and to tell the whole truth, I meant what I said. Even after I had left her, the thought of her was still with me, and I have even now to make an effort to be rid of it. (Laclos, 303)

Shaw's Don Juan is impressed only with the dangers of such a fall as Valmont experienced:

> Well, I found that when I had touched a woman's imagination, she would allow me to persuade myself that she loved me; but when my suit was granted she always said, first, "At last, the barriers are down," and second, "When will you come again?" . . . These two speeches always alarmed me; for the first meant that the lady's impulse had been solely to throw down my fortifications and gain my citadel; and the second openly announced that hence forth she regarded me as her property; and counted my time as already wholly at her disposal. (152f.)

He makes a great show of cynicism and would have us believe that there is no fidelity in his seductions. But what he fears is nothing other than being seduced. When he touches a woman's imagination so that she lets him have his way with her, she is having her way with him. He knows that then he is sunk, being more seduced than seducing.

The situation is even more complicated than this, for we cannot begin to seduce another until we have first seduced ourselves. At the very least, we need to convince ourselves that the risks of intimacy are worth the rewards it offers. We proceed by disclosing a piece of our soul. The clumsy seducer who is more aware of his own fears than his partner's soul reveals aspects of himself perhaps randomly, perhaps by starting with matters that most arouse his rejection anxieties. The more accomplished seducer reads his procedures in the soul of his partner. In that sense, she tells him precisely how she can be seduced. But that is her seduction of him; that is her disclosure of soul, which heightens his desire and draws him further into the process of lovemaking. The goal is to involve the whole being of both partners. Only then do we pass away in *fana*. Only then do we experience our own full identity and the full identity of our partner.

As in all other matters related to romantic love, the mystics have known these truths all along. In her great spiritual classic, *The Interior Castle*, Teresa of Ávila presents what might be taken as a blueprint for faithful seduction. It is a description of the stages that the mystic traverses in her growth in the love of God. The central metaphor is a castle comprised of a labyrinthine set of chambers arranged spiral fashion about a central room in which shines the pure light of divinity. God's love and enlightenment seduces the mystic into entering one chamber after another. From a psychological perspective, the Interior Castle is an image of the psyche and the labyrinthine course to the center a description of our discovery of Self. From the perspective of interpersonal relationship, it is a metaphor for the soul of the other whom I penetrate through my seductive discoveries and disclosures. And it is also an image of my own psyche whose Self I knit together in this process.

The mode of entry to the Interior Castle is prayer and reflection (Teresa, 38). Those who enter the first chambers may be individuals very much involved in the business of the world. But they reflect upon who they are, on the nature of things—"although in a rather hurried fashion"; and they pray. By "prayer," Teresa does not necessarily refer to a recitation of traditional formulas or an asking for favors or even an earnest conversation with an invisible listener. The essence of prayer is a certain *turning,* an orientation of consciousness toward the One. For these individuals, it means that they at least occasionally catch a glimpse of their deepest spiritual identity. There is a momentary "paradigm shift," and the hurly-burly of mundane preoccupations finds its humble place within the *ultimate* concerns of human existence. In the first chamber, this is only a momentary and dim recognition. "Hardly any of the light from the King's royal chamber reaches these first dwelling places" (ibid., 45), and distractions and temptations ("reptiles") abound.

In the second and third chambers, dwellers in the Interior Castle become progressively more serious in their quest for the center. At first they hear the Lord's calling through the words and examples of other people. Then they begin to suffer from dryness in prayer and a sense of their distance from God. Their growing conviction of the importance of their quest leads them to the realization that they have not yet given up everything for God. Their worldview oscillates back and forth between the mundane and the ultimate. They need the self-discipline of penance and seek it out. Although reason and intellect are still firmly in control of these individuals, they are beginning to use these faculties to serve their striving for the center.

When we translate this imagery into the language of relationship, the Interior Castle is the realm of intimacy. The reptiles of distraction and temptation—which abound outside the Castle and are to be found in decreasing numbers in the first few chambers—have to do with the pursuit of pleasure and power, where my partner exists to gratify my mundane needs. We begin to enter the Castle of Intimacy when our paradigm shifts and we catch a glimpse of the divine spark in our beloved. At first this may only be a momentary glimpse, but it changes our mind. It reorients us like prayer. We may forget these profound flashes, but they leave an impression. Now the business of intimacy becomes significant for us. We have discovered something essential about our beloved's soul. We want to know more and more about her (or him) and follow every gesture and word and inclination for further hints about that spark we have glimpsed. There are more than vestiges of self-interest in this quest. We hope our beloved will complete us, open us further and further to our own wholeness, which she helps us to realize. Self-interest is deepened and reoriented. We are ready to be generous and self-denying, but we still have not lost sight of our desire to possess our beloved. We are still thinking about our relationship in fairly conventional terms and plotting its success.

Only in the Fourth Dwelling Place does conventional, rational knowledge begin to give way to *gnosis,* to nonrational, experiential, mystical knowing. "There are things to see and understand so delicate that the intellect is incapable of devising a way to explain them" (Teresa, 67). Here we may begin to speak of the love potion, for a genuine union is finally being effected. Still, it is limited, for while "the soul is perhaps completely joined with Him . . . the mind is on the outskirts of the castle suffering from a thousand wild and poisonous beasts, and meriting by this suffering" (ibid., 71). True spiritual delights, possible for the first time in the fourth chamber, are like water from an abundant natural spring, produced by God with the greatest peace, quietness, and sweetness. Welling up in the interior parts of ourselves, they dilate our whole being (ibid., 74f.).

In the face of this dilation and change of heart, we are irresistible to our beloved. Infidelity is no longer possible once we enter the fourth chamber. Seduction sweeps us both along like a flood. Disclosure of our own soul and discovery of the beloved's become a single act. We know not whether we are drawn along by the beauty of the beloved's soul or by that of our own. We are free in a more profound way than we had ever imagined. Teresa says the soul loses all fear of hell and distaste for penance; its faith is more alive (82).

In the Fifth Dwelling Place, union falls short of betrothal, but the lovers are beyond any exchange of gifts (ibid., 103f.). We gaze at one another. We take so much delight in these matters of ultimate concern that we no longer need to deliberately reorient ourselves to the center. Now the divine spark is so real for us that there is no mistaking, forgetting, or becoming distracted. The lizards of suspicion cannot enter. The soul flies like a butterfly from a cocoon; how could it be happy walking step by step? "Union is always short and seems to the soul even much shorter than it probably is" (ibid., 89). It is not characterized by visionary experiences but by "a certitude remaining in the soul that only God can place there" (ibid.). Only a few of those who have tasted the love potion fail to enter this fifth chamber of Intimacy's Castle.

Those who enter the sixth chamber are said to be "betrothed" to their Spouse. Their union may be compared to the flames of two candles that burn as one when the candles are brought close together, but again become two when they are separate (ibid., 179). One finds oneself wounded with love for the Spouse and strives for more opportunities to be alone and to eliminate obstacles (ibid., 108). But they cannot be removed by our conscious efforts, they belong to our otherness from one another. They are a manifestation of the incompleteness of our union.

Because our love affair is our only orientation, our strangeness becomes quite apparent to others. Teresa says that God, in order to increase our love, sends us sufferings in the form of criticism and praise from our peers; doubting confessors; and, the most precious and painful suffering of all, a smoldering love that refuses to burst into flame (111–17). Amidst all this pain suffered on account of our distance from one another, there is also great joy and union. Now the soul experiences what Teresa calls "locutions" with God (119ff.). We converse with one another, generally without words, in the intimate depths of our souls. Amidst a profound quiet we may experience visions and ecstasies—and raptures in which our spirits sail off together at high speeds (ibid., 133).

Our souls are wed in the Seventh Dwelling Place, where the Spiritual Marriage takes place. Our union is like rain falling "from the sky into a river or fount; all is water" (ibid., 179). We are no longer distracted—even when apart from our Spouse and attending to affairs of the mundane world. The sense of presence we feel is not always like an intense light; sometimes it is like the awareness we have of another person who is with us in a dark room. Though we do not see him, we know he is there (ibid., 176). If in intimacy's sixth chamber we were tortured by the distance we experienced amidst our mutual presence to one another, then here in the seventh chamber the joy of our presence permeates our distance. We have passed away through one another and find ourselves resting in the One.

In this sense, faithful seduction is a "leading aside," a reorientation away from the habitual and mundane to the ultimate and eternal. Dmitry Karamazov underwent such a paradigm shift when he discovered the divine spark in Grushenka during their *Liebesnacht*: "Before, I was only tormented by those infernal curves of hers, but now I've taken all her soul into my soul and through her I've become a man myself!" (Dostoyevsky, 1958: 698). Grushenka's testimony at Dmitry's trial reflects the same "turning," the same discovery of sublime truth in the soul of her beloved: "What the prisoner tells you, you must believe. He is not the sort of man to tell a lie" (ibid., 833). Dmitry's prosecutor makes a mockery of these words, for the prisoner is a known and admitted drunkard, brawler, womanizer, and spendthrift. Surely Grushenka's words will not convince a jury; for how are they to know love had given her more perfect sight, and not just "blinded" her as love is so often reputed to do? We readers know that despite the demonic element in her relationship, what Grushenka says about Dmitry's soul is utterly dependable.

In their *Liebesnacht* Dmitry and Grushenka entered the fourth chamber of Intimacy's Castle, where further progress in seduction presumes fidelity. Before that, love was too undeveloped to know what it was agreeing to. In the first three chambers it glimpsed the spark, as through a glass darkly. But only as it grew into the fourth chamber did it become a reliable guide to the soul of the beloved as well as to one's own.

Every seduction, every "turning aside," raises the question: which course is most truly *mine*? A reliable test for whether an "in love" episode or a course of seduction is "real" or delusional is to examine what the adventure has done for me. Has it changed my course? Has it reoriented me? Am I more centered, more convinced, less distractible, calmer?

If we believe we have been betrayed in love, we should look to the quality of our connection with the betrayer. We must have been irresponsibly dependent on him or her. We cannot have been paying attention. We must have been looking at a mask rather than through a lens. We have not known love at all. We certainly have not entered Teresa's fourth chamber of intimacy. For there, a clear view of the divine spark and an orientation to Self and oneness brings us solid conviction and joyful fidelity. Seduction can be faithless only when the divine spark has been forgotten or perhaps has never been known at all.

8

Love Play:
Enabling Transcendence

Stories about romantic love reflect the reality we have all experienced of alternating union and separation. In seduction especially, where union is deliberately schemed for, a genuine separation is required. For only when we are fairly clear about who our beloved is, and are not covering her or him with the masks of our projections, do we know the beloved well enough to "lead her aside" from her habitual paths and into the garden of love. When we enter that garden we still cannot afford to let go of the sword of separation. We think of it as a garden of unity, where lovers play. But the very image of *play* implies a give and take, a me-against-you for the sake of us. Rumi knows this very well:

> Since we've seen each other, a game goes on.
> Secretly I move, and you respond.
> You're winning, you think it's funny.
>
> But look up from the board now, look how
> I've brought in furniture to this invisible place,
> so we can live here.
> (1984: quatrain 1245)

In love-play, as Rumi notes, there are generally two processes going on. At the more surface level, there are "moves" being plotted, perpetrated, and reacted to—amid much surprise, laughter, winning and losing. But at a deeper level a home is being prepared, a joint life. At one level we and our beloved are opponents while at another we are coconspirators.

One man reported an encounter with his "reluctant mistress" this way. They were sitting at a restaurant table engaged in one of their frequent quiet but charged conversations bearing only indirect reference to their affair. She was hunched over her ginger ale, trying to make her body language say they were just good friends and not lovers, when he dropped a word that linked the conversation with their relationship. At once her eyes softened and, as he reported, "It was as if a golden rainbow arched out of her breast, over her right shoulder, and cascaded directly through my chest like water." He felt the cascade as a bodily experience and said he had come as close as possible to *seeing* the rainbow with his bodily eyes. He believed their sense of unity at that moment was greater than anything they had achieved physically, while simultaneously they had an exquisite separateness that paradoxically seemed to add to their oneness. The initial body language and the apparently innocent conversation were the "moves" on the board game of their love-play. His dropped "word" pointed out the invisible dwelling place; the golden rainbow confirmed that the word had brought them both into a deeper stratum of their friendship.

Love-play need not always be joyous and tender. Its two-dimensionality may also be experienced in our quarrels with our beloved. We find ourselves in the midst of a seemingly hopeless wrangle. We have disappointed or been disappointed by some of the most habitual traits of our partner: his boorish, blunt bull-headedness, her fastidious demands for fine-tuned emotion. Just as there seems no way out of it, our attention may shift to the other level where we are deeply immersed in one another, where we realize there could be no quarrel if we did not understand one another so deeply. We see the quarrel as a nonsensical game we play while bringing furniture into the bedroom. Thus he says, "Why don't you just drop it and give me a hug?" Her shoulders relax and she asks him how he knew that was the right moment for such a boorish ploy? He does not know; he just saw the deeper level beneath the earnest game.

When a relationship loses its playfulness, its two levels collapse into one, and it becomes stuck and moribund. Thus in Lawrence's *Sons and Lovers,* Clara Dawes complains, "It seems as if you only loved me at night—as if you didn't love me in the daytime." And Paul Morel answers: "The night is free to you. In the daytime I want to be by myself" (1985[b]:348). As in his relationship with Miriam, Paul is terrified of losing his identity. He compromises with an arbitrary division of the twenty-four-hour day, and spontaneity dies. As soon as we cling to an artificial structure like that, the imaginative stream stops flowing. It is at this point that Clara and Paul begin to make love at the edges of rivers and public paths for the sake of novelty and exciting danger. They want a playful, conspiratorial togetherness; but preventing its natural emergence, they try to manufacture it artificially. Unfortunately though, the spontaneous and autonomous imagination cannot be led. Love-play occurs only when we learn to follow imagination's lead.

It is by imagination that we mask our beloved with rigid expectations; and it is by imagination, as well, that we bring our partner into focus. Imagination may be the glass through which we take snapshots, and it can also be a motion-picture lens through which we capture movement and change. Imagination is the faculty employed by anima and animus in both masking and clarifying activities. The general opinion in our culture is that imagination is precisely what is *not* real, that it is a wandering away from the factuality of the world into evanescent and disjointed whimsies. But this opinion has also no appreciation for the five-level structure of the soul and the "objectivity" of the archetypal dimensions of psyche.

When we speak of imagination in the same breath as anima or animus, we refer to the possibility that the image-generating faculty of the unconscious can be as true and objectively anchored as the Self-Self bond or as solipsistic as a masking projection. It is therefore by imagination that we focus on our beloved's soul and come to know realities that lie deeper than the ordinary reach of the sense organs and discursive thought. Because our imagination can be brought into harmony with our beloved's soul, it is directed by psychological facts that elude our more ego-centered faculties. When guided by the anima lens, imagination brings into focus who our beloved is, has been, and is becoming, as well. Through imagination's lens we can observe our beloved growing, showing us new aspects, realizing potentials. As our partner changes and we maintain our fidelity, ever entering more central chambers of intimacy, the love that binds us is transformed—and so are we.

When, on the contrary, we arbitrarily isolate imagination from life and from love, there is nothing left for it but to retire into a kind of alienated dreaminess. This is exactly what happens to Heathcliff in *Wuthering Heights*. Evidently his imagination flowed spontaneously during the few years of his childhood companionship with Catherine Earnshaw, but it certainly shut down during his single-minded obsession over uniting himself with her in death. During this latter period of his history, Brontë personifies his imagination in young Cathy Linton, the daughter of Catherine and Edgar, whom Heathcliff keeps captive, intending to use her marriage to acquire the Linton family estate. Young Cathy does the housework he requires in as minimal a fashion as possible and then retires *to carve birds and beasts out of turnip parings*. Her whimsical creations have the same dreamy repetitiveness and disposability of everything in the stultified world Heathcliff controls. The symbolism is too striking to be ignored. She has been so deadened by Heathcliff's obsession that the inborn releasing mechanisms, the denizens of the tiger pit, have been flattened into two-dimensional miniatures, lifeless and disposable. Her depression is so severe that she has lost her channel to the most important source of psychic energy, the instinct/archetypes. Imagination repeats like a trivial tape loop, adds nothing new, and has lost all creativity and vitality. Having been swept out of the center of life, imagination slumbers on the garbage heap with the turnip parings.

Imagination is the source of everything that is alive and changing and creative in romantic love. It is the "romantic" element in love, where psychological meaning and interpersonal possibility take precedence over dead facts. Primarily through imagination, romantic love rises above the biological instinct for procreation and becomes something new and spiritually fertile. Bare instinct (IRM) knows only tension and release, pain and pleasure. Imagination fills the blind, empty striving of the instinct/archetypes with richness, variety, and novelty. It brings into love's union the more highly developed and differentiated strata of the psyche—psychic levels where mythic themes and personal imagery emerge. Imagination creates an opening for freedom and transcendence.

The practitioners of Sahajiya Tantra in Bengal are aware of how biological determinism is transcended and psychological freedom given scope through imagination's variety and novelty. They express the opposition between determinism and freedom as the difference between marital love and adultery:

> *Svakyia* love (with one's legal wife). . . is meaningful only when procreation is the end in view; it is worthless for emotional or religious purposes, while *parakiya* love (adultery) corresponds to the path of non-involvement in the world and contact with God, being solely for erotic purposes. Procreative, *svakyia* love, conventional love, produces immortality through progeny; erotic, *parakiya*, religious love, offers immortality through Release. (O'Flaherty, 266)

Regardless of how literally the Bengali Tantrists may understand this doctrine, they are distinguishing two attitudes towards love. A couple need not be married to have their lovemaking dominated by the procreative urge; nor if they are married, need they be precluded from religious love. If in their relationship they are primarily preoccupied with social and economic security for themselves and achieving stability for their progeny, the transformative play of imagination may be largely missing. Denis de Rougemont's awareness of this psychological distinction underlay his contention that romantic love is incompatible with marriage. I think what he means is that romantic love is only possible as long as the lovers can continue to play. His assumption that play is incompatible with marital love is not necessarily justified. Love-play is surely very often lost a short time after the honeymoon, but it need not be. We need not be so single-minded.

The Hindu mythology of Shiva, god of yoga and sexuality, reveals a great deal of the spiritual meaning of love-play. In this mythology, the retention of sperm and the postponement of or refusal to enjoy the release of orgasm are central. It is, indeed, the mytho-theological foundation of Tantrism, discussed in chapter 6. The devotees of Shiva distinguish between procreative sexuality and love-play. The sexual act (*mahamaithuna*) involves intromission of sperm into vagina for the procreation of a child, while love-play (*ratiomatra* or *rati*) is something else (ibid., 263). Shiva, himself, engages only in love-play (*rati*) with his consort, usually Parvati, and generates such commotion and heat that the world seems in danger of destruction. (Shiva is also the god of destruction and of graveyards.) His love-play is extremely intense. One myth says he "swooned with lust merely from the touch of her body, and she was so ecstatic that she knew neither night nor day" (ibid., 269). In most of the myths, the other gods of the Hindu pantheon are eagerly awaiting the offspring of Shiva's lovemaking, a child who will be more powerful than the earth can bear, a son to kill the demon Taraka. But Shiva's love-play is as concentrated and beyond distraction as his yogic meditation. The gods finally realize they will not acquire the hero they want unless they interrupt Shiva's *rati*. In doing so, they incur the wrath of both Shiva and Parvati. Parvati curses the other gods with infertility, and Shiva's seed is spilled where it gestates outside the body of Parvati—often in the belly of the god Agni, who catches the ejaculation in his mouth.

The idea of an ascetic god who spends as much time in sexual play as in prayer and whose symbol is the erect phallus seems quite foreign to Judaic and Christian expectations. Rumi, however, whose *Mathnawi* is referred to as the "Persian Quran," tells several stories of heroes interrupted in their lovemaking. They rush off to battle and return without losing their erections. The erect phallus is, therefore, an image of powerful concentration. These knights have gone into battle without losing their loving concentration on their beloved, just as the lover of God goes about his daily affairs without losing his awareness of God's presence.

For Rumi, the erect phallus is an allegory; but Shiva, the phallic god, is too complex to be understood allegorically. One of today's most original and respected scholars of Indian mythology, Wendy Doniger O'Flaherty, has tackled this problem in her carefully argued and richly detailed book, *Siva: The Erotic Ascetic*.[1]

---

1. The difference in the spelling of the god's name is due to O'Flaherty's having used diacritical marks in her transliteration of Sanskrit words and names. There is an accent mark over the initial letter in O'Flaherty's spelling of the god's name. This indicates that the *s* should be pronounced as *sh* is pronounced in English.

Siva may be the cause of lust, the enemy of lust, the death of lust, or all of these at once. His character is in *some* way connected with this force, and it is neither a contradiction nor a paradox to say that he is both the creator of Kama (the god of desire) and his enemy: "Shiva *vai* Kamah"—there is something between them. (34)

When he is doing yoga, Shiva requires a wife who is a female ascetic (*yogini*); and when he is ready for *rati,* he needs her to be a *kamini,* a lustful mistress. The connection between these two activities and these two states is the heat generated by Shiva's concentration. *Tapas* is the heat generated by the ascetic within his body as he meditates, a raging fire that may be either creative or destructive; and *kama* is the heat of desire (ibid., 35). Thus, whether engaged in yoga or love-play, Shiva is generating an intense heat—enough to burn up the world.

The interchangeability of these two kinds of heat makes a great deal of sense in the context of romantic love. For we have seen repeatedly that the origin and goal of romantic love are to be found in the One, the divine spark. Hence, we may say that both in lovemaking and in meditation, Shiva contemplates the One. He symbolizes the transcendent meaning of sexuality. He is an illustration from the mythic stratum of the psyche, showing us the sublimity of love-play and how it is a vehicle of transcendent union.

The stories about Shiva illustrate both levels in Rumi's poem on love-play. In the erotic sport, the eighty-four million positions for sexual intercourse, the teasing, and the chase, he demonstrates the upper-level "moves" on Rumi's game board. In his *kama/tapas* heat, he inhabits the lower level of love-play: Rumi's dwelling place, the central-most chamber of Intimacy's Castle, where the fire of divine love burns with eternal steadiness. It is to this that the lover points when he asks his beloved to drop the quarrel and embrace. It is the golden rainbow cascading through the lover's chest.

Although far less sublime and differentiated a figure, the Greek Zeus shares some of Shiva's erotic characteristics. There is nothing about seed-retaining asceticism in the stories of Zeus' love-play. Zeus is ignorant of *rati,* but he knows *parakiya,* adulterous love, very well, indeed. A propensity for the lusty romp is built into his office as god of the sky, whence he is to fecundate the earth. Few goddesses, nymphs, or women are able to resist his seductions, but most make an effort—which is when the game begins in earnest.

Even with Hera, his wedded spouse and guardian of marital virtue, refusal gives rise to a spontaneous imaginative ploy on the part of Zeus. He changes himself into a half-frozen cuckoo to arouse Hera's pity. When she attempts to warm the bird against her breast, Zeus resumes his anthropomorphic form and ravishes her. Zeus, always too impatient for thousand-year-long dalliances, is more anxious to release his sexual tension than to follow its lead and explore its implications. What he misses in intensity and concentration, he compensates for with promiscuity. His love-play is serial and episodic rather than eternal and contemplative.

Hera is repelled by Zeus's promiscuity and demands marriage in return for her favors. Thus the primary representatives in Greek mythology of marital and of adulterous love are brought together for an eternity of wrangling. Their contentious union represents every one of us in our vacillation between social responsibility and the demands of romantic love. Hera and Zeus live in the souls of every individual. They represent the legitimate aims of persona and anima and express psyche's requirements at all its five strata: from the level of our personal goals, through the level of mythic longings, all the way down to the instinct/archetypes.

Zeus and Hera live not only in every one of us but in our relationships, as well. Every union of mortals replicates their Olympian struggle between the principles of familial stability and spiritual creativity. And, very much in the style of many human marriages, the divine couple has polarized itself—so that each partner identifies with only one of the opposites and rages against the other with blind self-righteousness. As long as Hera is unable to recognize and accept her adulterous shadow and Zeus represses his family-man shadow, there is no hope of reconciliation. In such a marriage the partners have dug in their heels and will not allow the whisper of change in one another. Imagination dries up. *Rati's* drive toward transformation and transcendence begins to look outside the marriage. The conventionality of the playless relationship becomes a dull boredom. Zeus's dissatisfaction extends even to the four offspring of his union with Hera: Hebe, Ares, Ilithyia, and Hephaestus. The bulk of his interest flows into his liaisons of *parakiya*—erotic, religious, adulterous love—and their offspring. One-night stands though they may have been, these affairs cannot have been trivial, for their progeny were highly significant deities, such as Athena, Hermes, Artemis, Apollo, Dionysus, and Persephone.

Psychologically speaking, the offspring of a union symbolize the quality of the interpersonal play of heat and imagination. One can infer that the liaison with Metis, goddess of Wisdom, must have been an extraordinary experience of aggression and philosophical transport to have produced the warrior goddess and intellectual powerhouse, Athena. In contrast, the Theban princess Semele coupled with Zeus in darkness and could only guess by the quality of the love-play that her partner was the king of the Olympians. Yet what transpired in that single night stretches the limits of conjecture, because its offspring was Dionysus, the god of fertility and of the vine, who liberates our emotions and fills us with joy and even frenzy. Like Christ and Osiris, he is a god of death and resurrection.

The power, variety, and profundity of Zeus's love-play may be gathered from the two liaisons that produced Athena and Dionysus. The discovery and disclosure of Self that must have taken place in those ardent moments were god-making as well as soul-making. The gods exist—not on some mountain top—but in ourselves. They are images and narratives that proceed from the mythic stratum of the psyche, expressing experiences and potentials that exist within each of us. The escapades of Zeus, therefore, as well as the thousand-year-long dalliances of Shiva, hint at what is available to us in our lovemaking.

Multidimensionality is the first characteristic of this adulterous/divine love-play. A middle-aged man describes an instance of *rati* about a year into his affair.

> Our attention had shifted about as often as our bodily positions, as we rolled over, sat up, paused to talk for a while, and so on. But at the moment I am remembering, there were at least three seemingly separate realities equally present in our awareness at the same time. In the first place was our bodies, burning up with a heat which could not have come from vigorous exercise but only from our ardor. It couldn't have been more than forty degrees

outside, and the window only inches from our heads was wide open, providing a continous refreshing stream playing over our faces, shoulders, and hips. This delighted us so that we commented on it and marveled at the heat. Of course we were aware, too, of our bodily parts and the delectable contact we were making with one another from our feet to our lips. But it was this sense of our being almost an exception to the laws of physics which arrested our bodily attention.

In a more personal or psychological sense, I was preeminently aware of gazing into her face, of the pink flush on her cheeks, of her extraordinarily relaxed attentiveness, and especially of the gray-green pools of her laughing eyes. I had the sense that I was peering into the deepest ocean and that I was seeing another universe with its own space and galaxies in eternal, timeless orbits. And somehow, inexplicably, this impersonal-seeming vision gave me the impression that I was coming to know the uniqueness of her soul. In one sense, I had known it all along, and yet in another I was seeing her gentleness, her generosity, her golden-heartedness for the very first time. Although in physical fact our bodies were barely moving, it seemed as I looked into those ocean pools that she was dancing a slow, elaborately choreographed dance which expressed the essence of her being; and I was dancing with her—remembering the choreography as though I had learned it before I was born and never thought about it until that afternoon.

If you can believe it, there was still another level of awareness in that same moment. For lack of a better term, I think of it as a union of spirits. There was a very strong sense—and this was a common experience with us which we had often discussed—that the coupling bodies on the bed and the dancing souls in that alternate universe of whirling galaxies were less "real" than something else. It was as though we were not the main couple in the room; we were just a manifestation of or an analogy for a spirit-pair who were achieving the "real" union. We were off-center, not the focal point of the spirit union, but below it and alongside it. These spirit beings were huge. Their bodiless forms filled the entire room and expanded past the boundaries of the ceiling, walls, and floor. We were in awe of this greater union and felt privileged to witness it, but we also felt—as we discussed later—that we were somehow left out. That, as intense and fulfilling as "our" union was, it was only a shadow of what was happening beyond our personal or interpersonal consciousness. Because we were "left out," this awesome experience carried a note of sadness with it. (Private communication)

Body, soul, and spirit; euphoria, awe, and sadness; contained, containing, and side-by-side; motionless and dancing: the variety and flow of imagination in this moment of *rati* hints at the density and clarity possible in a single instance of Zeus's one-night stands. The density and clarity suggest as well the diversity of psychological and interpersonal work that goes on during love-play. We discover new dimensions of ourselves, our partners, and our union. Such multidimensional encounters with another human being constitute one of the most powerful and dramatic ways to discover our own souls, to appreciate dimensions in ourselves of which we may not formerly have dreamed or which we may not have known how to reach.

Another characteristic of love-play has to do with the changes it takes us through. The mythology of Zeus provides a useful metaphor also for this second characteristic. In various of his seductions, Zeus assumes opportune shapes. He visited Danaë in the form of a golden shower; he seduced Europa in the shape of a bull and enticed her to ride. He coupled with Leda in the form of a swan and Dia as a horse. And to make love with Artemis's nymph Callisto, Zeus assumed the form of Artemis herself. Joseph Campbell rightly points out the underlying unity amid Zeus's changes:

> All of his goddesses were actually but aspects of the one, in a gown, so to speak, of changeable jade; while he in each of his epiphanies was as different from his last as was the goddess in the case from hers. (1964: 148f.)

Campbell's appeal to oneness refers to Rumi's dwelling place, the secret chamber the lovers are preparing even as they square off over the game board of love-play. Campbell is right to point out this deeper truth. But let us not disregard the shape-changing. No doubt change reveals the One beneath the flux, but there are important psychological reasons for the changes.

This becomes obvious when a Zeus-like god goes through several transformations in order to make a single conquest. The fullest example occurs in the *Brihadaranyaka Upanishad* (1.4.1-5), a Hindu scripture, which states that in the beginning of the universe there was only the self (Viraj) alone in the shape of a person. Desiring a mate, Viraj became the size of a man and woman in close embrace. He then divided his body in two and became husband and wife.

She reflected: "How can he unite with me after having produced me from himself? Well, let me hide myself." She became a cow, the other became a bull and was united with her; from that union cows were born. The one became a mare, the other became a stallion; the one became a she-ass, the other became a he-ass and was united with her; from that union one-hoofed animals were born. The one became a she-goat, the other became a he-goat; the one became a ewe, the other became a ram and was united with her; from that union goats and sheep were born. Thus, indeed, he produced everything that exists in pairs, down to the ants. (Nikhilananda, 190)

This is a story about how the universe came to be as we know it. It started out as a single point, a Self, and elaborated itself through a lengthy episode of love-play. Furthermore, although the play is made possible and driven, as it were, by the agency of the first (male) subject, his beloved mate introduces a variety without which the universe could not have become what it is. Through the exigencies of love-play, therefore, his beloved forces Viraj to actualize what he already potentially is. The asceticism of *rati*, we may say, requires him to acknowledge novelty in her and become something new himself.

Lawrence hints at this function of love-play in his novel, *Women in Love*, at the point when Gudrun's affair with Gerald is beginning to go sour. She more and more finds Gerald to be a stodgy stick-in-the-mud, entirely without imagination. At a ski resort she begins a flirtation with a playful German, named Loerke. Gerald is disgusted by it and unable to understand what is going on with this slippery, less-than-manly German.

The whole game was one of subtle intersuggestivity, and they wanted to keep it on the plane of suggestion. From their verbal and physical nuances they got the highest satisfaction in the nerves, from a queer interchange of half-suggested ideas, looks, expressions and gestures, which were quite intolerable though incomprehensible to Gerald. (1982: 546)

They talked a mixture of languages. The groundwork was French, in either case. But he ended most of his sentences in a stumble of English and a conclusion of German, she skillfully wove herself to her end in whatever phrase came to her. She took a peculiar delight in this conversation. It was full of odd, fantastic expression, double meanings, of evasions, of suggestive vagueness. It was a real physical pleasure to her to make this thread of conversation out of the different-coloured strands of three languages. (Ibid., 552)

Gudrun and Loerke are experiencing, here, some of the creativity of Viraj and his anima: a delightful coming into being of new dimensions of relationship and new aspects of themselves. Their love-play contrasts with Gerald's stuffed-shirted heaviness as day with night. Lawrence interweaves this episode of love-play with the dominant theme of the book, a passion for the ultimate quiet of death. Gerald, who accidentally and brutally murdered his brother as a teenager and courts death his whole life, is fascinated during this ski outing with the notion of murdering Gudrun:

But he kept the idea constant within him, what a perfect voluptuous consummation it would be to strangle her, to strangle every spark of life out of her, till she lay completely inert, soft, relaxed forever, a soft heap lying dead between his hands, utterly dead. Then he would have had her finally and forever; there would be such a perfect voluptuous finality. (Ibid., 560)

His need for control and possession is precisely the motive that love-play seeks to surpass.

There is a scene early in *Women in Love* in which Gerald forces a young horse to stand unflinching at a railway crossing, only a few feet from a speeding train. Lawrence refers to this incident several times later in the book. Clearly he wants us to see it as characteristic of Gerald's stance against natural and spontaneous life. In his professional career Gerald has succeeded in converting his father's inefficient paternalistic mining company into an impersonal money-making machine. Whereas his father had known the family of every one of his workers, Gerald knows the science and economics of mining. In attempting to apply this kind of control to his relationship with Gudrun, he has been continually frustrated by unexpected, and even whimsical, developments. Loerke represents the culmination of all of these. From Gerald's perspective Loerke represents the destructive potential of play, while in the eyes of Gudrun he embodies the transcendent promise of *rati*. This is again coherent with the mythology of Shiva:

> Among ascetics [Shiva] is a libertine and among libertines an ascetic; conflicts which they cannot resolve or can attempt to resolve only by compromise, he simply absorbs into himself. . . . Where there is excess, he opposes and controls it; where there is no action, he himself becomes excessively active. He emphasizes that aspect of himself which is unexpected, inappropriate, shattering any attempt to achieve a superficial reconciliation of the conflict through mere logical compromise. (O'Flaherty, 36)

In the moribund relationship of Gudrun and Gerald, Loerke's very name suggests the happy, whimsical bird whose name means transcendence in so much of English poetry. Just as Gudrun finds herself weighted down with the gloom of Gerald's possessiveness and control, a German-speaking Shiva falls trilling from the sky and invites her on a soul-restoring lark.

In relationship, life-giving change frequently appears as the "unexpected [and] inappropriate shattering [of] any attempt to achieve a superficial reconciliation." Love-play is the arena where old expectations are overthrown and staid roles dissolved. Our beloved continually becomes someone new, and we cannot remain what we were. We cannot cling to the comforts of yesterday, to an eternal unconscious oneness. Love-play is the stream of imagination that constantly challenges and renews. As we observe and act upon its apparent whimsies, we find our beloved changing, as well as the capacity to change within ourselves. Like Gudrun and Loerke, we find that transformation is fun: it entices us into dropping our defenses, lures us into becoming our greater selves. Love-play is above all the arena for this kind of challenge and growth.

Only the One in which love is anchored is beyond change. We, on the other hand, are both multidimensional in any moment and in flux over time. We take delight when our beloved's eye is caught by our attributes. We feel newly understood and appreciated. We are reassured that we are worthwhile—perhaps even fascinating. At the same time these newly appreciated attributes become more solidly integrated into our self-image. We gain in self-confidence, we feel healed and made whole. We begin to contemplate a brighter future. We feel more closely linked with our partner through an understanding and an intimacy that formerly was only implicit—if not wholly unknown. In this way our beloved, through the kaleidoscopic "moves" of love-play, sets us free from our former limitations. And by the same process we set her or him free. Love-play is the creative element in romantic love. In our *rati* we re-create one another, ourselves, and our relationship.

Love-play occurs during the spontaneous choreography of sexual intercourse, and especially foreplay. But it is by no means identical with sexual behavior. Whenever intercourse is dull and predictable, love-play is missing. But love-play is also not limited to physical, sexual relating. Love-play occurs in conversations, looks, and gestures, as well. Whenever we are caught by light glancing off new facets of our diamond beloved we are making a "move" on the game board of love. Love-play is the transcendent element in romantic love. Through its magic, we slip the coils of our old selves, our former limitations, the limitations we unconsciously placed on our beloved and on our relationship.

Rati enables us to transcend all of this. It is like a breath of fresh air. Like an underground stream, it secretly searches out depths and crannies and channels that lead us, smooth and tumultuous, to the vastness of the sea. Like a jet stream, it takes us sailing and weightless at unheard-of speeds. Birds of light burst from our chests, merge like candle flames, and disappear in the distance—hundreds of them, all single file, following the same course. Love-play is the stream of imagination that cascades miraculously out of our meeting. To observe it is to be inspired; to act upon it is to effect our own transformation.

When we oppose the flow of playfulness in love, our relationship seems to die, or at least get stuck. We become bored and irritated and we begin to think of escape. Our fancy turns to adultery, to *parakiya* love, to the erotic/religious playfulness that restores our soul. But we need not literally carry on an adulterous affair to achieve transcendence through *rati*. If *rati* seems impossible with our lawful spouse or other ongoing relationship, the reason is often to be found in our rigidity. We get stuck in the way we see our partner; and, inevitably, our partner gets stuck in how he or she sees us. It is as though we already know one another too well. We know exactly what to expect. The images we and our partner have of one another are as if carved in stone.

Getting stuck in the way we see our partners is a common difficulty. When we know our partner "too well," there is no mystery, no novelty, indeed no life left in our interactions. Growth and change have disappeared. Play is the gentle force of transcendence that can break up the logjam and thaw the ice. If we cannot welcome playfulness into our relationship, there are only two possibilities: either we resign ourselves to the dull prison of boredom, or the forces of change become disruptive, like the Shiva who opposes all quiescence with excess and all excess with inaction. Shiva can be almost cruel in his playful, pain-causing disruptions:

> Knowing of her egotism, Siva decided to reveal himself in such a way as to break her heart and remove her pride. He arrived surrounded by ghosts and goblins, riding on a bull, three-eyed, smeared with ashes, carrying a skull, wearing an elephant skin. (O'Flaherty, 217)

The ego-centered lover who cannot allow the spontaneous flow of love's playfulness may experience the horrific dimension of imagination as well as boredom. When, on the other hand, we value *rati* and allow ourselves to explore the intimate chambers it unlocks, we find ourselves challenged and enlarged. Here is where our souls dance an unremembered choreography while a spirit pair unites somewhere else. These are the moments when the formerly unthinkable becomes the touchstone of reality. We conceal the marvelous and divine aspects of our partners behind the masks we project upon them. In love-play we drop those masks and try on a whole series of guises (like those of Zeus and Viraj). We and our beloved appear to one another in new and surprising ways. Our old certainties finally become shaken, and our joint future opens up with new hope and promise. We begin to contemplate and to live adventures and roles that far exceed our habitual expectations. Something of this is hinted at in the mythology of Shiva:

> Although when he first made love to [Parvati] there was no biting of her lips and scratching of her breasts, later her hands were tremulous with pain, her lips marked with bites, and her thighs scarred with the traces of his nails. (Ibid., 233)

Love's madness makes the beautiful Parvati a horror to look at, her marred body a rebuke to all conventional expectations. But Parvati herself is not at all upset about the bruises and scratches on her body. Although she may not have wanted them while in a sober state of mind, once she had been overtaken by the heat of *kama,* the violence of Shiva's love became the vehicle that transported her to an altered state of consciousness. There, as the *Kama Sutra* says, the scars depend upon the depth and force of passion and are the "innumerable, varied and artistic . . . symbols of [one's] love" (Vatsyayana, 33). After the passion has passed, they become badges, as it were, of our partner's desire and respect. The *Kama Sutra* goes so far as to say that this kind of violent *rati* is the secret of love's continual renewal:

> When a man bites his mistress in the violence of love
> She should return his gesture with twice the force;
> Thus for a point she should tender a line of points
> And for a line of points—a broken cloud[2]—

---

2. "A bite in the form of an uneven circle—the unevenness being due to the shape and form of the teeth—is called the Broken Cloud" (Vatsyayana, 35).

And if breathless with passion she should accuse her lover
And provoke a lover's quarrel, seize him by the hair,
Bend his head and fiercely embrace his lower lip,
Then closing her eyes she should bite him all over his body
As an animal in the fury of passion does its mate.
Even in the daytime when her lover shows her the scars
She should smile, turn her head, then angrily show
The wounds his love has left on her.
Thus, if men and women act in mutual accord,
Their passion and desire for each other
Will not diminish even after a hundred years of love. (Ibid., 37)

We have touched upon three contributions that love-play makes to an erotic relationship. Its first achievement is to deepen, differentiate, and explore intimacy's chambers. In illustration of this we have considered such visionary experiences as the golden rainbow pouring through the lover's chest, the spontaneous choreography of imagination, and the union of spirit beings. Love-play's second contribution is its break with the past, which throws down all our former certainties. The third achievement is to call us gently into a new way of being. *Rati's* imaginative flow presents us with a vision of what is incipient in ourselves, in our partners, and in our union. We might call this last the "enjoyment body" of love-play.

By this expression, "enjoyment body," I refer to the doctrine in Buddhism that the Buddha had three bodies. The first is the flesh-and-blood body of the sage Siddhartha who was born around 560 B.C. and lived about eighty years, during which he attained enlightenment and taught its achievement to others. This earthly body (*nirmanakaya*) corresponds to the human body of Jesus of Nazareth, the carpenter and enlightened master of Christianity who died on a cross in about his thirty-third year. A second body of the Buddha (*dharmakaya*) is eternal and wholly beyond sense perception. It corresponds in Christianity to Christ the unchanging Son of God, coeternal with the Father. The "enjoyment body" of the Buddha (*sambhogakaya*) lies between the purely human and purely divine. The Buddha, in his "enjoyment body," appears to individual Buddhists to encourage their devotion and aid them in their quest for nirvana.

When the saint, in mystical trance, seems to encounter the Buddha and learns at first hand a new appreciation of old truths it is the *Sambhoga*-body of Buddhahood he has met. There are descriptions of the amazing forms in which this body appears to [the] faithful: it is resplendent in light and glory and the title given it, "Enjoy-ment-body," seems to indicate the belief that this "body" is in part the symbol of the conviction that the attainment of enlightened Buddhahood brings with it untroubled joy of a kind so different from any which the mere mortal can experience that we have no suitable words to describe it.

There are many stories of supernatural appearances of the Bud-dha and in general we may apply the term *Sambhogakaya* to them all. . . . It is in the form *Sambhogakaya* that the Buddha-Truth preaches most of the Mahayana *sutras* [scriptures appearing after the earliest period of Buddhism]. . . .

In short, the function of the *Sambhogakaya* is first to symbolize the self-enjoyment of Buddhahood and second to be the locus of mystical instruction and enlightenment. As such it is another link between the unimaginable Ultimate and the limping consciousness of the earthbound man. (Fox, 192f.)

The Buddhist doctrine of *sambhogakaya* clearly corresponds to the appearances of the resurrected Christ. Such an appearance to the disciples on the road to Emmaus (Luke 24:13-32) includes an explanation of how the events of Jesus' life fulfill the scriptures regarding the Messiah. When, in his breaking bread, they finally recognize him, they say, "Did we not feel our hearts on fire as he talked with us on the road and explained the scriptures to us?" All these events have as their common denominator an experience coming from elsewhere (God, Christ, the Buddha) but finely tuned to effect a transformation in the recipient. An "enjoyment body" experience, we may say, works as a kind of mirror for the individual soul, showing it precisely what it needs to know to recover from its stuckness and proceed upon its path. At the same time our accepting the challenge posed through the "enjoyment body" of our beloved enables us to approach our own "Buddhahood."

The Buddha's "enjoyment body" and Christ's resurrected body are instances of a divine love-play, calling us to transcend ourselves. Applied to human love-play, the "enjoyment body" of our beloved is how she or he appears, radiant and glorious, shot through with the light of the divine spark, resplendent in our mutual love. More than that, it is our beloved made new, recreated in the imaginative flow of *rati*, opening our eyes to the realities we have overlooked, and making our hearts "feel on fire." The "enjoyment body" of love-play is the "good news" that this particular friendship with this unique individual at this specific moment brings into our lives. Thousand-year-long frolics, such as Shiva and Parvati enjoy, must be studded with nearly a billion such epiphanies.

An epiphany is an "outward manifestation" of something usually hidden—especially an outward appearance of divinity. In the Christian tradition, the term *epiphany* is used almost exclusively for the fairly few instances in which Christ's divinity became manifest to onlookers. One thinks, for example, of the infancy narratives in which various groups or individuals recognized the divinity or messiahhood of Jesus: the shepherds, the Magi, Simeon, and so on. There was also the baptism by John in the Jordan, attended by a dove and a voice from heaven, as well as the several post-resurrection appearances. Perhaps the most striking instance is that of the "transfiguration":

> The appearance of his face changed and his clothes became dazzling white. Suddenly there were two men talking with him; these were Moses and Elijah, who appeared in glory and spoke of his departure, the destiny he was to fulfill in Jerusalem. . . . there came a cloud which cast a shadow over them; they were afraid as they entered the cloud, and from it there came a voice: "This is my Son, my Chosen; listen to him." When the voice had spoken, Jesus was seen to be alone. The disciples kept silence and at that time told nobody anything of what they had seen. (Luke 9:28–36).

When love-play is completely successful, every "move" on love's game board is an epiphany. Every step in our dance, every guise our beloved assumes and then drops, is a facet in the magnificent jewel of the Self, aglow from the divine spark within. The reason we laugh and slap our gaming pieces on the board with such gusto is that we know very well we have been dragging our bed into intimacy's central chamber.

9

The Lovers' Quarrel:
Fight for Renewal

It is no accident that Shiva and Parvati, the gods of love-play, are also renowned for their quarrels. O'Flaherty (311) shows that the structure of the quarrel myths parallels that of the myths of love-play: while playing a game of dice, they quarrel and part; subsequently Parvati seduces Shiva, and Shiva returns to *tapas,* his heat-generating meditation on the One. Parvati's complaints about Shiva are quite predictable, given the picture we have of him as the dissolute god of sex and meditation. She reviles him for his shamelessness, going about naked, unkempt, and covered with the ashes of the graveyard; for his improvidence as a householder, in that he holds no job but depends on begging like an ordinary mendicant monk; and for his fondness for drugs and low company. The quarrel polarizes the pair—as it often does, too, among mortals—until she stands for temporal values such as material comfort, respectability, and orientation to everyday details, and he, for his part, champions what stands outside of time—transcendental values, the One, and realities that lie beyond death and are inaccessible to ordinary states of consciousness.

In the lovers' quarrel, those matters that it is the business of relationship to harmonize and integrate fall into conflict with one another. The love potion's wonderful sense of unparalleled unity is suddenly called into question. Just yesterday we knew without a shadow of a doubt that our relationship was made in heaven and would survive forever. Our love made us immortal and indestructible. We felt we had returned to some original state of oneness for which we had longed all our lives without knowing it. We thought we had awakened from the twilight of a dreary dream into a glorious reality in which the dingy yellow light of the terrestrial sun had been

replaced by the pure white brilliance of the Sun of the Universe.
And now look at us, squabbling in the most demeaning and vicious
manner as though each of our very lives depended on annihilating
the other.

This is how matters must have appeared to Dido in Vergil's *Aeneid*.
The Trojan hero, Aeneas, had been directed by the gods through his
dreams to leave Troy, while the Greeks from the Trojan horse were
besieging the city, and to found a new civilization. He wanders from
one place to another until his dreams clarify that it is on the west
coast of Italy where he will establish the city of Rome—on the site
of the ancestral home of the Trojan founder, Dardanus. His mother,
Venus, intercedes with Jove to smooth his course, while Jove's wife,
Juno, does everything she can to impede Aeneas's progress.[1] These
warring forces drive his ship onto the coast of Libya, where Queen
Dido is building the city of Carthage, Rome's historic rival. Now
Juno and Venus collaborate to have Dido and Aeneas fall in love.
With these two goddesses cooperating, this could be a marriage that
combines both practical and transcendental love. Aeneas has just
about consented to help in the founding of Carthage, when Jove
sends Mercury to tell Aeneas to leave immediately for Italy. Aeneas
at once sets to work on his boats, without a word to Dido. Her rage
is withering:

> . . . No goddess was your mother!
> No noble Dardanus forebear of yours, you scum,
> But the foul Caucasus breached you out of its rocks,
> Hyrcanian tigresses gave you suck. . . .
> . . . Go. Go—seek Italy
> On the tempest, seek your realms over the storm-crests,
> And I pray if the gods are as true to themselves as their powers
> You shall be smashed on the rocks, calling on Dido's name;
> O, I will shadow your course like a black star
> And when cold death possesses my body and soul;
> I will haunt you wherever you go, you wicked creature,

---

1. Jove (or Jupiter) and Juno are the Roman counterparts of Zeus and Hera, and
they are having the same dispute over marital love versus illicit/religious love. The
Trojans represent *rati* insofar as it is their hero, Paris, who started the Trojan War by
abducting Helen, the wife of the Greek king, Menelaus.

I will see to your punishment. Report of you
Will filter down to me even among the dead . . .

(Vergil, 85)

That love can change its face so quickly from angelic bliss to fiendish spitefulness results from its being founded on our wounkedness. On the one hand, we are never so complete and so satisfied as when we are with the individual whose being and whose wound corresponds to our own. On the other hand, no one else is so capable of ripping open that wound as the one to whom we have given our heart. Indeed, before the fall into love we have typically learned to defend and protect our wound in a nearly automatic fashion. Not infrequently we succeed in convincing ourselves that we are whole and unwounded before meeting our beloved. Then, in *her* incomparable presence, we dare to rip off the bandage, like Tristan before his union in death with Isolde. We only brave this risk because we have already experienced some hint of the sublimity and peace we can obtain in union with her. And, for this very reason, we find our betrayal—as it seems—rocks the foundations of our world and calls into question our worth as a person.

Such, surely, was the condition of Dido. She had risked everything—including her reputation and her political position in Libya, whose powerful King Iarbus had wished to marry her and was enraged by her affair with Aeneas. Like Tristan and Isolde, like Shiva and Parvati, she has chosen romantic love over the social and political security of a sensible marriage. She has staked everything on the vision of Aeneas' soul she gained through her animus lens. That transcendental truth has the feel of eternity, and she expected a mutual *fana* with Aeneas.

Vergil makes it clear that Dido's love for Aeneas is a fatal wound:

>   . . . The fires
> Slinked mining through her marrow, the tacit wound
> Sucked inward from her breasts. Unhappy Dido
> In frenzy staggered and reeled through the whole city,
> Like a wild doe in the mountain groves of Crete
> A shepherd has shot at a venture, at long range,

And does not know his lucky shaft has stuck
And the flying barb clings like a burr in its wound—
And through the woods and plains of Dicte it reels
The deadly weapon fast in its dying flank.

(77)

We know that Aeneas' wound must be comparably grave. This son of the goddess of love has lived through the utter destruction of his homeland, his people murdered and enslaved—all for the love of a woman. In his many years of stumbling from one inhospitable shore to another, only Dido's Carthage opens its arms and invites him to become joint founder of a Libyan empire. His victories have been small and his losses, rejections, and devastation overwhelming. His dalliance in the cave with Dido must have been a monumental experience of timeless unity and surcease of temporal care. Vergil tells us that he abandoned his armor in her bedroom and never returned to claim it (ibid., 88).

We want to know how he could bring himself to break such a bond and expose again his wound, festering with abandonment and failure. Vergil tells us almighty Jove made the decision. In the language of the psyche, the mythic image of the king of the gods refers to the central organizing principle of the Self. Jove wants Aeneas to found the *Roman* Empire and not to mix Trojan blood with Libyan. Vergil leans too much on his political motives. He wants the *Aeneid* to make Romans proud of their heritage. We may therefore doubt whether he has done justice to the power of the bond between Dido and Aeneas. The poet might have sung a different story, had he taken Dido more seriously. But had he done so and still retained an episode in which Aeneas breaks the erotic bond, he would surely not have eliminated Jove. The image of Jove is a kind of shorthand notation to tell us that Aeneas had to have been powerfully moved from the very center of his soul to relinquish what had been achieved with Dido. Vergil leaves us no doubt of this, when he describes Aeneas' reaction to the appearance of Mercury bringing Jove's orders:

> Cowed by this apparition, terrified Aeneas
> Was dumb; his hair stood on end; his tongue clove;

He burned to escape, to quit these lotus-lands;
Thunderstruck with this stark ultimatum
From the god of gods.

(82)

Only after Jove has thundered from the center does Carthage seem to be a "lotus-land," a realm of debilitating oblivion. What a change in love's valuation! Is it the highest of human truths or a mind-numbing delusion? Very frequently this conflict lies at the heart of the lovers' quarrel. One partner, like Dido, fights to draw the other back into eternal oneness while the second, like Aeneas, struggles for heroic individuality, autonomy, and everyday accomplishment. The polarizing that occurs in the quarrel reveals the two major components that a successful love relationship needs to integrate.

This issue has come up in earlier chapters as the opposition between the love potion and the naked sword. A successful erotic relationship must take both demands seriously. Only the unity of two souls can open up the channels of the Self to the deep eternal bond that undergirds both the union itself and the two individuals, separately. But that unity becomes fusion, loss of identity, madness, and psychological death, unless we can each simultaneously redis-cover our own uniqueness. If the drive toward oneness is emphasized at the expense of that toward individuality, the union stultifies growth. When, on the other hand, individuality triumphs over union, relationship is dissolved. Only when the Dido principle and the Aeneas principle are integrated, without either of them losing its force, can relationship succeed.

The lovers' quarrel is fought over these two opposing principles. The story of Dido and Aeneas gives us a feel for the struggle, looked at from the outside. We know that both Dido's demand for devel-oping the transcendent oneness they have already begun to experi-ence and Aeneas' heroic sense of destiny are both important. And we know that Vergil's political purpose in creating a mythic justifi-cation for Roman hegemony caused him to use the story of romantic love to lend importance, dignity, and divine sanction to his hero's vocation. But he accomplishes this by letting us know very little about the inner life of Aeneas. We need a story that will take us inside the mind and heart of the lover who rejects the bliss of union.

The story of the troubadour Heinrich Tannhaeuser dramatizes the struggle very well—particularly because he has no heroic purpose, like Aeneas. He is moved to reject an eternal *rati* with Venus—not because he is called to some goal of worldly redemption or political accomplishment, but only because that one-sided eternal love was found to be unsatisfying purely on its own account. Tannhaeuser was an actual historical character, a *Minnesinger,* or wandering knight-minstrel, singing of courtly love (*Minne*). He was born around 1200, squandered his patrimony, participated in a crusade, and later wandered from one European court to another looking for a patron to support him. He was famous for his love of wine, food, women, and bathing twice a week. We follow, here, Richard Wagner's operatic version of the tale.

The Story of Tannhaeuser

The opera begins with a long, sensuous ballet in which scantily clad couples seem to be making languorous love on a dimly lit stage. The music in the orchestra is otherworldly, even spiritual. It seems to have no beginning and no end. A chorus of "sirens" occasionally calls from offstage urging hearers to come to this land, where the glowing arms of love will provide blissful release from care.

As attention gradually focuses on Tannhaeuser and Venus, lying in one another's arms at center stage, the atmosphere of love-play changes quickly to quarrel. Venus asks with loving concern where Tannhaeuser's mind has drifted. He responds as passionately and sharply as a slap in the face: "It's too much, too much! Oh, let me now awake!"[2] He has been dreaming of the old familiar sounds of earth and wonders how long he has been away. Here within the Venusberg (the "mountain of Venus," or, in Latin, *mons veneris*), there is no way to distinguish the passage of time: no sun, moon, or stars. Venus asks him if he is not happy to be like a god. He responds that he is

---

2. All quotations translated by me.

very glad for the gift of song she has given him but that unfortunately he is still a mortal and cannot handle so much bliss. Unlike the gods, he says, a man requires change. The quarrel goes on for some twenty minutes until Venus cries, "Return to me, I am your only salvation." In reply, he brings the scene to both dramatic and musical resolution, declaring: "My salvation lies in the Virgin Mary." This is an unprecedented pronouncement, for nothing distinctively Christian or in praise of chastity has been part of this argument. It immediately brings the scene to a close, and we find ourselves in a bucolic valley on earth.

It is May in the valley and a shepherd boy is singing about his dream of Lady Holda (Venus) as Tannhaeuser lies prostrate on the ground. A column of pilgrims passes through, singing with transcendent sadness of the burden of their sins. Tannhaeuser, glorious full-throated madman, praises God's wonder and mercy, which he hopes will help him bear his onerous guilt. To this end, he chooses a life of toil and trouble. A small group of minstrels enters. They recognize the prostrate Tannhaeuser as a former comrade who had feuded with them and left. If he is willing to befriend them, they urge him to mix his song with theirs so that Elisabeth, the Landgrave's beautiful niece, will again enter their Hall of Minstrels. She had retired since Tannhaeuser won her heart by his magic song and then departed the land of Thuringia. The name of this loveliest woman in the world rouses something powerful in Tannhaeuser. He sings out her name like a clarion bell that soars into the opera house and seems to absorb the whole orchestra into itself.

The second act opens with that paragon of beauty and saintliness emerging from seclusion into the Hall of the Minstrels. She says that, before his departure from the Hall, Tannhaeuser's song had awakened a new emotion in her breast. What previously had been dear to her had vanished before joys, pains, and longings she could not name. But in the months he was gone, her dreams were filled with anguish and her days haunted by pensive, gloomy shades.

The Landgrave enters and announces a song contest in

which the *Minnesinger* who best describes the nature of love will win Elisabeth's hand. Wolfram von Eschenbach[3] sings a tribute to Elisabeth to whom he kneels, in awe of an angelic beauty that he would never sully with reckless desires. Tannhaeuser is outraged by this pious claptrap. As words become more and more intemperate, he becomes a wild man, praising caresses and rapture until he is finally provoked into the mystic pagan strains of the Venusberg music. He praises Venus as the source of all that is beautiful and wondrous. Only he who has enjoyed her passionate arms can know what love is. "So," he spits in derision at his antagonists, "go to Venusberg!" The whole Hall of Minstrels comes down on him. As chorus and principals all sing different phrases, righteous and vengeful melodic fragments pierce the babel of sounds, while Tannhaeuser's penitent tones roll uncertainly about like black fog. Swords are drawn, and Elisabeth's commanding soprano calls for forgiveness and charity. The Landgrave says there may be hope yet if Tannhaeuser can get the pope to absolve his sins. Tannhaeuser ends the act with a heroically determined but strangely gloomy, "To Rome!"

The third act finds us back in the bucolic valley, which resonates with a penitent yet triumphant melody sung by a column of pilgrims returning, gratefully shriven, from Rome. Because Tannhaeuser is not one of them, Elisabeth is very disturbed and prays to the Virgin that she might waste away to death in expiation for her *Minnesinger's* guilt. After she leaves the stage, Tannhaeuser appears, alone, ragged, and defeated. Although his austerities have been as single-minded and excessive as his former liberties, the pope has condemned him to eternal damnation. He has fed the demonic flames of Venusian delight and therefore stands as little chance of salvation as the pope's barren staff of putting forth flower or leaf. What a turning point! His eyes are open, and he is disgusted by pious

---

3. Also a historical character (1170–1220), author of famous verse epics and love lyrics. In his christening of pagan legends, he glorifies married love and sane affection over the far less tame tradition of courtly love. He is a favorite whipping boy for Wagner, who has him lose another song contest in his last opera, *Die Meistersinger von Nürnberg*. Wagner portrays him as an uninspired plodder, good-hearted but arrogant, an observer of the letter of the law who has never experienced its spirit.

Christian deceptions. They turn his soul to ice. He looks instead for the bliss-filled, warm, and magic nights of Venus. As his voice soars again into the ardor of the Venusberg music, the love goddess's cave materializes upstage; and she herself, raven-haired personification of otherworldly beauty and rapture, welcomes her prodigal with open arms.

In a frenzy Tannhaeuser is straining up the path to the Venusberg when Wolfram sings out the name of the Landgrave's niece, that angel who has hovered in blessing over her sinful troubadour and brought him redemption. Again the name of the blond exemplar of all that is pure and holy in love pulls Tannhaeuser up short; he sings out, *Elisabeth!* in the ringing tones of a man finally come to his senses. Venusberg fades as pallbearers enter with Elisabeth's coffin. Tannhaeuser stumbles to her bier and sinks to death himself, asking the holy Elisabeth to pray for him. Pilgrims arrive from Rome bearing the pope's staff, bursting with blossoms and leaves.

In having Tannhaeuser saved by the saintly Elisabeth, Wagner has taken liberties with the medieval legend. There the pope's staff blooms three days after the *Minnesinger* returns to Venusberg—a shockingly un-Christian resolution, which implicitly links the libertine's three days in the cave of sexual delights with Christ's three days in the tomb, whence, in the words of the Apostle's Creed, "He descended into hell." In my view, both outcomes are unsatisfying. The medieval legend rejects Christian puritanism in favor of sensuality while Wagner seems to do the reverse. But Tannhaeuser's central problem is how to reconcile these apparent opposites.

The Venusberg music, which plays throughout the balletic prologue and the long quarrel between the goddess and the minstrel, has the shimmering, leaping quality of flames, without any sense of burning up or consumption. These are spiritual flames that occasion no pain but transport and transform the soul. They are the divine presence that Moses saw in the burning bush. We experience them in those moments of joyful clarity when our whole being gently meets the being of our beloved and we find that the solid earthy substance of our body has fallen away and our anatomy has become pure flame.

The music has the sound and feel of rapture. And yet it somehow insinuates a subtle dreariness, as though a line has been crossed between a paradisal eternity that knows no time and the malaise of time without end. On the blessed side of that line, we look up from our couch to see with dismay that only three hours of dalliance remain before we have to dress for work. What has happened, we wonder, to that glorious stretch of time we had so carefully set aside? Could seven hours have passed so wholly unnoticed? Once the line is crossed into tedium, however, even fifteen minutes seems unendurable. We find ourselves restless, preoccupied with the concerns of the day, held back, raring to go. Solidity returns to our flesh so that the silken flames that glided over one another so easily become sticky skin in need of a bath. We have a crick in our back from lying so long supine. Our lover no longer has anything fresh to say, nor do we. It is time for a change.

Tannhaeuser has crossed that line. He needs to become reacquainted with the seasons of the year, the movements of the heavens, the death and rebirth of the land. Venus offers him the softest of pillows and freedom from all discomfort. He retorts that only a god can dwell in bliss, that he needs pain as well as pleasure. This is no slight to her charms, for she is the source of all beauty and wonder. The flame in his heart will burn always and only for her. He will sing her praises from one end of the earth to the other, but he cannot stay. Her presence is too powerful for it; he is in danger of being absorbed. He must struggle, even though it bring about his death. In fact he would even embrace death, if that is what it takes to escape Venusberg.

Such sentiments lie at the heart of every quarrel between lovers. Every outburst of anger, every aggressive move is an attempt to reconstitute ourselves. When we find ourselves threatened, only two options are open to us: fight and flight. When we flee the challenge, we react with depression and sadness, as we mourn our loss of territory, standing, prestige. When we fight, we use our anger to recoup our losses. This is what happens, too, in the lovers' quarrel. One partner feels he has lost something, given up too much, or especially is in danger of losing identity. No amount of comfort and bliss can erase Tannhaeuser's need for the struggles that establish and maintain his identity. If he remains too long with Venus, he loses his own autonomy and becomes her slave. He loves her deeply and will never cease to sing her praises; he is grateful for what he has received from her—his gift of song and the delights of love; but he cannot stay without losing his equality. He is afraid he will become nothing but an adjunct to her.

We imagine Tannhaeuser may even be surprised at this turn of events, for in the first timeless months of his dalliance he must have felt he was discovering himself. This is, anyway, what we are led to gather from his argument in the song contest. Had he not experienced the sensual and spiritual bliss of Venusberg, he could not have been so recklessly sure of himself, so confident that the pieties of the Landgrave's minstrels were missing the point about love—and indeed of human relationship itself.

In his early novel, *The Joke*, Milan Kundera gives us a very good idea of what the surcease of temporal care through romantic love can provide an individual. Young Ludvik has gotten himself into serious trouble with the Czech authorities by sending a crudely satirical postcard to a girlfriend away at a kind of summer training camp. He finds himself sentenced to hard labor and stripped for life of all opportunity for professional achievement and social respectability. He is in the doldrums, almost suicidal, but too listless to initiate anything. In this situation, he meets a very strange girl, Lucie, psychologically damaged by childhood abuse and almost completely lacking in social adaptation. She walks with a slowness that radiates resignation, as though there could never be anywhere worth hurrying to. She sits as though waiting to be called in for surgery, and waves her hand as though she has learned that is what people do when they separate. She is capable of waiting weeks between Ludvik's furlough days and still greet him as though they had just parted the day before.

In meeting this girl who lives outside of time, Ludvik says he feels "inhabited" again. Regarding the tragedy of losing his career, he says:

Lucie had a miraculous effect on that deep pain. All I needed was to feel her close to me, feel the warmth of her way of life, a life outside the issues of cosmopolitanism and internationalism, vigilance and the class struggle, and what constitutes the dictatorship of the proletariat—a life outside the whole gamut of politics, its strategy and tactics. (Kundera, 60)

She knew nothing of the *major problems of our times,* the problems she lived with were *trivial and eternal.* And suddenly I'd been released; Lucie had come to take me off to her *gray paradise,* and the step that until such a short time before had seemed unthinkable, the step enabling me to "make my exit from history," was suddenly a cause for relief and rejoicing. Lucie held me shyly by the arm, and I let myself be led. (Ibid., 61)

Tannhaeuser, too, must have let himself be led. For what is even a mad genius who sings like an angel compared to the goddess of love? She has to have led him on tracks he could never have found for himself, and he must have found them liberating.

The tracks along which Venus led her *Minnesinger* belong to the archetypal levels of the psyche: the realm of the mythic image, the preimagistic Self, and the instinct/archetypes. Here, there is no sense of time; it is always *now.* One is overwhelmingly impressed with the interrelatedness of all things. A sense of Oneness on the Self-level oscillates with the roaring chaos of the tiger pit. There is no sense of ego or personhood, no history, no personal memory, no "style," nothing characteristic; for these things belong to the conscious individual and to the personal unconscious.

As he was led into this archetypal realm, Tannhaeuser must have been delighted to have found the "depth dimension" of his song-making, his lovemaking, and his "bumming around" from one European court to another. This is what he had sung about and searched for, always catching just a glimpse of something compelling, always feeling that he had fallen just short of the transcending experience in which his soul could find its missing half and be able to relax into fulfillment. Like the first troubadour, William of Poitier and Aquitaine, Tannhaeuser must have found his august lady to be his completion, that obedience to her was equivalent to perfect fidelity to himself, that she was the sole source of his salvation. But now, after he has been in Venusberg for days or years or centuries, something has changed. He repudiates her declaration, "Return to me, I am your only salvation," with that puzzling reference to the Virgin Mary.

A recent interpretation (von Rhein) of the opera by Peter Sellars solves the puzzle of Tannhaeuser's conflict too easily by making Tannhaeuser a fallen television evangelist. Accordingly, the Venusberg becomes a sleazy motel somewhere in the Bible Belt; Venus is a prostitute; and the bucolic valley of penitence and reconciliation is replaced by O'Hare airport with an American Airlines tarmac in the background. Here the drama depends on conflict between the irreconcilable principles of compulsive, sensual sinfulness and idealized, letter-of-the-law perfectionism. I think it misses the point of Tannhaeuser's struggle. Sellars's televangelist enters the Venusberg cynically or naughtily for a diverting debauch, while the *Minnesinger* enters honestly in quest of wholeness and truth.

Wagner's Venus is not a bawdy temptress; she exists on a different plane from the Christian literalism of Wolfram von Eschenbach and the Landgrave's other minstrels. As in his other operas, Wagner is striving for a vision of a higher integration. Because the pope's staff, in blooming, repudiates the pontiff's arrogant puritanism, neither Wagner nor Tannhaeuser puritanically condemns Venus. She is not repudiated as evil, but transcended as incomplete. Goddess though she may be, she suffers an abandonment very much like that of Dido. Tannhaeuser has gone on to something else.

Ironically, Venusberg is both "too much" and not enough for Tannhaeuser. The painfulness of the quarrel depends on there being no clear alternatives of right and wrong. There would be no quarrel if the lovers were not bound to one another very deeply at the level of Self. Fighting erupts when one of the partners finds that this archetypal bond is not sufficient or that it is threatening to his autonomy and identity. The conflict is not between good and evil but between two goods that are incomplete and in search of reconciliation. In order to make this point clearer, we can consider the very well-documented[4] love affair between the American novelist Thomas Wolfe and the stage designer Aline Bernstein.

---

4. Not only do we have biographies of both partners (cf. Donald and Klein) but also their love letters (Stutman) and fiction by both parties, which describes the affair with only the most superficial alteration of facts.

They met in 1925, when she was forty-four and he twenty-five. He describes her as a matronly woman, energetic, with a fresh, ruddy face, whom few people passing on the street would have given a second glance. Yet she became for him "the creature of incomparable loveliness to whom all other women in the world must be compared" (1973[a]: 312–14). For her part, she felt she had "already known" this awkward, passionate giant. In her novel about the affair, *The Journey Down,* Bernstein says that right at the beginning they experienced an inadvertent merging and began to marshall their defenses against it (1938/87: 15).

Wolfe was eloquent in his praise of Bernstein or Esther Jack, as he calls her in his last two novels. He found her rich in joy, dignity, and imagination, a real contrast with the general run of people who "have little power of living in themselves" (1973[a]: 380). She transferred this energy directly into his blood:

And instead of the old confusion, weariness, despair, and desolation of the spirit, instead of the old and horrible sensation of drowning, smothering, in the numberless manswarm of the earth, he knew nothing but triumphant joy and power. (Ibid., 447)

"For the first time in his whole life he mattered deeply, earnestly, to someone else" (ibid., 389). The great city of New York, which had formerly terrified this small-town southerner, came together for him in Aline. "She was the city he had longed to know" (ibid., 390), and the "world" (ibid., 405). Whereas he lived in disorder and confusion and could not seem to get either his life or his career together, her life was the very model of the clarity, control, hope, and integrity that a great artist required (ibid, 463).

Tom's importance to Aline was no less significant. At their first meeting, when he began to praise her beauty and to kiss her, she thought she must leap into the sea and drown, for life could only be downhill from that moment on (1938/87: 24). She was in love with his passion, violence, and neediness; his ability to write and to see and remember so marvelously. "Darling you must never be not wild, but naturally I like to be wild with you—I should like to go like lightning somewhere" (Stutman, 45).

Their relationship flourished as long as his writing went well (Donald, 164); their course was rocky. After a fairly successful tour of Europe together in the summer of 1926, he stayed on in England in order to be away from her to finish his book. Although he wrote a great deal, he felt alone and lost, like a phantom in the world of people, or a person in a world of phantoms (Stutman, 82), writing her letters of colossal length and then not believing in the mails to get them to her (ibid., 86). Still, as he headed home, he wrote in his notebook, "What rut of life with the Jew, now?" (ibid., 143).

The big quarrel marking the turning point of their relatonship occurred about nineteen months after they had met. Aline appeared radiant and cheerful, as usual, one day when Tom was particularly depressed. He immediately felt betrayed. He was entangled in her web;[5] she was "entombed in his flesh" (Wolfe, 1973[a]: 556), absorbing all his thoughts and energies while he was sunk in doubt, suspicion, and madness. Perhaps he was just one of many young men whose blood she sucked. He had given her his youth and she had very likely never loved him at all. He accused her of this and of being as depraved as any in the world of the theater—being the daughter of a travelling actor and promiscuous playboy. There was an element of truth in this taunt, and Aline raged in a sobbing voice that she would smash his face in for maligning her family. *His* family, though—and here she spoke the truth his *Look Homeward, Angel* denies and which he was never able to face—did not care whether Tom lived or died. Worst of all she attacked the father he needed to believe was a "great man":

> "Yes, a great bum!" she jeered. "A great whiskey drinker! A great woman chaser! That's what he was! He gave you a fine home, didn't he? He left you a large fortune, didn't he? You ought to thank him for all he's done for you! Thank him for making you an outcast and a wanderer! Thank him for filling your heart with hate and poison against all the people who have loved you! Thank him

---

5. Before his death, Wolfe had thought he was working on a single novel, with the title, *The Web and the Rock*. As the city and the world, Aline was the *rock* of the title; and as his opponent she spun the *web*. After his death, his editor separated the gargantuan collection of manuscript fragments into two novels and named the second *You Can't Go Home Again*.

for your black, twisted soul and all the hate in your mad brain! Thank him for making you hate yourself and your own life! Thank him for making a monster of you who stabs his friends to the heart and then deserts them! And then see if you can't be as much like him as you can! Since that's what you want, follow in his footsteps, and see if you can't be as vile a man as he was! (Ibid., 566)

He threw her out of the apartment and a few minutes later went running after her, thinking that he was just a grumbling baby while she cheerfully did the work of a titan. They had a noisy, argumentative reunion in the street, in which he accused her of making the bystanders laugh at him.

There is always a struggle in romantic love between oneness and separation, though perhaps not always so violent as in this affair. Typically, too, when a struggle does emerge, there is a polarization of the two parties. Although both lovers want unity with the other *and* a separate life and identity, the quarrel results in their identifying with only one of the poles and forgetting or even fearing their need for the other. As Tom tries to break free of Aline's "web," she is doing all in her power to further and champion their oneness and the archetypal dimension of timelessness. In her short story about the affair, she wishes "they could just freeze like this, turn to stone, never be forced to go to some inevitable end" (Bernstein, 1933/88: 56). She delighted in experiencing him as "all encompassing"; "he had wrapped her in a cloud, and taken her up and away and beyond all other people" (1938/87: 272). Because she had a husband and two children in a comfortable brownstone, as well as acclaim in her profession, she could afford to long for timeless hours of undifferentiated oneness. Because her life was so well-organized and efficient, she could aspire to share in his wildness. Things were quite different from Tom's perspective. For him, unity was a trap that stripped him of his individuality. He was determined to separate himself, with violence if need be, "from the sense of ruin, desolation, and loss unutterable which had possessed and conquered him" (Wolfe, 1973[a]: 614).

The foundation of Wolfe's problem was that he needed love and unity so badly that he found it all but irresistible. His father had been distant, both physically and emotionally, and his mother's affections had been treacherous for him. One moment she would smother him, longing for release from her own loneliness, and the next she would push him away. In the words of the lesbian poet Audre Lorde, he *needed* love but could not afford to *want* it:

> To the first woman I ever courted and left. She taught me that women who want without needing are expensive and sometimes wasteful, but women who need without wanting are dangerous—they suck you in and pretend not to notice. (5)

This phenomenon is of course not limited to women. When we need to fuse too much, the draw becomes terrifyingly powerful. Then, like Thomas Wolfe, we *want* above all to be separate and to avoid that suction. We will clutch at any means to pull away. In her novel, *The Ravishing of Lol Stein*, Marguerite Duras presents a dramatic instance of this cold will to break free from the prison of unity:

> "In a certain state of mind, all trace of feeling is banished. Whenever I remain silent in a certain way, I don't love you, have you noticed that?"
> "Yes, I've noticed."
> She stretches, laughs.
> "And then I begin to breathe again," she says. (129)

The initiative toward separation is taken by the partner who more acutely feels his sense of identity threatened. The quarrel is a battle between the needs for unity and for separate identity, between eternity and time, between the archetypal and the personal, between "us" and "me." It is a battle to reestablish the relationship on a different basis. For all his drive toward individuality, Tom, as much as Aline, found their union fulfilling and whole-making. He does not want to lose this completely, only to renew himself, reestablish his own personality and equality with this powerful partner of his. Tom wants to renew their separateness—and threatens to do so with his very first move in the quarrel. Aline is then forced to defend the principle of unification. For her the quarrel, itself, is the threat that inspires her attempt to renew their oneness.

Really both are right: they need a new unity that will respect their individuality and a new sense of individuality that will respect their unity. But because the situation has become polarized, they can each see only one side of the picture. Each is aware, above all, of his own wound. For example, Aline speaks of the fibers, dangling, bleeding from her wound, tendrils that used to grow into him, before he tore them free. The suffering would be unbearable, except for her "unconquerable golden knowledge" (Bernstein, 1938/87: 209), that is, the knowledge of his undying love, which she has at the archetypal levels of her psyche. He has this knowledge, also; it is the reason he cannot bear to have her refer to their love. He knows it and needs it too well; thus he *wants* above all to deny it.

As a result, they are engaged in constant plotting. He plots to keep them occupied with their moves on the surface of the gaming board, while she plots to remind him of that bedroom down below into which she has been dragging furniture. She uses the most subtle tricks to bind him: "She moved her arm so that her hand lay against the pulsing heart, and so made one more channel for him to flow to her" (Bernstein, 1933/88: 56). And he used the coarsest techniques to prevent her: "I am ugly, cruel, and mad in a way you know nothing about; if another loves me I torture them, curse and revile them, and try to drive them away"[6] (Donald, 258). He was able to admit his love for her only when they were separated by thousands of miles. He terminated her regular Thursday noontime visits in January of 1932, when he arranged to have her met by his mother. In the last six and a half years before Tom's death,[7] they met fairly infrequently—usually in connection with a cry for help from him. His last words were, "Where's Aline . . .I want Aline. . .I want my Jew" (Klein, 316).

In hindsight it appears that Thomas Wolfe was incapable of sustaining a deep, intimate, and balanced relationship. He was

---

6. These words were uttered to Claire Zyve, Tom's lover for a brief period in Paris. His warning was clearly based on his experience with Aline.

7. He died of a tuberculosis infestation of the brain after what his doctor had diagnosed as a bout of pneumonia.

capable of momentary fusion and great dependency as well as a slashing, brutal drive to break free of the bonding that drew him so inexorably. Generally he indulged this with prostitutes and in one-night stands with the women who pursued his celebrity status. In these liaisons he defended himself very well. According to his biographer (Donald, 364), he showed a total absence of affection or interest in his partners. He told Aline she had ruined him for making love with anyone else (ibid., 332). Thus he was not at all free of his union with her, but only tried to pretend he was. Evidently he was capable of only two dimensions of erotic experience: fusion and fighting fusion with the quarrel.

It appears that Bernstein was capable of a great deal more—although she also manifested great weakness. She was hospitalized at least twice for psychosomatic reactions to Tom's mistreatment and had some severe bouts of drunkenness and at least one nearly successful suicide attempt. She gives three accounts of how she eventually recovered from her obsession with Wolfe. In a letter to Tom in February, 1934, she says that she was brought to a transcendental realization through intense pain in a dental chair:

> . . . suddenly I knew that the pain was hurting nobody but myself. Here was a man, so close that I could feel the human warmth exuding from him, and he could not feel my pain. . . . I was an entity, a body so complete and so perfectly made that no one need know what I felt or thought if I did not choose to show it. I felt godhead in me and at once the tenseness of my muscles relaxed. (Stutman, 370)

In *The Journey Down* she uses very similar words—albeit in the third person. She won this realization through a pain like broken glass in her chest, incurred upon attempting suicide, about the same time as the dental incident:

> She had reached the point the other side of pain, and she had found supreme peace, the calm that an angel might know; and if she lived, that would remain with her forever, a precious talisman.
> "Nobody knows what I am like," she thought. . . . "Nobody

knows what I am made of, not a soul knows what is in my mind and heart, maybe I must live longer to tell it." (Bernstein, 1938/87: 304)

The third account is placed four years later, in February 1938, just six months before Wolfe's death. He had stormed up to the Bernstein apartment, drunk and enraged by her published account of their affair in *The Journey Down*. Among other intemperate words, he called for three cheers for Adolf Hitler; and she knocked him out with a punch in the nose. She told a friend afterwards:

It was the most sickening experience of my life; horrible, but it succeeded in finally freeing me from the spell. . . . I have always protected him . . . and . . . allowed for his behavior because of a certain greatness I have felt about him; but this was too much. (Donald, 444)

It is clear that, although Aline had discovered the divine spark in this novelist whom Dos Passos had called a "gigantic baby" (ibid., 353), she was, for almost the whole of the thirteen years she knew Tom, unable to live sanely, integratedly, and as a whole person. She and Tom were demon lovers for one another. Quarreling was an attempt to curb the excesses of their mutual obsession, but it succeeded only in truncating the process and keeping it unresolved. The erotic bond held them because it promised and provided a taste for a transcending unity at the level of Self. They reveled in the feeling it gave them of being engaged in a whole-making and fulfilling enterprise. Although there were surely moments when they passed away *(fana)* into one another and, like Shiva, contemplated the One in the midst of their love-play, only Aline reached a point of calm and fairly self-sufficient resolution. But unfortunately she had to do it alone, by a unilateral acceptance of the sword of separation. She discovered the godhead in herself and the indomitable foolishness in him, which she had been trying for thirteen years to excuse.

Tom probably experienced the spiritual flames of Wagner's Venusberg, as Aline certainy did. But it is evident that his neurotic defenses frequently converted them into the bumps and grinds of Peter Sellars's Venusberg Motel. He apparently could never accept the notion that people he knew slept together (ibid., 126). Women he knew as having a sexual life were sometimes indistinguishable from prostitutes for him. Wolfe's biographers seem to be agreed that he was a narcissistic personality who suffered so severely and constantly from his wound that he was rendered incapable of a sustained and sustaining erotic relationship. He tried to style his rejecton of Aline after the heroic realization of an Aeneas, sadly leaving Dido to pursue a nobler destiny:

> For he had learned tonight that love was not enough. There had to be a higher devotion than all the developments of this fond imprisonment. . . . So now he knew that if he was ever to succeed in writing the books he felt were in him, he must turn about and lift his face up to some nobler height. (1973[b]: 249)

I have little doubt that this was his honest assessment of the situation. But the question is still open for me as to whether almighty Jove lay behind his separation from Aline. If it *was* a command from the center of his psyche, it must have sounded like resignation: "This erotic struggle is too great for you; you have learned and striven enough; it is time to settle down to tasks you can perform with confidence."

We have considered three titanic quarrels, Aeneas with Dido, Tannhaeuser with Venus, and Thomas Wolfe with Aline Bernstein. It is clear that in all cases, the participants parted with great sorrow and that their fight was for renewal. Generally one partner wants to renew his individuality while the other wants to renew their unity. One fights for archetypal, eternal values, while the other struggles to assert the necessities of personal differences and the realities of every day. Insofar as each finds the other's position an annihilating threat to his own, they have fallen victim to the trap of polarization. In each case considered here, the quarrel eventually brought an end to the relationship. Ideally, it need not do so. It is not beyond the powers of human relationship to reconcile the heroic search for individual meaning with unitive contemplation of the divine spark.

10
Worthy Opponents: Love's Refinement

Accounts of the affair between Aline Bernstein and Thomas Wolfe occasionally contain indications of what might have been, if relations had not been severed so obstinately. For example, Bernstein describes a sultry Brooklyn noon hour in Wolfe's basement apartment, sitting beside his bed as he sleeps, enjoying their nearness and afraid to wake him lest he prove irascible and rejecting. She thinks, "Before I die I must break the distorted mirrors where he sees me" (1938/87: 208). We catch her sense of injustice and being misunderstood as well as the patience to wait, and almost—but not quite—to accept him on his own terms. Although there is some violence suggested in the image of breaking, it is not directed against him but against his "mirrors." She has a sense for what she believes to be "reality" over against his "distortions." She would like to have it out with him, if only it were safe. From her point of view, it is not safe because her smallest demands might provoke him to sever the very minimal contact that remains between them.

Wolfe was scared, too; but differently. He simultaneously feared his destruction and deemed her his "destiny," for she was "beyond comparison the most determined, resolute, and formidable antagonist he had ever known" (1973[a]: 613). It is only unfortunate that he had to hold her at such a distance with explosive quarrels. Progress in their relationship required that each affect and be affected by the other. Antagonism, if it did not manifest itself too formidably, might have accomplished a great deal. But for this it was necessary that some flexibility be allowed both in his sense of identity and in her sense for their union.

An erotic relationship may very well flourish beyond the fireworks of the quarrel. A squabble is an indicator of problems in perceptions and behavior between the partners. A quarrel indicates these irritants are beginning to feel intolerable. But rather than a flare-up in which the partners slap each other down with complaints, protests, and defenses, the relationship would be served by stretching the antagonism out into a calmer conflict of longer duration.

Tom and Aline needed a sustained opposition in which each not only expressed his grievances but heard those of the other. Patience and flexibility were required on both sides, so that they might find opportunity for changes in their perceptions of one another and shifts in their standpoints. They needed a commitment, each to allow himself to be changed, and not only to try to change the other party. They needed to be one another's "worthy opponent," each standing up for his own vision, but tolerantly.

There are as many different styles of worthy opposition as there are couples. In some cases conflict may become tenacious and almost savage, whereas in others it may be so slow and quiet as to be nearly unnoticeable. As an example of one of the more slow-moving and distanced cases of worthy opposition, we may consider Blanca Trueba and Pedro Tercero from Isabel Allende's recent novel, *The House of the Spirits*. Their relationship began in childhood, very much like that of Cathy and Heathcliff in *Wuthering Heights*. She was the daughter of the landowner and he was a son of the servant-manager. As children, they were one another's primary interest; and they became sexual partners as soon as she entered adolescence. She was married appropriately for her class, and he became a charismatic Marxist revolutionary. Like Cathy Earnshaw and Aline Bernstein holding on to their respectable marriages, Blanca wanted to be able to continue with Pedro Tercero as the primary relationship of her life—purely on the strength of their bond at the level of Self. She believed that there should be no conflict between this relationship and the commitments and events of her everyday world.

Pedro Tercero did not find this solution acceptable, and his way of life did not permit anything like a standard connubial arrangement. At bottom, though, he fled sustained intimacy—albeit less frantically than Thomas Wolfe. "He discovered many roads and many bodies trying to distance himself from her, but at the moment of greatest intimacy, the exact point of loneliness and the foreknowledge of death, Blanca was always the only one" (Allende, 264). We do not learn much more than this about the erotic development of Pedro Tercero. But this is quite a bit. We know that he is at least partially conscious of the nature of his bond with Blanca.

About her we learn somewhat more:

> The only man in her life was Pedro Tercero. . . . The strength of this immutable desire saved her from the mediocrity and sadness of her fate. She was faithful to him even in those moments when he lost himself in a sea of straight-haired, long-boned nymphs, and never loved him any the less for his digressions. At first she thought she would die every time he moved away from her, but she soon realized that his absences were only as long as a sigh and that he invariably returned more in love and sweeter than ever. (Ibid.)

Probably few would endorse this as an ideal relationship. Blanca and Pedro Tercero have achieved more than Aline and Tom, in part by reducing their expectations. Still there is the very clear suggestion that each is growing and that their moments of union are becoming more rewarding; such was surely not the case with Wolfe and Bernstein. By allowing Pedro Tercero a great deal of latitude, Blanca enjoys him more and arrives more gently at a sense of her own self-sufficiency than did Aline.

The quarrel manifests a particular stage in the joint woundedness of the lovers. Typically, there is a three-stage process. In the beginning, when all seems glorious, the conjoining of the two wounds seems to promise eternal happiness. Audre Lorde came to understand this very well through her affair with a woman named Muriel:

> Each one of us had been starved for love for so long that we wanted to believe that love, once found, was all-powerful. We wanted to believe that it could give word to my inchoate pain and rages; that it could enable Muriel to face the world and get a job; that it could free our writings, cure racism, end homophobia and adolescent acne. We were like starving women who came to believe that food will cure all present pains, as well as heal all the deficiency sores of long standing. (209f.)

The next stage in our joint woundedness, the quarrel, is designed to destroy this illusion. For at least one of the parties, quarreling is the means to reassert individuality over against the relationship's tendency toward fusion and loss of identity. The expression "to fall in love" suggests a passive movement. We find ourselves opened and drawn in by a force that is not our own. In the quarrel, we try to pull ourselves out of this centripetal collapse. But the quarrel can only accomplish a break. Thomas Wolfe is driven to deny the value of union—and indeed of love itself—in order to recover his personal resolve.

Something different occurs between Blanca and Pedro Tercero. They do not attack, deny, or injure the archetypal foundation of their union, their oneness at the level of Self. Respecting and honoring it, they each explore ways to develop their own individuality while giving the other scope to do the same. This is the third stage in romantic love, when a more creative and conscious stance is taken toward our joint woundedness. Worthy opposition distinguishes itself from the quarrel in precisely these two ways: (1) it is patient enough to realize that solutions cannot be achieved overnight; and (2) it builds on the bedrock provided by the love potion. Worthy opponents may surely engage in a great deal of arguing and negotiating. These may be the means of their communicating their needs to one another. They may even require the assistance of a referee, in the form of a marriage counselor. These matters differ from couple to couple, but the essential mark of worthy opposition is the recognition that the erotic bond at the level of Self is a pearl of great price, the precondition of a fulfilling relationship.

In order to sketch an overview of what worthy opposition can accomplish, let us consider another of the lais of Marie de France.

The Story of Yonec

In Britain there was once a rich old man, the Lord of Caerwent, who took a wife in order to have heirs. He loved her for her great beauty and nobility, but out of jealousy kept her locked in a tower so that she could not even go to church. After seven years of this misery, and still childless, she cursed her parents who had consigned her to this fate and cried in anguish to God to send a knight to free her. At this, a giant hawk flew into the room and changed into the form of the handsomest and noblest knight she had ever seen. He declared he had long been in love with her but required her asking before he could leave his own country and come to her. He requested that they be lovers; and she agreed, providing he believed in God who would make their love possible. To test his word, the Lady of Caerwent called her chaplain, and the hawk-knight took on her lovely form and received the sacrament. Then they made love. As he departed, again in the form of a hawk, the knight declared he would visit her within the hour of any request she might make—only warning her to observe moderation, that they be not discovered.

The lady's mood was now joyously transformed, and she became content in her prison cell. Her old husband noticed the change and had his widowed sister spy on his wife when the younger woman thought she was alone. The old man very shortly learned the truth and prepared a trap of iron spikes, which he fixed outside his lady's window.

On his next passage through that window, the hawk-knight mortally wounded his breast on one of the razor-sharp points. With his blood soaking into her sheets, he told his beloved that she was with child and would give birth to a boy who would avenge his death. She was to name the lad Yonec. With this, the hawk-knight left her. Reeling with joy, sorrow, and despair, the noble lady jumped twenty feet to the ground and followed the trail of blood through a hollow hill to a walled city of silver and into the palace. She found him pale, weak, and near the end, stretched out in a golden bedroom. He embraced and comforted her tenderly but then sent her back to her husband. She was frightened and begged to be allowed to stay with him in his kingdom and even to die with him rather than to return. He was adamant that she had to return. But to make it easier for her, he gave her a ring that would make her husband forget what had happened and free her from the tower. The knight also gave her a sword to keep for Yonec's vengeance.

One day when Yonec had grown up and been dubbed a

knight, the first family of Caerwent found themselves
guests at a marvelous fair castle on the feast of St. Aaron.
On being shown about the court by a monk, the three
encountered a tomb covered with a cloth of gold brocade
and honored with twenty candles and continually burning
incense. Tearful inhabitants of the town explained that this
was the tomb of their last and greatest king, who had
been killed at Caerwent for the love of a lady. At this
news, the lady pulled out the sword she had kept hidden
for nearly two decades and handed it to her son, declaring
that this was the tomb of Yonec's father who had been
killed by her husband's treachery. As she fell dead across
the tomb, her son believed her and beheaded his step-
father.

The people laid the Lady of Caerwent in the royal tomb
with her knight-lover and made Yonec their king.

The story opens with the depiction of a relationship in grave need
of renewal. The wife, who wed to fulfill the expectations of her
parents and social class, experiences the marriage as a prison. Indeed,
it is a union in name only, for there appears to be no affection or
psychological connection between the two. The husband's interest is
centered on the bodily and social attractions that make his wife an
excellent ornament for him. She is not a person for him, but only a
possession, a device to further his acquisitive purposes by providing
him with heirs. Apparently, because of their failure to relate, even
this aim goes unrealized, and the lady is barren for seven years. Very
likely she is as psychologically infertile as he is sterile.

Things begin to change when the wife prays to God, that is,
consults the Self-level of the psyche. She is rewarded almost immediately with the Lohengrin-like figure of the hawk-knight. She tests
him, somewhat as the citizens of Brabant tested the swan-knight, to
see if he comes from God. This means she is determined not to fall
for the same kind of superficial connection as she did the first time.

When we take a tale like this as a psychological document, we
need to ask ourselves what the story accomplishes. The Story of
Yonec begins with a dissatisfied, acquisitive old man, almost wholly
ignorant of his desperate need of relationship. In his unconscious,

however, lives the repressed and misunderstood anima/wife who is capable of making the connections he so badly requires. She conjures up the kingly hawk-knight who, being a figure of the Self, personifies everything the stultified old man lacks. The old greedy attitude represses even this, but not before something new and hidden is produced in the unconscious. Yonec, the child, represents a new attitude, which requires a long maturation before it is prepared to replace the old, tired point of view. Thus the Story of Yonec is about how an inadequate approach to life is replaced by a fresh, vital, and far more comprehensive attitude.

The means for this transformation is depicted in the story as the struggle against a limiting and imprisoning marriage. It is clear that the crucial first move toward change is Lady Caerwent's prayer, her appeal to the divine spark that appears to be missing in her marriage. That it is not wholly missing, we know from the subsequent appearance of the hawk-knight. But he does not live long. The wound in his breast is caused, we may say, by her narcissistic defenses; for the iron spikes come from the same parental complex that led her into an imprisoning marriage in the first place. She has not dared to be herself or to consult her own feelings, much less to explore the deeper dimensions of interpersonal union. She has kept herself from becoming familiar with these realities by clinging to values handed down from her parents and supported by the proprieties of the social order. They function to defend her wound and to keep her ignorant of her very deep needs. That it works for seven miserable years testifies to the terror her wound inspires in her and the gravity of her dependency on her defenses.

It is clear that even the hawk-knight is not immune to these automatic, cruel, and highly effective defenses. As is nearly always the case, the narcissistically excessive defense of *her* wound results in *his* being struck to the heart. A pair of lovers always shares a distinctive woundedness. Worthy opposition begins with the attitude we take toward our joint woundedness. Whereas quarrelers would turn their backs on one another and stumble off in opposite directions, accusing one another and trying to bandage their bleeding wounds with their anger, worthy opponents attempt to use their pain to come to a new understanding of themselves and one another. Lady Caerwent, for example, follows the trail of her lover's blood.

Her sensitization to his wound gets her out of her narcissistic cocoon, and she finds a leap out of her tower window no longer unthinkable. Suddenly the imprisoning defense is a manageable obstacle.

That she wants to die with him in his kingdom, however, rather than returning to her own life situation, means she wants to rest in a timeless archetypal realm—the love-death or the Venusberg. There is no opposition in this eternal dimension of relationship, and the hawk-knight cannot permit her to rest here for long. Personifying the wisdom and harmony of the Self, he offers her two principles that balance one another and make it possible for her to establish a worthy opposition: the ring and the sword. The ring symbolizes transcendental union around the divine spark. Her dawning realization of this has already begun to free her from the rigid defenses that have been preventing love. Thus the ring keeps her connected with the Self-level of the psyche. The sword, on the other hand, is the tool she needs in order to bring discrimination, definition, and clarity to the everyday world of space, time, and individual differences.

With the sword of discrimination, she can begin to live in the real world. As the sword sunders illusion from necessity, she can begin to see that what imprisons her is a false picture she has cultivated of her husband's absolute authority. She projects this image onto him like a mask and awaits the maturity of Yonec until that projection can be beheaded and she can begin to consult the authority of her own feelings, intuitions, and ideas.

Yonec is simultaneously a symbol of her living union with the hawk-knight and the hero who takes on the tasks of the real world for Lady Caerwent. While the other sword, the naked sword of separation, keeps her alone with her memories of her union with the hawk-knight, the process of her soul's journey to find her is symbolized by her sons' maturation.

It is significant that he begins his knightly and royal career on the feast of St. Aaron. It is a hint that his kingship has something to do with the Exodus of Israel. Aaron was God's spokesman, brother of Moses the stutterer, and coexpositor of the Mosaic vision. It was above all Moses and Aaron who preached the oneness and authority of God as the foundation of the people of Israel and of Israel's destiny. Similarly Yonec is the product of a union ordained by God to express the transcendent foundation of a fulfilling relationship. In the story this is symbolized, too, at the end, when he unites his people, seeming almost to bring them back to life. Psychologically speaking, these dejected and uncentered people are the fragments of a personality that have been kept apart by overweening narcissistic defenses. Yonec leads them across the Red Sea of psychological transformation to a land flowing with the milk and honey of integration and intrapsychic cooperation.

It is no accident, either, that Lady Caerwent dies at this moment across the tomb of her lover. This is a very complicated love-death. Isolde's *Liebestod* occurs at the same time as Tristan's death, and that is the point of the story—the primacy of eternal, transcendent union over the requirements of the social order. In the Story of Yonec, however, the love-death is postponed some two decades after the hero's death because the tale describes not simply the importance of Self-level union, but the higher achievement whereby that eternal union is integrated with the temporal and personal differentiation that makes the partners unique individuals. It is not a modern story; consequently we learn none of the details of those two decades during which the psychological maturation and integration is taking place. We know only that Lady Caerwent remained steadfast to the twin principles of the ring and the sword. And we know that she died at the same time as Lord Caerwent. This means that once the sword has vanquished the illusory and narcissistic defense that prevented a deep and fulfilling love, she can finally enter the sacred precincts of eternal union. Finally, her death means that the anima has been "withdrawn" and needs no longer to be projected. In Jung's words, she is transformed "into a function of relationship between the conscious and the unconscious" (1928/35: par. 374). The new attitude, which has been incubating in the unconscious for two decades, Yonec, now becomes the conscious personality and Lady Caerwent functions as an integrated anima, as mediatrix between ego and Self.

It would have been convenient for our argument if Marie de France had been able to give us some details about how Lord and Lady Caerwent had lived during the two decades of Yonec's matura-tion, for that was the period when they were worthy opponents.

Perhaps they fought a great deal—violently passionate arguments like those of Wolfe and Bernstein—but without losing sight of the ring and the sword. Perhaps they found a referee, something like a modern marriage counselor, who could help them contain and refocus their conflict. Or perhaps, like Blanca and Pedro Tercero, they had to take separate paths—a peculiar kind of faithful infidelity in which they came to understand and enrich their own relationship through their interactions with third parties.

Gabriel García Márquez tells a story of this last type in his novel, *Love in the Time of Cholera*. The central narrative concerns Florentino Ariza's sixty-year pursuit of Fermina Daza. At the beginning of the story seventeen-year-old Florentino was almost rooted to a park bench, where he could see Fermina, age thirteen, and her duenna pass by on their way to and from school. Between her passings, he read sentimental love poetry and wrote voluminous letters he dared not send. Eventually, when they did start leaving notes for one another in hollow trees and under stones, he wrote every night, sometimes all night long. Her letters were short, distracted, and "intended to keep the coals alive without putting her hand in the fire, while Florentino Ariza burned himself alive in every line" (69). In a year's time, he learned to play the violin well enough that he could serenade her from the choir loft at Sunday mass. When she was fifteen he proposed marriage, to which she replied after a very long delay: "Very well, I will marry you if you promise not to make me eat eggplant" (ibid., 71). Her father took Fermina away with him for two years, but Florentino became a telegraph operator and continued to manage their correspondence. The idyll ended shortly after her return, one day in a shop:

> She turned her head and saw, a hand's breadth from her eyes, those other glacial eyes, that livid face, those lips petrified with fear, just as she had seen them in the crowd at Midnight Mass the first time he was so close to her, but now, instead of the commotion of love, she felt the abyss of disenchantment. In an instant, the magnitude of her own mistake was revealed to her, and she asked herself, appalled, how she could have nurtured such a chimera in her heart for so long and with so much ferocity. (Ibid., 102)

She married the respectable Dr. Juvenal Urbino, and never knew or dared to ask if their marriage was based on love or convenience. Still, she reached a kind of oneness with him: "they felt uncomfortable at the frequency with which they guessed each other's thoughts without intending to" (ibid., 224). Fifty-one years, nine months, and four days later, Urbino died and Florentino took over management of the funeral details with firmness and subtlety. When everyone had gone, he stayed behind to tell Fermina that he was still waiting for her. This was the first time in their lives that they had ever been alone together. She threw him out in a rage.

The relationship between these two strong-minded people developed through three distinct phases: four years of puppy love, fifty-two years of estrangement, and the final stage after Dr. Urbino's death. Florentino lived more than two-thirds of his life in dialogue with her silence. He found it a worthy opponent and teacher.

His education began while he was still a telegraph operator, when—in order to get out of the room he shared with his mother—he moved into a bordello owned by his boss. His virginity was neither tempted nor embarrassed by the naked women who shared their daily lives with him. Nor did they challenge his devotion to the image of Fermina Daza. This quiet period of reading and love letters ended when he was raped by a naked woman on a riverboat. "At the height of pleasure he had experienced a revelation that he could not believe, that he even refused to admit, which was that his illusionary love for Fermina Daza could be replaced by an earthly passion" (ibid., 143).

At home, Florentino's mother provided him with an easy opportunity for an affair with the Widow Nazaret. Although she turned out to be "an uninspired lay" (ibid., 151), they remained intermittent lovers for thirty years and taught one another a great deal. He taught her that nothing is immoral if it perpetuates love, and he developed an unerring eye to spot the one woman in a crowd who was waiting for him. He also began the first of twenty-five notebooks in which he gathered and collated the data from his 622 affairs during the fifty-two years of his separation from Fermina Daza. Although he met with his regular mistresses "in strict rotation" (ibid., 218), he enjoyed a distinctively different intimacy with each. He wept when they travelled on or died, though after a few hours the memory of Fermina Daza "once again occupied all his space" (ibid., 270).

He learned, too, from his rare encounters with Fermina. Perhaps the most important of these occurred when she was pregnant with her first child and he could see what a woman of the world she had become. He immediately determined "to win fame and fortune in order to deserve her" (ibid., 165). He gave up telegraphy and became a shipping clerk for his uncle, gradually rising in the river trading firm until he became its president. His mercantile correspondence, however, had an amorous lilt unless he exerted the utmost discipline to eliminate poetic phrases and rhymes. These latter he indulged in the Arcade of the Scribes, where he wrote love letters for inarticulate lovers—sometimes writing both sides of a correspondence. What he learned from these activities, he developed into a massive manuscript, a *Lovers' Companion*. He imagined all the situations in which he and Fermina Daza might find themselves and described as many alternative stratagems as he could devise (ibid., 172).

Fermina Daza was not satisfied throwing Florentino Ariza out of her house on the day of her husband's funeral; she followed up with several pages of vituperation that he read as a love letter. Mastering the typewriter more easily than he had the violin sixty years earlier, he began a series of epistles that, after the passage of a month, he began to number. They amounted to extensive meditations on the relations between men and women, couched as an old man's memories. They actually comprised a new *Lovers' Companion,* designed to "teach her to think of love as a state of grace; not the means to anything but the alpha and omega, an end in itself" (ibid., 293).

Until he began visiting her regularly on Tuesday afternoons, he did not know whether she was even reading his letters. She studied them. They gave her "serious and thoughtful reasons to go on living" (ibid., 298). Soon the Urbino house rang with their quarrels, and eventually he talked her into a cruise on one of his trading company's riverboats. García Márquez leads us to believe they will sail up and down the river forever.

In my view, García Márquez has succeeded far better than Peter Sellars in giving us a modern version of the *Tannhaeuser* legend. For what is Florentino Ariza but a minstrel of love, an alchemist of the erotic, in search of the ultimate integration of flesh and spirit? His odyssey encompasses an amazing set of transformations. He moves from puppy love's dreamy enclosure in its own narcissistic cocoon to an ability to read Fermina's unconscious demands and direct the details of her husband's funeral empathically, efficiently, and unobtrusively. He grows beyond the "whipped dog" and "disgraced rabbi" persona of his youth into a distinguished president of the river trading company. He begins in an abysmal state of anima possession, overwhelmed by undifferentiated sexual and emotional needs, but becomes a refined and considered septuagenarian wooer.

As he moves from telegrapher, to clerk, to chief executive officer, he never loses his anchorage in the timeless unity of the Self. That is the "given," the unchanging touchstone of reality. His transformations take place in the everyday realm of space and time, where he becomes not only more and more adequately adapted to the realities of commerce, but to those of sexual and emotional communication, as well. Like Tannhaeuser, he could never have become the extraordinary mad genius of his magic song, had he fulfilled his original intention of honoring her with perpetual virginity. Had he done that, he would still have been a sexual and emotional teenager when his "unknown lady" had become a seventy-year-old widow. It is important, too, that he began with the physical and emotional nudity of the bordello to depotentiate the youth's overvaluation of sex and to learn the primacy of interpersonal intimacy. His subsequent sexual explorations were built upon this foundation. García Márquez emphasizes again and again that what Florentino and his mistresses enjoyed above all was being naked together, sharing their deepest interests, joys and sadnesses.

His entire education is characterized by dialogue: response to the unvoiced demands of Fermina Daza and reply to the verbal and bodily communications of his lovers. The seriousness with which he took this intercourse is suggested by the twenty-five notebooks, wherein he rendered his life of dialogue conscious. A similar development is represented by the love letters he wrote for strangers. There he had to explore not only the full range of his own emotions but also the plight of his individual clients, so as to be able to adapt poetic sentimentalities to real-life situations. Simultaneously, he was working to extricate his professional correspondence from his romantic obsession and thereby to develop an ego that knew the difference between the two.

The *Lovers' Companion,* in its two versions, represents the culmination of this work of consciousness-making. Here he brought together the exploration of his own psyche and the many encounters with his idiosyncratic partner and clients. But, in using his imagination to push beyond his own experience, he creatively opened up a worthy opposition with the Fermina Daza of his fantasies. By this means he prepared himself for anything the real woman might concoct. I am inclined to believe that the thoroughness and sensitiveness of his work on the *Companion* is proven by the success of his final wooing.

Most impressive is his ability to read evidence of the erotic bond hidden behind the insults and provocations of the letter she wrote him after his proposal at her husband's funeral. She herself saw it as "the vilest act of her long life" (García Márquez, 284). To Florentino it seemed "that Fermina Daza's misfortune glorified her, that her anger beautified her, and that her rancor with the world had given her back the untamed character she had displayed at the age of twenty" (ibid., 322). Here, it seems to me, Florentino's vision has been so clarified that his anima is now functioning as a lens. He does not let the superficial display of her anger distract him from the deeper issues in her soul, and he does not let cherished fantasies about what he would like her to be cover her identity like a mask.

His typewritten letters carry this project forward. In them, he is undoubtedly disclosing his own soul in the most gentle and seductive manner possible—that is, not in the form of crude and sensational confessions that may titillate and disarm but discourage reciprocity. Rather, as he discloses his own soul, he feels his way into hers. It is a project of active empathy that goes beyond merely understanding her as she deliberately represents herself. He probes his way into recesses of her soul that she herself does not yet know. This is why she finds his letters so interesting and helpful. That he can do this without alarming her and mobilizing her defenses is a tribute to what fifty-two years of worthy opposition have accomplished in his capacity for empathy.

When he has wooed her close enough, their quarrels begin. This is evidence that the work of worthy opposition is not complete—

indeed, it will never be complete so long as a relationship is still vital. He finds their disputes exasperatingly familiar: every time he tries to move their relationship forward, she blocks the way. For example, at one point, he reminds her that they had used the familiar form, *tú,* "before." As soon as the word *before* is out of his mouth, he knows he has made a mistake, reminded her of the past and of his wooing. She says nothing is the same as it was. He says *he* is the same, is she not also? She says it does not matter, as she is seventy-two.

> Florentino Ariza felt the blow in the very center of his heart. He would have liked to find a reply as rapid and well aimed as an arrow, but the burden of his age defeated him: he had never been so exhausted by so brief a conversation, he felt pain in his heart, and each beat echoed with a metallic resonance in his arteries. He felt old, forlorn, useless, and his desire to cry was so urgent that he could not speak. (Ibid., 309)

It is a shame they have to go on hurting one another like this. Perhaps they can learn to soften the blows somewhat; but as long as they are two individuals attempting to hold both the ring and the sword, emotional blood will be shed. Florentino's refusal to let go of the ring is what enables him to bear the pain and come back for more.

Three pages before the end of the book, as the lovers are concluding their first up-river voyage, García Márquez emphasizes the eternal, Self-level unity they have attained: "It is as if they had leapt over the arduous calvary of conjugal love and gone straight to the heart of love" (ibid., 345). García Márquez is convincing, here, only to the extent we accept the possibility that his characters can continue indefinitely sailing up and down the Magdalena River under a yellow cholera flag—totally outside of real space and time. It is again the image of the love-death. For, short of a quarreling breakup like that between Wolfe and Bernstein, death is the only way to avoid worthy opposition.

Death, too, is the solution in Wagner's *Tannhaeuser*. The errant *Minnesinger* is saved by Elisabeth's self-sacrifice and dies beside her bier, an apparent love-death, in which the two attain eternal oneness on the other shore. The reason this is disappointing is that Tannhaeuser had already tried immortality on Venusberg and found it wanting. The structure of the opera is as follows. Tannhaeuser, bored with the eternal sameness of Venusberg (A), quarrels with Venus, and leaves in search of the temporal world (B). He takes up penitence (C) in order to put Venusberg behind him, but this only keeps him suspended in an unresolved limbo without vigor or memory. The name of Elisabeth (D) brings him to his senses and gives him a reason to live; but he offends her social world (B) by referring in the song contest to his experience in Venusberg (A). Elisabeth sends him back to penitence (C), which again fails. In the end she saves him herself: her name (D) calls him to his senses again, and her willing death (A) saves his soul.

The story oscillates between eternity (A) and time (B), between archetypal and personal relationship. Tannhaeuser's task is to integrate the two dimensions, but apart from Elisabeth's sacrifice, the narrative provides only two images for how this might be accomplished. One is the name (D), and by implication, the person of Elisabeth. Musically, the most powerful moments in the opera occur when Tannhaeuser sings that magic name and awakens from his confusion. Clearly, Elisabeth personifies the integration for which Tannhaeuser is searching. For him, she is an image of what might yet be, if only he can find a way to live what she represents. His faux pas in the song contest was to refer too frankly to the depth (A) with which he understands this integration—that it cannot be some ethereal, angelic platitude. Love is not in the stars, as Wolfram would have us believe, but in our earthly, bodily selves. And we, through the body and soul of our union, can scale spiritual heights Wolfram only prates of.

This is too dangerous a truth for society to tolerate. As wife of the next ruler of Thuringia, Elisabeth cannot be party to such subversive notions. Psychologically, this means that we cannot simply marry the piece we need to complete our wholeness. We have to develop it in ourselves. Tannhaeuser has to "become" Elisabeth, just as Majnun "becomes" Layla. He needs to be sent away from her to suffer the "sword of separation" for the same reason Florentino Ariza has to fill his notebooks and write love letters for strangers.

Elisabeth sends him on a penitential pilgrimage "To Rome!" (C), and he embraces the option with the whole orchestra. "*Nach Rom!*" is sung on the note that resolves the harmonic tensions of act 2. It plays a similar role as does the name "*Elisabeth!*" in acts 1 and 3. Elisabeth and penitence are the two means offered to Tannhaeuser to try to resolve the tension and integrate the archetypal and personal dimensions of life. He might have accomplished this with Elisabeth (D) if they had been able to become worthy opponents. But as that was politically not feasible, Tannhaeuser is sent outside the civil domain to the church, the preserver of society's myth and source of political investiture. If the pope can forgive him, it will be safe for the state to accept his marriage to Elisabeth. The means to the pope's forgiveness is penitence (C).

The incompatibility between Tannhaeuser and penitence is unmistakable in Wagner's music. The *Minnesinger* is a heroic and inspired madman, ranting and soaring, rough-hewn but audacious, a loner who is utterly convinced of the truth of his experience. The chorus of pilgrims, on the other hand, surges along, hugging the ground like a stray tongue of sea, without individuality, confident only in its collectivity. Unlike the humble Florentino Ariza, Tannhaeuser throws himself as heroically into penitence as into the song contest. He inflicts the most austere measures on himself, goes the longest time without water, carries the heaviest burdens. There is no room for dialogue in this. No opponent is worthy of this endearing but bull-headed hero.

The purpose of penitence is to tame the heroic tendencies of the ego, to expose its vulnerabilities, to acquaint us with the pain our grandiose defenses hide—even from ourselves. But Tannhaeuser wants to win his pardon on the model of a knightly joust; consequently he never submits to the discipline of loneliness and inner struggle. He seeks to flee his pain rather than to understand it and learn from it. Pain is the very stock-in-trade of relationship. We are joined by our common experience of pain, find relief when our wounds "fit" one another like a key in a lock, quarrel when our wound is irritated, and become worthy opponents when we decide to accept the challenge of our joint woundedness. A proper penitence would have revealed this to Tannhaeuser. But his penitence is a kind of "ego-trip," a kind of self-hypnosis that keeps him in a limbo in which both Venus and Elisabeth are vague dreamy memories, confusion reigns, and he has lost all conviction.

In the last analysis, Elisabeth's self-sacrifice is disappointing because it saves Tannhaeuser from the task life has set him. Indeed, *he* is the individual who needs to undergo sacrifice. His heroic ego understands only glorious combat where laurels await the winner and knows nothing of a worthy opposition that goes on for years and exploits the strength hidden in vulnerability. He has not realized that to know and be known by our beloved, we must be in an important sense alone while we are together. Relationship moves forward by a dialogue that continually circumambulates the wound that is the secret source of our bond. Worthy opponents carry on that dialogue by remaining conscious of their unity at the level of Self while exploring the differences in their personal needs and aspirations.

11
Love's Angel:
The Creative Third

This book is, from beginning to end, a phenomenology of romantic love, a description of what it feels like to be a lover, and an exploration of dimensions of erotic experience that may not immediately be apparent to the individual in its grip. I have hoped to achieve more than the aesthetic joy of producing a truthful and engaging portrait of love. I hope, as well, to challenge the reader morally and practically by articulating psychological principles that constitute the foundation of an attitude toward and a praxis of romantic love. There have been several indications of this in previous chapters. For example, chapter 5 argues that the appearance of the demon lover and the resulting tendency to obsessive behavior is by no means an indication that love has gone wrong—only that the striving for wholeness has undergone a distortion. Chapter 6 argues that such a neurotic distortion can be worked through, if the couple can remain faithful to the truth of their union and to their accurate and love-inspired perception of one another. Chapters 9 and 10 reinterpret opposition between the partners as a search for renewal in the relationship. This implies that each couple will have to find its own distinctive mode of battle so that the partners can refine their perceptions of themselves and one another, reexamine their needs, and in effect revise the unwritten contract of their common life. Chapter 8 presents amorous play in a similar light, as an opportunity for the partners to expand and renew their images of and expectations for one another. If such images and their related feelings are truly appreciated, they will change the way we conduct our relationships. In this sense, moral implications have always been very near the surface in this book.

In these last four chapters we take up such practical and moral themes more explicitly. An issue that has been avoided in the previous chapters as "too complicated" to address is nevertheless central to the everyday decisions and judgments we have to make in the conduct of our relationships. We may find ourselves at sea when it comes to choosing between the potion and the sword or between the incapacitating obsessions inspired by the demon lover and the seeming chimera of resolution through an unholy marriage. In a situation like that of Thomas Wolfe, we may find ourselves torn between the inclination to hang on to an expanding, deepening soul-connection, which seems to be the very reason for living and, on the other hand, a need to express, write, and publish, without which, Wolfe believed, living could never transcend itself.

There is no easy way of addressing these issues. There is no single answer to any question. Each issue is specific to a unique couple with a singular set of conditions. Nothing less than a unique solution would be adequate. I can therefore hardly hope to spell out such solutions in detail and must remain content if I can articulate fundamental principles with sufficient emotional valence and com- pelling imagery to suggest what it feels like to be on the right track.

Getting "the feel" of a thing is familiar to us in a physical sense if we have ever learned how to ride a bicycle, drive a car, hit a golf ball, or indeed walk. We become so accustomed to these things that we forget there was a time when we had not yet had the experience. Mystics say the same about spiritual experience. We fall silent if a nonrider or nonmystic should ask us to say what it is like. How can we find the words when the context cannot be taken for granted? Jung made such an attempt in *The Psychology of the Transference,* where he tried to describe how the premises of an analytical relation- ship change as each partner takes the other progressively more seriously. It is not his most accessible book, and he must have known the difficulties he was creating for his readers, because he identifies with the alchemist who wrote, "Only he who knows how to make the philosopher's stone can understand their [the adepts'] words about it" (1946: par. 498). Those who know how to make the stone project their own experience into their reading and fill out the author's images with their own blood and breath. Jung filled the alchemists' images with his experience as an analyst who had not been able to avoid involvement in a rather erotic rapport with a few of his patients.

I ask my readers to fill out the images in these next four chapters with some of their most refined and subtle experiences. The argument of the first four chapters can, I hope, be followed by anyone who has ever been in love. In the seventh through tenth chapters, the lover needs to have discovered the unique and changeable otherness of his beloved in order to follow the argument. All lovers do not make this discovery. Some remain in a narcissistic cocoon from which their beloved is never appreciated in her or his unique otherness. What they see instead is the anima (or animus) mask they project onto her (or him). It proceeds from their wound and glorifies their beloved almost to the status of divinity, thus making possible a very compelling experience of oneness. But it does not tolerate the real human individuality of the beloved. It draws nourishment only from the eternal sphere and fails at integration with the everyday world. This very common state of affairs is what has given romantic love a bad name as neurotic, destructive, and unrealistic.

Romantic love that has not emerged from a narcissistic stage may be said to be "unipolar" in the sense that there is no real, effective other. The individual remains shut up in a cocoon of self-reference, contemplating the images of his own unconscious as though they were the real partner and the outer world. We are all capable of remaining stuck at this stage of love, even while we pay lip service to love's bipolarity. Intellectually, we know that love involves two people, two sets of needs and expectations, two sets of fears and neurotic defenses, and two drives toward autonomy. Because this is all self-evident, I have been confident that the argument of the previous chapters would not present the reader with conceptual difficulties.

Now I need to introduce a much less widely understood concept, the notion that there are not simply two autonomous factors in an interpersonal relationship (the lover and the beloved) but also a Third. Popular culture recognizes a bit of this reality in the imagery of Cupid, whereby a couple will not fall in love unless their hearts are pierced by arrows from the cherub's bow. It implies that the initiative comes from elsewhere, that there is an autonomous but invisible third agent whom the two lovers follow. The imagery of the Third is frequently to be found in love poetry. For example, a recent collection of translations of Rumi's verses (1987) bears the title, taken from one of his lines, *We Are Three*. Pablo Neruda describes a vision of threeness in the last verse of his poem "September 8th":

> Between you and me a new door opened
> and someone, still faceless,
> was waiting for us there.
>
> (9)

This expresses an awareness probably most lovers have had, that there is something mysterious but definite that encounters the two of us. It is as though our openness to one another lets some Third being into the room.

In a much more abstract and rational manner, Edmund Husserl and his followers in the philosophical school of phenomenology speak of two individuals sharing a *Mitwelt*, a coworld. It is a joint project of the two related individuals, brought about primarily through their respective unconscious intentions. It cannot exist without the two individuals and cannot be reduced to either of them. Although changeable according to the interaction of the partners who share it, every *Mitwelt* has a givenness, an objectivity that influences the perceptions and behavior of the individuals who share it. In this sense it acts almost as a third member of the relationship. For example, people who have been married a long time may often feel their *Mitwelt* as confining and limiting. Assumptions and expectations have taken on such a tone of inevitability that the partners can no longer imagine alternative ways of seeing and behaving. They need a dose of love-play or a bout of worthy opposition to loosen a *Mitwelt* that has come to function almost as a policeman.

A couple newly in love will very likely experience the Third as a marvelous, transformative presence that, perhaps, bathes the whole world in glorious light. Such is the experience of Alfred and Violetta in Giuseppe Verdi's opera *La Traviata*. Again and again in arias and duets, they sing to a soaring, rapturous melody, "I sense that love is the heartbeat of the whole universe; mysterious, lofty, the pain and delight of the heart."[1] Sometimes, naively, it seems to us that all of this glory is granted through the person of our beloved. Neruda, for example, speaks of countries and rivers being in his beloved's eyes and lighting his world (33). In this imagery, it seems as if two individuals were enough to produce the marvel. But if, as is highly likely, his beloved is experiencing the same thing, we seem to have two recipients and no initiator of the phenomenon. The imagery of the Third arises to account for the creative agent when both lovers feel themselves on the receiving end.

I think we may even take it as a rule that whenever we feel a blast of energy or light from our beloved it is not that she has unloosed a psychological cannon on us; for she feels the same blast we do. We do not blast one another, we find ourselves blasted by a Third. Such was surely the case between the pair of lovers who felt a golden rainbow arching between them and pouring through their chests (chapter 8), or another who each experienced an inexhaustible supply of light pouring out of their chests, or a third who found themselves enclosed together in a cocoon of whirling red and gold light fibers. This kind of phenomenon occurs also in the analytic hour. Severely narcissistic patients have once or twice accused me of having invaded their bodies by some magical means extending through the several feet of empty space between us. There is a sexual tone to the accusation. Clearly the patient feels violated and believes I have deliberately perpetrated an indignity and that I am able to stop doing it at will. Invariably I am experiencing an identical sensation, an ecstatic probing in my abdomen. It feels to me as though she is doing this to me, while in actuality neither of us is "doing it." We are both being done to. The agent is the Third.

These experiences make it clear that the Third is closely associated with a mystical participation at the Self-level of the psyche. What sets it apart from other experiences of this type is our conviction

---

1. My translation. The Italian is almost intelligible to a reader of English without translation:

> Sentia che amore e palpito
> Dell' universo intero,
> Misterioso, altero,
> Pena e delizia al cor.

that an impersonal agency attends the Third. It never acts for my good or for yours, but in behalf of purposes probably neither of us has guessed. It takes us both by the hand, shoots us both with its arrow, frustrates the whims of both of us.

Another characteristic of the Third is that it is autonomous in the sense that it cannot be deliberately manipulated by either of the partners. It implies mutuality as much as impersonality. It guides the two of us and resists some of our intentions. It seems as much to have its own mind as another person would. True, the archetypes, wherever they are found, have a certain numinous autonomy. But sometimes they can be read or manipulated for one's own purposes. If so, these are phenomena that do not belong to the Third. As an example, we might consider another couple from Isabel Allende's novel *The House of the Spirits*. The landowner Esteban Trueba, who had become rich and powerful by arrogantly taking possession of anything he wished—including, especially, the peasant women on his land—fell hopelessly in love with and married Clara, a woman who lived much more in the world of the spirits than on the temporal plane. Although Esteban had hoped to possess and control Clara's psychic powers, he was no match for her.

> Esteban had bouts of despair because Clara treated him with the same kindness she displayed toward everybody else. She spoke to him in the same cajoling tones she used to address her cats, and was incapable of telling whether he was tired, sad, euphoric, or eager to make love. However from the color of his rays she knew at a glance whether he was hatching a swindle, and she could defuse one of his tantrums with a few simple and mocking words. (111)

Here we see one partner (Esteban) fascinated by the phenomena of archetypal interaction while the other uses them for her own purposes. There is no mutuality between these people. They live in wholly separate worlds, she being as controlling and autocratic in the world of psyche as he in the material world. Her use of imagery from the mythic-image level of the psyche indicates only a bipolar relationship. She is not only not "fused" with her husband in a narcissistic manner, she is hardly connected at all. Thus archetypal phenomena constitute no certain indication of the presence of a Third, although the Third does depend for its existence on a Self-level connection between the partners.

Careful observation, therefore, reveals to lovers a "third" agency in their relationship. It seems to be a transpersonal, autonomous, directing intelligence, mutual to the two partners, somehow constituted by their union, and yet not reducible to either of them nor directly manipulable. Philosophers have advanced a similar notion, the *Mitwelt*, not an intelligence but a joint project that takes on a distinct autonomy in relation to the pair of lovers. The notion of the Third is to be found in the writings of the mystics, as well. Meister Eckhart has said, "The eye with which I see God is the same as that with which he sees me" (Happold, 67). Clearly he means that in some sense God and I are not distinct. Although we are two, there is some place, moment, or act in which the distinction is lost. He says, "There is something in the soul so closely akin to God that it is already one with Him and need never be united to Him" (Dupre, 461). Following this concept, it appears that the joining point in our love-union with God resembles a Third, constituted by the two of us and yet distinct. It bears no small resemblance to the Christian doctrine of the Trinity: three "persons" in one God. Theologically this has been "explained" as having been brought about by two "processions." The Son proceeds from the Father as a manifestation of divine *truth*, while the Holy Spirit proceeds from the Father *and* the Son as a manifestation of divine *love* (McBrien, 358f.). Thus the love between the Father and Son is nothing less than a coequal, Third divine person.

From the perspective of psychology, theological statements like these are evidence not so much of God in his heaven as of the shape of the human soul. For it is we humans who arrive at such conclusions. What we claim for God, we can only have learned from our own experience. If we see God needing a triune relationship, surely we require it, too.

I find Ibn al-Arabi's doctrine of angels to be the most fascinating treatment of the notion of a Third entity in the relationship between the human individual and God. In his view an angel constitutes a metaphysical link between each individual and God[2]. He distinguishes five levels of being, two wholly divine, two wholly human, and an intermediate angelic level. The human pole admits distinction into body (the lowest of the five levels) and soul. As for the divine pole, Ibn al-Arabi distinguishes between the absolute, wholly transcendent Allah and the "lord" whom each of us serves. Each individual's life bears witness to a different lord, a different facet of the inexhaustible and irrepresentable Allah. Between each soul and its lord is a specific angel, the Third for that human-divine love affair.

Ibn al-Arabi's thinking begins with what is probably the most frequently quoted saying (*hadith*) of the prophet Muhammad: "I was a Hidden Treasure and I wanted to be known. So I created the world so that I might be known." The godhead is speaking of itself, here, in the first person, as always in Muhammad's prophetic utterances. The assertion that creation is a divine self-manifestation implies that, if only we know how to see the world as it really is, we will be able to apprehend God. Ibn al-Arabi goes so far as to claim that creation itself is on a kind of continuum with its Creator: the Absolute at one end and matter at the other. Creation proceeds through five stages of emanation or embodiment, bearing no small resemblance to the Gnostic tradition in Christianity or the Jewish Kabbalah's doctrine of redeeming the divine sparks, which we discussed in chapter 6. The Absolute manifests itself first as an indefinite (almost infinite) number of lords, each of which—like the Quran's ninety-nine Names of God—reveals one aspect of the infinite Truth about God. Each of these lords, in turn, manifests as an angel, each angel as a soul, and each soul as a bodily individual. Thus, each created being (be it mineral, plant, animal, or human) is so constituted that it cannot help but reveal an aspect of God to anyone who can see through its bodily form to the soul, angel, and lord that it embodies. And each human being has the additional

---

2. In this argument I am following the language of Henry Corbin. Toshihiko Izutsu's exposition of the same doctrine uses the expression "permanent archetype," where Corbin speaks of "angel." Corbin emphasizes the philosophical and mythological context out of which Ibn al-Arabi writes and is particularly concerned to explicate the Sufi writer's initiation into mastership by an invisible guide (angel), named Khidr. For Ibn al-Arabi the angel or archetype is not an abstract principle but a personal experience of the Third.

benefit of self-consciousness, whereby we can each come to know the lord we reflect.

In all of this, the angel is pivotal. It is the form according to which the godhead knows itself and reveals itself differently in each one of us. We need the angel in order to be connected with God, and God needs the angel in order to be known. Henry Corbin explicates this doctrine of Ibn al-Arabi's by referring to the Jewish mystic Joseph ben Judah, who says the soul needs to struggle with its angel as Jacob did, in order to be freed from the darkness that would otherwise imprison it. And "the Angel needs the response of a soul if his being is to become what it has to be" (35). This is a notion very close to that of Eckhart: God and I seeing one another through the same eye. Eckhart's "eye" is like Ibn al-Arabi's "angel," except that the Muslim sage emphasizes God's dependency. He thereby brings the human/divine relationship even closer to our experience of romantic love. In this he resembles the Christian mystic Angelus Silesius (1624–1677), whose collection of aphorisms, *The Cherubinic Wanderer,* contains some surprising observations. For example:

> I know that without me the life of God were lost,
> Were I destroyed, he must perforce give up the ghost.
>
> (1, 8)

And:

> God shelters me as much as I do shelter Him;
> His Being I sustain, sustained I am therein.
>
> (1, 100)

And:

> That God shall have no end, I never will admit,
> Behold, He seeks my soul, that He may rest in it.
>
> (1, 277)

Where do mystics get such notions? A Christian would not hesitate to answer that they come from the Holy Spirit, the divine Third, the indwelling source of all inspiration. In Islam, the agency may typically be ascribed to angels. The prophet Muhammad received the very words of the Quran directly from the Angel Gabriel, and Ibn al-Arabi owed his initiation as a Sufi sheikh to the angel Khidr. Ibn al-Arabi follows in the tradition of the philosopher Avicenna (980–1037) regarding angels. Angels are the source of prophetic inspiration and visions of God—"the foundation of an intermediate world of pure Imagination" between terrestrial and celestial spheres (Corbin, 12). By Ibn al-Arabi's birth (1165), the Avicennan theory had already been eclipsed by the criticism of Averroes (1126–1198), who had pointed out that a doctrine of personal revelation through angels threatened orthodox authority (ibid., 62). Thus, half a millennium after the angel-inspired prophet had established Islam, its authorities suppressed the doctrine of angels. It is the same fate suffered by the Holy Spirit in Christianity, and for the same reason.

Ibn al-Arabi, however, did not participate in the suppression. His invisible guide, Khidr, the "Green One," is traditionally believed to be the same angel who became Moses' guide in the Quran's story (18: 61-83). When Moses meets the angel, he asks if he may be allowed to follow him and learn from him. The angel resists, saying that Moses lacks the wherewithal to understand angelic actions, in that they are informed by a knowledge of God that is far beyond Moses' attainments. Finally he agrees to let Moses tag along on condition that he ask no questions. The angel then proceeds to poke a hole in the hull of a ship, kill a boy, and repair without asking remuneration a crumbling wall in a town that had refused hospitality to the two travellers. In each case Moses cannot resist asking for an explanation. On the third occasion the angel forbids Moses to follow any further. Then he explains that by sinking the ship he was saving it for its poor owners from a king who was seizing all seaworthy vessels; by killing the boy he was saving the faith of the parents; and by repairing the wall he was insuring that a treasure hidden at its base would not be found before the orphan boys who would inherit it had grown big enough to claim it.

Clearly Khidr is the repository of a wisdom that comes directly from God and is superior to orthodox law; for, although Moses is the preeminent lawgiver who met God face-to-face on Mount Sinai, he is no match for Khidr. Khidr teaches a mystical truth that surprises mortal ken. The Quran calls him, "one of Our slaves, unto whom We had given mercy from Us, and had taught him knowledge from Our presence" (18: 66). Here lies the scriptural foundation for Ibn al-Arabi's doctrine of the Third. It is a claim for transcendent sublimity.

But Averroes was not wrong; a doctrine of personal inspiration spells serious trouble for communal orthodoxy. The angel does not destroy the law; he only finds exceptions. But even this is troubling. For although the godhead cannot be at odds with itself, the idea of an inspiring angel possessed of transcendent wisdom can be a dangerous tool in the hands of the naive or the unscrupulous.

Likewise my doctrine of following the Third in a relationship of romantic love admits of misuse. It will be safer and more secure to rely on a community consensus for guidelines in pursuing our relationships. Furthermore, such a consensus does not arise arbitrarily but generally represents conclusions drawn from long experience. Still, the Quranic Khidr has shown us that there are sometimes very important exceptions that must be made. The couple who elect to follow the guidance of the Third may end up bearing a significant tension. It may occasionally happen that our guide pulls us in a different direction from that of collective morality. Before addressing these difficulties, however, we will consider one more symbol of the Third.

One of the most widely known and mysterious symbols of western culture in the last thousand years is that of the Holy Grail. Scholars agree only that the origins of the Grail legends are lost somewhere deep in pre-Christian Celtic mythology and that Christianized French compilations appeared late in the twelfth century. In what follows, I have used two main sources, *The Quest of the Holy Grail,* which is an excerpt from a huge French compilation known as the Prose *Lancelot,* and Thomas Malory's *Le Morte d'Arthur,* which is a condensation and revision of the Lancelot material, placing King Arthur in the central role and emphasizing the tragic inevitability of Camelot's fall.

The Grail is generally pictured as a plate, bowl, or cup;[3] usually it is either the cup Jesus used at the Last Supper, in which wine was

---

3. Wolfram von Eschenbach describes it as a stone on which all the names of the knights of the Round Table have been inscribed.

changed into his blood, or it is the bowl in which Joseph of Arimathea (mentioned in all four canonical gospels as the burier of Jesus) collected blood shed by Jesus while hanging on the cross. Legend relates that the Grail is brought to Britain by Joseph of Arimathea whence it is abstracted into a magic kingdom because the people of Britain prove themselves unworthy of it. This kingdom becomes a wasteland because its king draws too near the sacred vessel and is punished. His land becomes barren, and King Mordrain himself is wounded (usually in the thigh), blinded, weakened, and suffers great pain and will continue to languish for four hundred years until Galahad shall find the Grail.

The holy vessel is the central object in a masslike liturgy performed daily in the Grail Kingdom by Josephus, son of Joseph of Arimathea and priest of the Grail. Its rare appearances in the world of space and time are generally attended by extraordinary weather phenomena: darkenings, brightenings, thunderclaps, and dramatic changes in the wind. The fact that it is nearly always borne by a maiden, together with the sexual taint implied in the Grail King's wound, suggests an erotic dimension. Referring to the Eschenbach version of the tale, Emma Jung and Marie-Louise von Franz conclude that the Grail "prescribes" which woman a man should marry. The Grail King, Anfortas in this version, suffers the wound to his thigh for having chosen a woman of whom the Grail disapproved:

> As the fate of Anfortas shows, the moment of individual choice is fraught with great danger. The Grail nevertheless appears to have acted as a guiding symbol in the midst of entanglements engendered by the anima, in that, as an image of the absolute totality of the individual, it established the process of the latter's development in the service of a higher goal. (155)

The authors seem to mean that, whatever pain this experience may have caused Anfortas, he ultimately *gained* by having his attention directed from an unworthy mistress to the worthiest object of all— and that this will make him "whole." Emma Jung and von Franz become obscure near the end of the passage because they also wish to imply—without saying so directly—that this lesson is valid for us all. Whenever life provides us erotic "entanglements," we have an opportunity to find our way to the center, the highest goal, personal wholeness. If we get snagged along the way on some lesser goal, the pain this causes is never too high a price. This is a radical view but hardly shocking when we consider the meaning of Khidr and the dangerousness of the Holy Spirit.

The Grail is not only the center of attention, it always occupies the physical center of a scene: the Round Table, the altar, and so on. It emits a heavenly radiance of light and sweet fragrance. When it nourishes, it supplies each communicant with the very food and drink that most completely satisfies, not only the body's appetite but the spirit's as well. The Grail heals illness, wounds, and souls; maintains life; and preserves youth. In the story of Anfortas, we have already seen that it discriminates good from evil—sometimes in a quite unpredictable and ungentle manner. But it expresses divine will more literally than that, for it sometimes appears covered with writing that is understood to be decrees and commands from God. Its appearance also constitutes a test of faith and moral probity for potential witnesses, as it is invisible to sinners and the unbaptized. The Grail particularly favors virginity in discursive passages of the *Quest* and *Le Morte d'Arthur,* while narrative passages are likely to suggest a different attitude toward sexuality.

In the *Quest,* every adventure is followed by one of the protagonists encountering a holy man or woman who explains the spiritual meaning of the events that have just transpired. One hermit assures Lancelot that the quest of the Grail is a venture for heavenly, not earthly things: "Be assured that your prowess as a knight will avail you nothing in this Quest unless the Holy Ghost first pave your way in all the adventures that you meet with" (134). Other passages suggest that the Grail, itself, is the Holy Spirit. It first appears to Arthur's Round Table on the feast of Pentecost, which celebrates the coming of the Holy Spirit to Jesus' disciples who were shut up in the upper room of the Last Supper out of fear of the authorities who had killed Jesus. Likewise, Arthur's knights were in an upper hall of the palace:

When they all were seated and the noise was hushed, there came a clap of thunder so loud and terrible that they thought the palace must fall. Suddenly the hall was lit by a sunbeam which shed a radiance through the palace seven times brighter than had been seen before. In this moment they were all illumined as it might be by the grace of the Holy Ghost, and they began to look at one another, uncertain and perplexed. But not one of those present could utter a word, for all had been struck dumb, without respect of person. (Ibid., 43)

In Christianizing the pagan legend of the Grail, the authors make the greatest of claims for the holy vessel. It is also said that a trio of great priests—Christ, Josephus, and Galahad—preside over three great fellowships, the table of the Last Supper, the table of the Holy Grail, and the Round Table (ibid., 9f.). All of this suggests that an appearance of the Grail brings with it a foretaste of the Second Coming of Christ, when the faithful will enjoy a sublime oneness and peace, what the New Testament calls the Parousia.

As anima-connected guide, symbol of the Holy Spirit, and foundation of the parousial *Mitwelt*, the Grail is the ultimate image of the Third for the recent millennium of western civilization. It remains for us now to see how the Grail works as a guide for the knights who ride in quest of it. We have already seen that they need to be free of sin or "thoroughly shriven," lest the quest bring about their humiliation or even their death. Sin implies an attachment to something less than ultimate. The Ten Commandments, for example, assert God's ultimacy and then list as prohibitions some of the typical ways we get sidetracked. Therefore, to say that he must be free of sin means that the Grail knight must eschew all distractions from his meditation on the center, both in intention and in action. As a symbol of the center, the Grail will never be found by those who do not in their own lives know the difference between the center and the periphery. Whether they intend to do evil or not, they are the sinners whom the hermits and anchoresses of the *Quest* warn against.

To be free of sin, though, is a negative requirement. The Grail knight needs some active kind of guidance if he is to find what other Christians, regardless of their holiness, have missed for twelve or thirteen hundred years. It is surely not to be found well-marked on any of the highways of medieval life, nor even on the byways. Indeed, the knights ride separately into the deepest and darkest parts of the forest, avoiding the quotidian paths. They really do not know where they are going or how to get there. On meeting a woman riding a white palfrey who asks where he is going, Lancelot replies: "In truth, young lady, I do not rightly know, save there where fortune takes me. For I have no notion of the wherabouts of what I seek" (*Quest*, 146).

It takes a great deal of humility and trust to throw your life into a quest that is so uncertain and undefined. In romantic love we often try to save ourselves from this uncertainty by clinging to an image of where our relationship is going. For example, our union at the archetypal level always carries with it a sense of eternality. It is natural to take this impression literally and to assume that the fact of our connection means that we should marry and live happily ever after. But this is not always a valid conclusion. Our connection at the level of the Self may be realized in a great variety of forms, and to cling too rigidly to any one image of a goal is to limit the guiding Third. As human beings we are "condemned," as it were, to entertain images for where our lives are headed. We cannot be involved with a partner and not imagine a goal toward which our affair is tending. But it is the function of love-play and worthy opposition constantly to challenge these images and to introduce alternatives. If there is anything we can learn from the Knights of the Holy Grail, it is to entertain images of the goal without becoming attached to them. For only such a detached involvement can allow room for the Third to influence our course.

When we take them literally, images of the goal can cause us to jump ahead to conclusions that the relationship itself does not warrant. We should rather view such images as heuristic symbols, that is, as clues to help us in our search for the meaning of our involvement. Even a successful marriage is not relieved of the requirement of following the Third and of examining the images that it provides. When we think we know where we are and where we are going, we should be skeptical. It is too easy to live in an imagined future, contemplating how things are going to be or how they "should" be, rather than to stay in the present moment. More than anything else, relationship requires that we be present to one another, right now. Rumi makes this requirement definitive, too, of the love of God:

> I love the half a coin that I have already in my hand
> from yesterday more than the *promise* of a whole one
> today, or the promise of a hundred tomorrow.
> A Sufi is the child of *this* moment.
>
> (1988: 13)

When lovers are helped to stay in the present moment through their love-play and worthy opposition, each is allowing his own state of mind to be transformed by the needs, fancies, and inspirations of the other. The "not knowing" of which Lancelot speaks is a kind of receptivity. Meister Eckhart calls it *Gelassenheit*,[4] the quiet, contained state of mind in which one maintains a psychic balance between acting and being acted upon. In the *Quest* this attitude is expressed in the knights' search for "adventure." What they mean by *adventure* is the fortuitous, unpremeditated element in life, usually coming in the form of a challenge to their courage, honor, or faith. It might be a fight with lance and sword or the rescue of a damsel in distress. But the *Quest* is always clear that ultimately it is God, the Holy Spirit, who chooses the adventures and matches them with the individual knights.

This is an exact analogy for what I mean by following the lead of the Third. To "follow the relationship," in this sense, means to be aware that we do not know the outcome in advance. Rather our course is revealed to us gradually in every individual moment of our mutual presence with one another. We entertain and take seriously all the images of and feelings about ourselves and one another. We pay attention, too, to the images, feelings, and intuitions that occur to us regarding the relationship itself. Nothing is discarded a priori; everything is taken seriously and playfully. We "hang in there," actively clarifying and receptively awaiting clarification.

In this way we maintain a state of active receptivity, *Gelassenheit*.

---

4. So does Heidegger. His *Discourse on Thinking* bears the original title, *Gelassenheit*. My understanding of the term is derived in part from Heidegger.

But how do we know what we are looking for amid all these images and feelings? This is the central question, the task of tasks. A pretty good starting point for addressing this issue is provided by a parable about a lost camel, which Rumi tells in his *Mathnawi*. A man who is searching for his lost camel is joined by a second man who *pretends* to have lost a camel so that he can tag along for a while and then lay claim to the first man's beast when it is found. The man who really lost a camel, however, behaves quite differently from the pretender. He recognizes scents the other does not smell and finds clues the other does not see. He knows his camel's smell and habits. Above all, he knows what it is like to be close to finding a lost camel, while the pretender has no inkling.

There is a "stinger" to this tale. Unbeknownst to himself, the pretender has also lost a camel. And as he tags along after the first man in his ignorant greed, suddenly he sees his own camel standing a few feet before him. It is quite a shock and quite a recognition. Now he, too, becomes a seeker (Rumi, 1988: 29f.).

We can draw at least three conclusions from Rumi's parable. First, staying "on track" when we follow our relationship means recognizing clues that are intimately familiar to us. It means stalking scents we have come to know so well that we forget them the way we forget our ears when we listen to music. The second lesson in Rumi's parable is that if we have not lost our camel, there is no point in searching for it. There will be no clues to recognize. A couple searching for a camel they did not lose would correspond to the knight who goes unshriven to the quest. Even though they think they are searching for the Grail of relationship, they have gotten attached to a less than ultimate goal. They want a camel they have no right to: their false image of the goal. We only get to know the goal that fulfills and expresses the essence of our relationship by getting to know the relationship itself. That is to say, we have to attend to what we are perceiving and feeling right now—as well as to who our beloved is, what mood she or he is in, what world she or he inhabits.

The third lesson in Rumi's parable is that even if we think we have lost no camel—even if we think we have never owned one—there is a camel out there that belongs to us. Sometimes we are on the track of our relationship without ever guessing that there are scents to follow. Perhaps we have been living in an unconscious state of oneness that we have been taking for granted. The fact that we have not opened our eyes to see it does not mean there is no divine spark in our union. Rumi probably addressed this parable to his followers who had only the faintest glimmering of what a spiritual life might be. He invites them to follow the Sufis who *know* that they have lost God's presence. When they recite the *dhikr,* perhaps a phrase about God's presence repeated over and over, and begin to whirl in the dervish dance, they might encounter their camel. In Ibn al-Arabi's language, their camel is the angel who connects them with their lord. The camel is another image for the Third person in the relationship. In the same way we—if we act like real lovers and stay in the moment—may encounter the Khidr of our union.

When we finally encounter the camel we did not know we had, we get a "feel" for having a camel. In the same way, we can get a feel for when we are following the relationship. Rumi has found many ways to express this in images and words:

> When you do things from your soul,
> you feel a river moving in you, a joy.
>
> When actions come from another section,
> the feeling disappears.
> . . . .
> Don't insist on going where you think you want to go.
> *Ask* the way to the Spring.
>
> Your living pieces will form a harmony.
>
> (1987: 44)

Rumi points, here, to a principle of harmonious integration, evidently what Jung means by the Self. When we are in harmony with that Self, it is as though a joyful river were flowing through us. But beware; for following that river is not always the same as doing what our ego thinks it wants to do. The joyful river results from the confluence of our several living pieces.

In Rumi's few lines we have a powerful and moving description of the process that Jung calls individuation, "the model and guiding principle" (1919/48: par. 187) of analytical psychology. It is "a process in the psyche that seeks its goal independently of external factors" (1944/52: par. 4) and that greatly differentiates and combines collective functions and faculties (1928/35: par. 267) so that we become "our innermost, last, and incomparable uniqueness . . . [our] own self" (ibid., par. 266). It is "a course of development arising out of the conflict between two fundamental psychic facts" (1939: par. 523): the ego's conscious decision and the Self's unconscious intentionality.

Individuation is the organic unfolding of one's being in which imaginative phenomena (fantasies) fill out and compensate for the incompleteness of conscious attitudes. As orchestrated by the Self, fantasy is nothing other than one's own existence revealing itself. Every dream, for example, is a compensation, a momentary adjustment of the conscious imbalance. "But with deeper insight and experience, these apparently separate acts of compensation arrange themselves into a kind of plan . . . subordinated to a common goal" (Jung, 1945/48: par. 550). In this process, the ego experiences itself "as object of an unknown and supraordinate subject" (1928/35: par. 405), called the "transcendent function," "whose power is as great as that of the instincts" (1928/48: par. 96) and "leads to the revelation of the essential man" (1917/43: par. 186).

"Following the relationship" is parallel in every detail to "individuation." In relationship, integration and harmony are achieved by a Third, which resembles the transcendent function in its powerful, joyful-flowing-river quality, as it reconciles conscious goals with an unconscious vision of wholeness. The Third, whether we call it Khidr, the Holy Spirit, or the Holy Grail, is the "transcendent function" at work in relationship. Its job is to reconcile and balance the various pairs of opposites: the potion and the sword, the eternal and the temporal, the archetypal and the personal, ego decisiveness and expectant receptivity, unity and individuality, mine and yours.

This describes the principle of the Third, as the guiding spirit in a relationship. It is almost like a third partner, a creative principle that draws its intentionality from the unity we have with our beloved. To follow the Third, we need to keep one foot in the archetypal, eternal dimension of the union and the other in the practical, everyday, personal world of me and you. To find a balance between opposing demands and desires is a ticklish affair for which we need to acquire a "feel." But we will never do so if we do not take a few risks. The Knights of the Holy Grail show us that these risks are not to be pursued recklessly, but only as we find life (the Third) presents us with "adventures." Many of these will seem too humble and demeaning, others of questionable propriety. Each couple's course on the quest will be unique. No path has been carved for it. We have to carve our own.

12

Love's Quest:
Following the Relationship

Falling in love is a matter of luck or grace. Life simply grants us a favor. Although we may be able to look back on an incident of falling in love and appreciate the extent to which our woundedness had prepared us for it, it never appears that we in any way earned or deserved it. In its early stages romantic love almost always seems to be a wonder and a blessing—like the arrival of the swan-knight or the hawk-knight in answer to a maiden's prayer. As time passes, however, we may become less and less sanguine in our descriptions of our relationship. Difficulties rooted deep in our respective wounds begin to surface, and it may seem that the trials of love demand far more effort than love's pleasures can recompense. What seemed to pull us out of the doldrums now takes us more deeply into them. We want to escape. We may even laugh scornfully at love and its chimerical promises. Very likely, though, we are stuck, feeling it too painful to go on and impossible to pull out.

We like to think of love as a kind of huckleberry raft or ethereal cruise ship afloat between reality's shores. But this respite from everyday concerns usually seems to betray us, for it seduces us into confrontation with some of the deepest conflicts of our lives. Until we are so seduced, we tend to believe we have successfully resolved or avoided such conflicts. No wonder love's reputation is clouded. Those who can successfully end their entanglement with a quarrel or walk away without regrets seem to be fortunate, indeed. If they can lead their lives happily without having to wrestle with the stickiness and pain that Eros unearths, the rest of us may envy them. But we who cannot change course so easily find ourselves condemned to work through our difficulties. There is nothing left for us but to accept the challenge and *live* our romantic life.

In the previous chapter, we have tried to formulate an attitude about this. We have concluded that the course of romantic love is unique for every couple, so that pratical precepts and guidelines are bound to be misleading. The one common denominator is that every couple must "follow the relationship." This implies that there is a guiding third principle, like Khidr, the Holy Spirit, or the Holy Grail, to which the partners open themselves in a kind of active receptivity. Because of their alert attention and their active participation, we may say that they "tend" the relationship as much as "follow" it. They resist sliding into unconsciousness and by no means abdicate moral responsibility. Following the relationship is a moral undertaking of the highest and subtlest order.

To flesh out this abstract picture, we shall consider the careers of three knights as they go in quest of the Holy Grail: Galahad, who enjoyed supreme success; Gawain, who was unable even to get started; and Lancelot, the only successful knight to have returned to the real world. Unless otherwise noted, this material comes from *The Quest of the Holy Grail*.

Galahad's Quest

On the eve of a certain Pentecost, Lancelot is called out of Camelot by a young woman and taken to a nunnery. There he meets for the first time his own son, Galahad, whom the nuns want dubbed a knight. Lancelot does so Pentecost morning.

Arriving at Camelot about noon, Galahad pulls a magic sword from a stone and then becomes the designated occupant of the famous Seat Perilous, which had gone empty since the founding of the Round Table. Then he jousts—shieldless—with the finest of King Arthur's knights, demonstrating extraordinary prowess. That evening the Grail appears in the center of the Round Table, and all one hundred fifty knights vow to go on the Quest.

As Galahad begins the Quest, he wins a shield designed for "the finest knight in Christendom," casts the devil out of a blessed graveyard, and frees a large number of impris-

oned ladies from the Castle of the Maidens. Later he
battles with Lancelot, Perceval, and Gawain—all unrecog-
nized. He unhorses his father, and almost kills the other
two.

Next a maiden, who turns out to be the sister of Perceval, conducts Galahad to a magic ship in which the two
of them set sail together with Perceval and Bors. They find
another marvelous sword on board, and the ship takes
them to the Castle of Carcelois in Scotland, where they
are attacked by ten knights, whom they kill. They learn
that these ten are guilty of incest with and the murder of
their sister. At another castle, they fight seventy knights to
save Perceval's sister from being bled to cure a leprosy
from which the lady of the castle suffers. On learning the
cause of the battle, the saintly maiden volunteers to be
bled, and asks to have her body placed in a boat at the first
port they come to. The boat will take her to the city of
Sarras—the end of the Quest—ahead of the three knights.

The knights travel on in separate directions. Galahad
finds the abbey where King Mordrain is suffering from
four hundred years of weakness and blindness after having
approached too near the Grail. Galahad's presence restores
his sight, and he dies in Galahad's arms. Galahad then
meets Perceval and the two of them travel about Britain
for five years putting an end to preternatural (pagan)
phenomena, such as boiling springs and flaming tombs.
At the end of this time, they meet up with Bors, and the
three of them come to the Castle of Corbenic, the Grail
Castle, where Galahad restores the broken sword of
Joseph of Arimathea. At the table of the Grail, Josephus,
"the first Christian bishop," is borne down from heaven
by four angels; and Christ, naked with bleeding hands
and feet, distributes communion. Galahad is bidden to
heal the Maimed King[1] with blood from the lance that
pierced the side of Christ. Then the three companions are
ordered to take the Grail out of Britain to the City of
Sarras, again using the magic ship.

---

1. In this version of the Grail story, there are three different Grail kings. Pelles, the
Fisher King, reigns at Corbenic. King Mordrain has been languishing in an abbey.
And now, a Maimed King appears. It looks as though three traditions have been
insufficiently harmonized.

In Sarras, an evil king imprisons the companions, and they are fed miraculously by the Grail for a year until the king dies. A voice tells the people to select Galahad for their king. But before this can happen, another Grail service is celebrated by Josephus, who invites Galahad to look into the Grail. The vision, not described to the reader, is so impressive that Galahad resolves to die on the spot. A hand reaches down from heaven and takes the Grail up with it. Perceval also dies, and Bors buries him beside his sister and Galahad. Bors returns alone to Camelot to tell the story.

Galahad, "the Good Knight," appears full grown on the Arthurian stage, virtually without preparation and coming out of nowhere. His mother Elaine, along with Viviane, Morgaine, and Morgan, is one of the magical Ladies of the Lake who, in an earlier age, were Celtic goddesses. Everything about him sets him apart from ordinary mortals: the sword, the shield, the Seat Perilous, his virginity.

Some details mark him out as a new Arthur, particularly the favor of the Ladies of the Lake, the sword pulled out of a stone, and the second sword discovered in a magic ship. There are many more, however, that mark him as a second Christ. He has a secret childhood, a short public life, and an early, voluntary death. He heals King Mordrain and others. He ends the pagan era, ushering in the era of Christianity. Above all, he is a virgin and preserved from sin. Even in portraying the violent life of a knight, the narrator rarely allows Galahad's blows to be fatal. If they are, he immediately reassures us that the knights Galahad killed were among the most heinous individuals on the face of the earth.

A magic ship seems to carry him through his entire life—not only when he is travelling by sea. He lives entirely in the eternal, archetypal world, like Lohengrin. Such experience is by no means foreign to romantic love. We considered the stone-in-the-pocket kind of phenomenon at some length in chapter 3. When we are in an unconscious harmony, a mystical oneness, events glide by frictionlessly: it is inspirational; it bonds us with our beloved; it reveals to us something about the profundity of the human soul; it may open the lens of our anima or animus and bring into focus the being of our beloved. All these things are very important. They guide our relationship, give it ballast, reinforce the certainty of our trust in one another. They shed light, too, on issues that arise in the personal, temporal realm of our joint life.

Sometimes we enjoy minutes or hours, even weeks, in this archetypal realm where everything seems to be divinely ordered. Sometimes a couple can seem to spend years this way—particularly when they live quite different lives and spend fairly little time together. A moment's glimpse of our Self-level connection can nourish us for weeks, reassuring us of the depth and eternality of our love. We catch one another up on the news from our respective lives, and we even pay some attention to the details; but all of this is really a vehicle for our reconnecting at a deeper level. Our meetings are radiant, glowing from within with the light of the divine spark. They are instances of love-play. We take delight in the new facets of one another's soul that have been brought out during the time we have been separated. We delight in our union, a kind of conspiracy of affection and inspiration. Each of us provides the matrix for the other's growth and transformation, because we do not cling to specific images of one another and insist that certain expectations be filled. We look forward to each meeting receptively, as to a spiritual adventure where we will be delighted to find more intriguing inspiration. It seems as the years go by that we are eternally the same and yet forever different. The breadth of our connectedness grows, seems to burst our chests in a most subtle ecstasy of joining ever more satisfyingly.

Probably we all experience something like this—if only in nearly missed glimpses. For this is the Self-level bond, always the same and yet always unique with every couple. It is rare, indeed, for such experience to dominate in a relationship that lasts for decades. "Real life" with all of its mundane details is eventually bound to intrude, bringing with it conflicting demands and personal difficulties that we may very well regret. But, regret them or not, we have little control over their appearance. They are part of our very being as mortals. And, as we have explored in chapter 10, these differences can even be a blessing in disguise if we become worthy opponents and treat them as opportunities for growth rather than as indications that our union will never work.

In any event, when temporality and personal differences intrude into the paradisal eternality of our union, we will probably find that the example of Galahad provides little help. His divinely privileged origins and goal preserved him from the practical frustrations we have no hope ever of escaping. His value for us ordinary mortals is to remind us that there *is* a level of Self-Self union outside of space and time. As we have seen in the discussion on worthy opponents, the dimension of eternal union can operate as a kind of anchor amid the passionate storms brought on by our individual needs. We *could* follow our relationship in the Galahad manner, if only we could free ourselves of our nonultimate attachments. Perhaps it is impossible for us not to have spasms of inordinate need for security, nurture, or independence. But the example of Galahad indicates the higher and clearer-eyed alternative. To have gained this kind of perspective already attenuates our nonultimate spasms. A vision of following the relationship as smoothly as Galahad in his magic ship helps us to see our union as a whole and keeps us from getting stuck on the same old snags. Or when we do get stuck in spite of ourselves, a Galahad vision makes it easier for us to detach ourselves from those snags.

The translator of the *Quest*, Pauline Matarasso, tells us in one of her very well-informed footnotes (296, n. 56) that Galahad's boat represents Christian mysticism. In view of our discussion in the previous chapter, we can be more specific than that. The magic boat represents what Meister Eckhart calls *Gelassenheit*, the mystic's attitude of actively holding oneself open for the guidance of the Holy Spirit, the Holy Grail, or any other personification of the Third. Galahad himself represents more than saintliness, because—apart from the mother of Jesus—no human has been preserved from sin as he. His quest of the Grail represents following a relationship with supernatural clarity. If, as lovers, we had Galahad's enhanced vision, we would never lose sight of our beloved as she appears through the lens of our anima or animus. Despite our difficulties, we would keep our relationship anchored in the essential core of our beloved, the divine spark that justifies our relationship ultimately.

It is very possible to see that core and to fail to see the mundane issues that can lead to quarrels and worthy opposition. It does indicate a bit of perhaps willful blindness, but most couples who see

230

through their anima and animus lenses can enjoy periods of time in a Venusberg of eternal joy. They might find that such interludes give them the strength and courage to struggle with their mundane issues. But I have seen couples, too, who have clung to their Venusberg interludes as though they were the whole of the relationship—and denied the validity of their quarrels. There is a certain seductiveness to the eternal dimension of romantic love. It has a quality of being "realer" than real life, a quality of givenness, as though God has ordered things this way just for us. I have heard people describe their relationships this way, concluding that really nothing can go wrong, that the eternal, spiritual dimension of their union is so strong that it is bound to overcome all difficulties on the apparently less significant personal plane.

We know how people can come to have a view like this, for the archetypal dimension of relationship is often the most powerful experience of the psyche that individuals ever have. But with a modicum of exposure to the difficulties, we also know how easy it is to overlook and devalue the importance of the personal. Furthermore, as the story of Thomas Wolfe makes clear, there are other archetypal realities to reconcile with our relationship—a need for personal autonomy and accomplishment, for example. When an archetypal requirement like one of these begins to make itself felt, it invariably picks up on some of the overlooked and devalued personal whims and individual differences we fooled ourselves into thinking we had overcome.

In general, I have more hope for the renewal and salvation of a relationship in which the couple too much favors their archetypal connection over the personal, than for a relationship in which the couple has never taken the archetypal dimension seriously. Nevertheless, this in itself is not adequate. It is very possible for the archetypally conscious relationship to fall apart even as the partners are denying evidence of failure.

In the real world it is not possible to live by archetypal vision alone. It is possible, though, for the lovers to cultivate a Galahad-like vision that ignores interpersonal difficulties until they become large enough to be stumbling blocks. If then, in a kind of saintly earnestness, they accept the mundane challenge their personal differences offer them and value one another's complaints, the relationship can still move forward.

It will never move as smoothly and effortlessly as Galahad's magic ship, but the partners will experience an intermittent "divine" guidance. Their rootedness in their Self-Self bond will continue to give them ballast and balance, and it will relativize the snags they meet and give them the sense that these limitations are not insuperable. Therefore if they go to work on these difficulties with a good will, they may make the adjustments required and fall back relieved and triumphantly into their archetypal current. Such a relationship does not proceed so much like Galahad's magic boat's track over a glassy ocean as like the tumultuous course of an inflated raft on a white-water river. They shoot ahead, get hung up on boulders and fallen trees, spin rear-foremost for several heart-in-mouth moments, and perhaps even overturn once or twice. But they are wearing their archetypal lifevests; and if they do not lose their hold on the line that attaches them to the raft, they will likely be able to right their craft and clamber back aboard. Then, after some laborious pushing, prying, and poling with the paddles, they may be able to shoot forward again in a spirit of eternal joy, while their muscles tremble with exhaustion and horror at their recent close call.

Such starry-eyed lovers and sometime worthy opponents do not so much resemble the Galahad of the *Quest* as the pure fool, Parzival, in the Grail story of Wolfram von Eschenbach. Parzival's purity results from his Self-level vision and his foolishness from his ignorance of mundane affairs. What saves him and enables him to cure the Maimed King and restore the Wasteland is the archetypal purity of his intentions, the way he brings himself back onto the track of the Third after the mistakes that lead him foolishly astray.

Foolish or not, it really helps to be able to sail like Galahad in a magic boat and keep our focus on our beloved's transcendent individuality. Our battles are worth the trouble precisely on account of the beauty of our beloved's soul and the fulfillment we experience in our union. Indeed unions sometimes fail for no other reason than that the partners have forgotten the archetypal perspective on one another that they used to enjoy. Without nourishment from the Self, they can come to feel that their battles with one another are wearing them out. Such a couple's struggle with the issues of relationship resembles more the plight of Gawain than Galahad's privileged course.

The Frustrations of Gawain

On Pentecost weekend, before the Quest is officially opened, Gawain obeys the order of King Arthur—against his own better judgment—and attempts to remove the magic sword from the floating stone, which only Galahad can attempt without punishment. When the Quest is declared, he is the first to vow wholehearted participation. Nevertheless, when Arthur expresses his sorrow that the Quest will take away his best knights, Gawain "would gladly have gone back on his word had he dared, but the occasion had been too public to permit it" (*Quest*, 45).

On the Quest, Gawain continually misses adventures and comes upon Galahad's achievements a day or two too late to observe them or to participate in them. Eventually he meets Hector of the Marsh, and they compare notes. They cannot understand why they are not encountering any important adventures. Gawain has killed ten challengers without any hint leading to the Grail, and Hector has met twenty of Arthur's knights—all complaining of lack of adventure.

On being challenged by an unknown knight, Gawain wounds him severely, and he and Hector carry the man to the Hermit Nascien to be healed. He dies as Gawain extracts the spearhead. Nascien then explains dreams and visions the two knights have had, telling them that they will never meet adventures of the Holy Grail as long as they are in a state of sin. He advises them to return to Camelot. Unwilling to accept this, Hector rides away. Gawain tells the hermit that he would like to talk more, but that he needs to catch up with his companion.

In one of only two other references to Gawain, he enters a fray outside a castle while, unbeknownst to him, Galahad enters on the other side. The Good Knight, wielding the magic sword Gawain had touched against his better judgment, slays Gawain's horse, which falls dead on top of its rider.

The author of the *Quest* says of Gawain, "Beyond doubt he enjoyed a more widespread popularity than any man alive" (209). He and Lancelot are the knights King Arthur loves the most. Both the *Quest* and *Le Morte d'Arthur* portray Gawain as a generous, open-hearted, enthusiastic, brave, and loyal soul. His impetuosity springs from these sources and is therefore generally quite endearing. However, it also leads him to commit a very grave and humiliating sin against chivalry and, indeed, humanity, early in *Morte*. He battles with a knight who has slain his hunting hounds. At the last moment the knight's lady throws herself between the combatants, and Gawain is unable to stop his sword from beheading her (Malory: bk. 1, 101f.). Such is typical of how the good-hearted Gawain stumbles unconsciously into sin. He is forever capable of breaking our hearts, and we are constantly ready to forgive him.

At the beginning of the Quest, too, he shows his endearing but limited colors, as he is the first to declare for the Quest and then the first to regret his oath, out of allegiance to King Arthur. Finally, he cannot go back on his pledge because so many people have witnessed it. All of this reveals him to be a man primarily concerned with literal, political reality and collective values. Whereas Galahad is motivated by the Holy Spirit moving within him, Gawain is motivated by the political and social allegiances that surround him. Even his desire to participate in the Quest comes essentially from his persona. He sees it as just another test of honor and courage. It is a large and celebrated test, but still subordinate to the duties and ideals of chivalry. This is why his sentimental impulse to abandon his oath for the sake of the continuance of the Round Table is really stronger than his desire to quest after the Grail. For him, the Grail is just another sporting event, while the Round Table is the source and goal of his knightly oath.

Gawain is mundane man at his best: high principled, loyal, skillful, dedicated, boisterously good-natured. But he has no talent or sensitivity for the spiritual life. He finds no "adventure" because he is not following the Third. Like most of the knights (Hector has met twenty of them), Gawain has no ear for the voice of the Holy Spirit. In Nascien's terms, Gawain is a sinner. This does not mean he is a bad man. He is good as gold. The problem is, he does not know how to distinguish the center from the periphery. His sin is to mistake the less-than-ultimate ideals of chivalry for the absolute objective of his life's dedication. In religious language, he is idolatrous. He cannot see beyond the idol of chivalry to the One, which is the origin and aim of his heart's deepest longing.

We fall into the attitude of a Gawain in our relationships when we look primarily to collective expectations and rules to guide our outlook and behavior. There is no doubt that these rules ought to be taken seriously, for they have been developed over centuries, if not millennia, of human experience. There is a genuine wisdom in them. But it is a statistical wisdom—what is best for the average individual. Unfortunately, none of us is entirely average, and life has a way of leading us into situations that fall between the cracks of our society's mainstream ethics. Gawain finds himself in such a difficulty when he cannot make a resolute judgment regarding the Quest. The theological and mystical element in his society's ethos impels him to be first in line to sign up for the Quest, while the chivalric ideal of fealty to his earthly lord pulls him in the opposite direction. Both ideals are good and admirable, both are supported by Gawain's society. The issue is that he seems to have no inner criterion for prioritizing these conflicting claims on his allegiance.

We do this, too, in our relationships when we get caught between conflicting demands and cannot bear the tension that gives the Third its opportunity. We want an immediate solution, so we appeal to the rules everybody knows and to the experience of our friends. We go to a counselor to be advised what to do. Gawain-style issues and questions constitute nearly a hundred percent of readers' letters to newspaper advice columnists. We assume there must be a "right" way to do things that will cement our security in the matrix of society's approval. Since our "god," the highest principle in our outlook on life, is identical with the status quo in society, we have no "ear" for the voice of a Third like the intractable Holy Spirit or Khidr. Our relationship trudges along in the most ordinary and uninspiring way, and we begin to wonder, perhaps, whether there is some way to recover the interest in one another that we have lost. Still, when risky opportunities arise, we look first to collective notions of propriety or else feel ourselves wicked for leaving the straight and narrow.

Gawain tends to relieve life's ordinariness by throwing himself wholeheartedly into one lofty project after another. No challenge is too great for his enthusiasm and energy, provided he can be sure of society's approval. He obtains his greatest satisfaction, in fact, from his enthusiastic excesses. His killing is an example of this. Both *Morte* and *Quest* agree that, although he may kill the wrong man or woman, he does it with the best of intentions and cheerful good-heartedness. But he is very much a killer. The sword of his clumsy, flat-footed good deeds swings with a momentum that carries it too far. His short-sightedness results in a net decrease in life.

Our relationships should add to our lives. When we are guided by the Third, they shimmer with the light of the divine spark, they connect us with the One. This is what the hermit was trying to tell Gawain. When our relationships are so much in the dark that we are absolutely ignorant of the Third, it is time to stop riding in search of adventure. It is time to examine ourselves.

Gawain provides very little help in our search for an understanding of what it means to "follow the relationship." He never comes near to following the Grail. Lancelot begins his Quest in somewhat the same condition, but he listens to the hermit and stays on to effect an inner transformation. Lancelot is the whole man, comprised both of instinct and of spirit. Galahad and Gawain each represent a half of Lancelot.

Lancelot's Quest

After dubbing Galahad and returning to Camelot, Lancelot wisely refuses Arthur's order to try to remove Galahad's magic sword from its floating stone. He is the second, after Gawain, to declare his dedication to the Quest. In his first adventure he is unhorsed by Galahad. Then he enters the thick of the forest without benefit of a path and is the first to encounter the Holy Grail.

He has lain down for the night, with his head on his shield and passes into a kind of waking catalepsy in which he cannot move or speak. He sees the Maimed King carried up on a litter before a small chapel. As the king groans for release from his suffering, the Holy Grail issues from the chapel on a silver table. The king drags himself

up to it by the strength of his arms and obtains relief
by kissing the silver table. During all of this Lancelot gives
no sign of recognizing what he sees. The restored king's
squire speculates that the immobile Lancelot "committed
a grave sin, of which he was never shriven" (*Quest*, 84).
He then arms the king in Lancelot's armor and seats him
on Lancelot's horse.

Lancelot then spends a good deal of time with hermits
who preach to him about the sinlessness required for the
Quest. Lancelot confesses his decades-long affair with
Queen Guinevere and dons a penitential hair shirt. When
he returns to the active Quest, he comes upon a tournament in which a group of black knights is losing to a
group of white knights. Lancelot joins on the side of the
losers and is taken prisoner for the first time in his life.
After he escapes, he finds himself hemmed in on all sides:
a deep river in front, cliffs on either side, and a treacherous forest behind. A black knight on a black charger
emerges from the river and kills Lancelot's horse. Lancelot
decides to pray and await God's mercy.

In the middle of the night, a voice commands Lancelot
to gather his arms and enter a boat. It turns out to be
the boat carrying the corpse of Perceval's sister. Lancelot
rides it for nine months, six together with Galahad, having many strange adventures and enjoying the "grace of
the Holy Ghost who was their constant aid and succour"
(*Quest*, 259). About a month after Galahad leaves the
boat, it brings Lancelot to the Castle of the Grail, and he
finds his way to the room where the Grail is kept. From
the doorway he sees Josephus celebrating mass, surrounded by ministering angels. Lancelot has a vision of
the Holy Trinity at the elevation of the host. As the priest
struggles with the weight of the body of Christ, Lancelot
starts forward to help. A blast of flaming wind scorches
him, and hands throw him out. He lies inert for twenty-
four days, and when he awakes he wishes his visions could
continue. A maiden brings him a white garment and tells
him he no longer needs his hair shirt, now that his Quest
is ended. He returns to Britain and Camelot.

Lancelot is a little less impatient than Gawain and a good deal
wiser. When he perceives a supernatural influence at work in the

phenomenon of the sword in the stone, he knows that—king or not—Arthur has no authority to command his involvement. Very likely, this ability to distinguish center from periphery qualifies him to glimpse the Grail. But failure to respond to his first view of the Grail is Lancelot's greatest sin in the *Quest*. For when we have the vision of a Galahad, it is sinful to act with the thickheadedness of a Gawain.

In this Lancelot resembles us, when we recognize the divine spark in our beloved and remain strangely unmoved. It is an indication of sin, that is, of some lesser attachment. For example, we may be gratified by this glimpse of the spark, but we do not want to be distracted from our goal of persuading our beloved to marry us. Or perhaps the glimpse frightens us, because we are terrified that submission means a passing away from which there is no turning back. We have all kinds of good reasons for fearing this plunge into the abyss of *fana*. Like Thomas Wolfe, we may fear losing our identity, our autonomy, our ability to pursue our daily activities, our professional competence. We take comfort in the known—even when it torments us or bores us to death—so that the prospect of *fana*'s transformation impresses us first with what we may have to give up. We cling so tightly to what we have known ourselves to be, that there is no possibility for transformation.

If, on the other hand, we are overly impressed with the kind of temporal and accidental considerations with which everyday anxieties and daydreams bombard us, we may never even guess that such a thing as a Third could exist. For example, we may be so taken up with our concern for financial stability that we resist all efforts to rock the boat when things are going well for us monetarily. When we feel insecure, we escalate our demands, even threaten to break off the relationship if our partner cannot be more responsive to our needs. We become so taken up with these anxieties that they isolate us from one another. Similar diversions can result from our sexual and emotional needs. We almost seem to retreat from one another into a frantic flutter, searching for a smooth path out of our difficulties. We long for Galahad's boat, but we are looking entirely in the wrong direction. For if our interest in our beloved is overshadowed by carnal, financial, or ornamental considerations, the Grail of transcendent intimacy will never appear. This would be the sin of a

Gawain. Lancelot's sin is that he knows he is seeing the Grail and still does not let himself pass away.

But unlike Gawain, Lancelot submits to the regimen of penitence that the hermits recommend. This indicates that he has appreciated his sinfulness, that he has seen that his attachments have been keeping him closed to the Grail. Although his failure to act is a more serious sin than Gawain's, something has dawned on Lancelot that passed Gawain by. Still the work of repentance is not done when he dons the hair shirt, because he is aware of his blindness still in a merely theoretical manner. Apparently he continues to believe he can follow the Grail on the strength of his knightly prowess, now augmented by his repentance. Extraordinary knightly prowess is an ambiguous virtue in an individual like Lancelot. On the one hand, his success in tournaments and war is accepted as an indication that God favors his cause—like the *Gottesgericht*, the divine judgment in *Lohengrin*. But even in *Lohengrin*, the question of whether the dream-knight has been sent by God or relies on magic, is central. Lancelot's prowess is comprised both of physical skill and spiritual talent and dedication. When he defeats those who accuse the queen of adultery, should we take this as God's condoning or even favoring of the adulterous affair; or should we take the more cynical perspective of Mark Twain's *Connecticut Yankee*, that Lancelot was a star athlete and a colossal brute who justified his behavior with naive theology?

The *Quest* addresses these issues directly. By his cataleptic immobility on first sighting the Holy Grail, it tells us that he is more than a brute, more even than a good-hearted and enthusiastic citizen like Gawain. Lancelot has an eye for Galahad visions, but something stands in the way. He has not yet sufficiently differentiated his spiritual from his knightly prowess. He accepts this in a theoretical way when he sits at the feet of the hermits, but he does not really come to grips with the implications of this insight in an emotional and practical manner until his knightly powers fail him. He needs to ride into a formidable cul-de-sac in order to realize finally that the following of the Grail is not something that falls into the bailiwick of his ego. This realization becomes undeniable when his horse is killed.

Lancelot spends a good deal of his time unhorsed in the *Quest*.

The "greatest knight in Christendom" is unconquerable on the field of chivalry but cannot stay mounted on the Quest. The horse represents an animal, instinctual, carnal power—precisely what needs to be transcended in order to exercise *Gelassenheit*. Thus Lancelot, having been converted in his thinking, saddles up and rides directly into an impasse where he loses his horse, becomes completely immobile, and is reduced to prayer as a last resort. He needs to experience his own helplessness and his dependence on God before he can begin to travel on a magic boat with Galahad.

We, too, are like this in our relationships when we think that progress depends on negotiation and compromise—as though we could work out in an intellectual manner issues that are rooted deeply in our woundedness and set about with emotional confusion. Although common wisdom tells us that each of us has to yield "fifty percent," in actual practice this rarely works. Jung refers to the individual's inner "Third" as the "transcendent function" precisely because it transcends impasses that the conscious mind cannot solve. In Jung's language, we must bear the tension of the opposites and simply stand still until the transcendent function provides us an illogical but forward-moving alternative. This is exactly what happens to Lancelot when he kneels to pray in the cul-de-sac beside his dead horse. And out of the darkness of midnight comes the magic boat of the Third. In just this way, a couple must have the patience to reject no alternatives and force no solutions, but wait in a spirit of *Gelassenheit* for the Third to guide them onward. The best exercise in preparation for this would be the process of recollection Lancelot underwent in hermitage: a process of renewing his dedication to the Ultimate.

With all of this as background, it seems that Lancelot's actual encounter with the Holy Grail in the Castle of Corbenic is the author's way of ratifying the knight's earlier process of humiliation and transformation. He gets the reward, and this verifies his methods of following the Grail. The vision itself is almost an anticlimax. From our perspective, the most important element in this episode is his regret at awakening from the twenty-four days of trance and his return to Britain. This is the issue that Galahad never solved for us: how to integrate a vision of transcendental beauty with the everyday world. Aside from Bors, Lancelot is the only knight to see the Grail and return to Camelot. But Bors is a minor character; Lancelot, alone, commanded the storyteller's interest. Therefore we need to follow the story further to determine what effect the vision of the Grail has had on Lancelot's own relationship of romantic love—or, indeed, on his everyday life in general.

13

Love's Labor:
Ordinary Time

In the previous chapter we studied *The Quest of the Holy Grail* in order to find guidelines for what it means to follow a Third. Relationship always involves not only two individuals who have a connection with one another, but also the relationship itself or the spirit of the relationship, which acts with relative autonomy, as though it were a third person. In fact, it acts in the relationship analogously as the Self within a single individual. It is a transpersonal factor that imposes itself on the two partners equally and mutually, and it has a wholeness to it by which it distinguishes itself from the one-sidedness or privatized quality of each individual partner. We have been arguing that a relationship has, as it were, a mind of its own and that this mind is more comprehensive than the conscious mentality of either of the partners. Therefore when we get involved in a relationship, we allow ourselves to participate in something that is not only larger than either of us, but has an intentionality that is more comprehensive. If we are to avoid the pushing and shoving, the narrowness and shallowness of my will against yours, we have to consult this "wiser" participant in the relationship—very much as the individual can consult his greater psyche, his Self, in order to get a more holistic perspective on the conduct of his life.

This "Third" has a number of analogs in the various traditions of human culture: the Holy Spirit, Khidr, the Tao, and the Holy Grail. The last of these has played an extremely important role in western thought over the past millennium. We have therefore chosen to examine it to see what kind of clues it can give us about following the relationship. In particular, we have tagged along with the three most important knights, as the Grail story is told in the anonymous *Quest*: Gawain, Galahad, and Lancelot. The *Quest* has taught us something about the attitude of *Gelassenheit*, whereby we actively keep ourselves in a state of receptivity for what may occur to us.

Gawain had none of that attitude and therefore met with no "adventures" in his Quest for the Grail. Eventually he saw the handwriting on the wall and gave up. He might have gone on, but only if he had the patience to sit still for perhaps a lengthy period of time and examine his conscience in order to determine what his goals really were. He had to learn to distinguish central matters from peripheral concerns and to perceive that the Quest was an undertaking of a wholly different order from the usual challenges of knight-errantry. He remained from first to last a very mundane individual. His less-than-ultimate concerns so dominated his consciousness that he was not able to recognize the more subtle issues that pointed to the Ultimate. His instructive value for us is that he embodies values that we all have, particularly values consonant with the social order. These are very important values, without which society could not survive. Besides this, as social beings we find ourselves off balance and frighteningly alone when we go against the collective mentality of our society. We begin to doubt ourselves and assume—not without justification—that we may be mistaken; for how do we dare set ourselves up as more reliable authorities than the society that has supported us and made us what we are?

Galahad, called "the Good Knight" by the author of the *Quest*, takes an opposite perspective. He was raised and trained outside of society by nuns, the Ladies of the Lake, or Celtic goddesses, depending on which layer of the tradition we follow. He enters the Arthurian cycle on the day before the Quest begins, and the Quest ends with his death. He is privileged from first to last and a saintly virgin. Either the Christian God or the Celtic goddesses prepare his course very carefully. They make sure that, with little foresight on his part, he commits no sin, kills no virtuous knight, and falls in love with no lady or maid. He performs miracles like Jesus and finds guidance from ladies on white palfreys and magic boats that take him through difficulties he never has to face. Because of the privileges he enjoys, he is not a very useful model for following the Third. But he does give us a good notion of what it would be like for us, if only we did not have to deal with the limitations of the human condition—especially our tendency to get confused about our priorities. If only we could "lock on" to the Third in our relationship, much as an airplane's automatic pilot locks on to electronic beams in the sky, we would be able to proceed as easily as Galahad. Galahad gives us a hint for what it must feel like to be on intimate terms with the Holy Spirit.

If Gawain and Galahad primarily show us what to avoid on the one hand and what we can hardly aspire to on the other, Lancelot provides a more realistic model for us to consider. He begins somewhat in the style of Gawain, but with the addition of having a sense for the spiritual and especially for the Third. Due to his long-term erotic relationship with Guinevere, we might guess that he has learned something about following a Third. But clearly he has not learned enough, for his first encounter with the Holy Grail leaves him thoroughly anesthetized and in a state of catalepsy. This experience, however, is enough to build his resolve to get to the bottom of his sinfulness, that is, to his habitual tendency to accept contingent values as though they were ultimate. He spends a good deal of time seeking for no adventure at all, but sitting at the feet of hermits who instruct him in the spiritual life and bring about in him a change of heart, a conversion, a *metanoia* in the language of the New Testament. He returns to the active Quest wearing a hair shirt but gets almost no distance at all before he finds himself in a formidable cul-de-sac standing beside his dead horse. At this point he finally relinquishes his reliance on his own knightly prowess and places himself in the hands of God. His *fana* is rewarded by the appearance of a magic boat (and the companionship of his son Galahad), which carries him to the Grail Castle where he enjoys twenty-four days of sublime visions.

While it is wonderful that Lancelot has succeeded quite well in the Quest, it is too bad for us that his double conversion (once at the feet of the hermits and again when his knightly resources failed him) has led only to another Galahad-like magic boat. We conclude from this that to follow the Third is something like riding in a mystic barque. But we still do not know what to do with this insight. How do we cultivate a knack for following the Third and still have a *real* life? To pursue this question, we shall follow the career of Lancelot after he returns to Camelot and resumes his relationship with Guinevere.

It is the task of this chapter to enter "ordinary time." This felicitous phrase has been used by many of the Christian denominations to refer to those parts of the liturgical year when no cycle of supernatural events is being celebrated. From around the first of December until the middle of January, the Church celebrates the coming of Christ and the first major events of Jesus' life. Then from the middle of February until around the first of June, the Church remembers the passion, death, resurrection, and ascension of Christ and then the coming of the Holy Spirit on Pentecost. The rest of the year is "ordinary time." Particularly in the summer, after celebrating Pentecost, the Sundays are designated with numbers: Fourteenth Sunday in Ordinary Time, Fifteenth, and so on. Once the Holy Spirit has come at Pentecost to guide the Apostles, they go about the work of establishing the Church as an institution to carry on the project Jesus started. The special times are past, when we saw Christ face-to-face or felt his Spirit come over us in the form of tongues of fire. Now we are in Ordinary Space and Ordinary Time, trying to get along in our spiritual labors by following just the "ordinary" indications that the Holy Spirit gives. The Third is no longer a pillar of fire by night and a column of smoke by day. Now we need to follow the Holy Spirit by looking within ourselves, by relying on our intuitions and those of our partner.

Lancelot enters "ordinary time" when he returns from the Quest. If we follow his post-Grail career, when he resumes his relationship with Guinevere, we will get an indication of how the integration of the eternal and the personal can be accomplished by following the Third. But we will have to change texts, because *The Quest of the Holy Grail* ends with the burial of Perceval. To follow Lancelot, we must rely on *Le Morte d'Arthur* alone, of which the story of the Quest occupies only about fifteen percent of the narrative. The final quarter of *Morte* is devoted almost exclusively to the activities of Lancelot on his return from the Quest. The second paragraph after the termination of Grail narrative again takes up the issue of Lancelot and Guinevere:

Then, as the book saith, Sir Launcelot began to resort unto Queen Guenever again, and forgat the promise and the perfection that he made in the quest. For, as the book saith, had not Sir Launcelot been in his privy thoughts and in his minds so set inwardly to the queen as he was in seeming outward to God, there had been no knight passed him in the quest of the Sangrail; but ever his thoughts were privily on the queen, and so they loved together more hotter than they did toforehand, and had such privy draughts together, that many in the court spake of it, and in especial Sir Agravain, Sir Gawain's brother, for he was ever open-mouthed. (Malory: bk. 2, 373)

Twice in one short paragraph, Malory distances himself from the theme by his phrase, "as the book saith." It is not *his* viewpoint, rather his sources insist. It is a difficult problem. Throughout *Morte* Malory emphasizes the extraordinary virtue in Lancelot's faithfulness to Guinevere. In his very first mention of Lancelot, he says, "He loved the queen again above all other ladies damosels of his life, and for her he did many deeds of arms, and saved her from the fire through his noble chivalry" (ibid.: bk. 1, 194). He places his final tribute in the mouth of Lancelot's brother Hector, "And thou were the truest lover of a sinful man that ever loved a woman" (ibid.: bk. 2, 530). Regarding Guinevere, he says, "While she lived she was a true lover, and therefore she had a good end" (ibid., 426).

Lancelot resists the seductions of four queens, one of them the formidable Morgan le Fay, winning their praise: "Thou art the noblest knight living, and as we know well there can no lady have thy love but one, and that is Queen Guenever" (ibid.: bk. 1, 198). He succumbs to Elaine, a humanized Lady of the Lake and Galahad's mother, only because she employs an enchantress to make her resemble the queen; and Lancelot is honestly fooled. Indeed, Arthur's queen discovers them in flagrante only because Lancelot, still unaware of his error, is babbling in his sleep of the love he has for Guinevere (ibid.: bk. 2, 202). When he learns what he has done, he leaps out a window and goes mad, living like an animal in the forest. Eventually he is cured by the Holy Grail, as he wanders into Elaine's father's castle, Corbenic (ibid., 220f.). Finally, when Elaine announces the birth of Galahad and identifies Lancelot as the father, a white dove bearing a miniature golden censer in her bill comes down from heaven and the Holy Grail feeds all the assembled.

Clearly Galahad is a bastard in the style of Jesus. The Holy Spirit is very intimately involved in the unnatural unions that generate both heroes. The events and the images of the narrative, therefore, indicate that the problematic union between Lancelot and Guinevere is favored by God. The hermits do not know the Spirit which "bloweth where it listeth" (John 3:8) or Khidr. They are the spokesmen of orthodoxy when they tell Lancelot that the devil entered Guinevere to seduce him (*Quest*, 142) and that she "loves you little and esteems you less" (ibid, 136). The Third does not always respect orthodoxy of religious belief.

The Christianizers of this ancient collection of legends have used the Quest episodes to inject a doctrinal apologia into the Arthurian cycle. But according to the stories the narrative relates, the Holy Spirit guides romantic love as much as it guides the Quest. The Quest, indeed, is in a position to further the erotic bond between Lancelot and Guinevere—insofar as Lancelot can bring what he learned about following the Third into his relationship with the queen. This is, indeed, why we have resorted to the final books of *Morte*, to see whether and how the Third of the Quest can be integrated into a relationship of romantic love.

I can accept that perhaps Lancelot and Guinevere "loved more hotter than they did toforehand"; but I cannot accept Malory's statement that Lancelot had been only "outwardly" devoted to God, while "privily" obsessed with his lady. Does God judge by outward appearances? Did Lancelot trick God into showing him the Grail? If he had wanted to see the Grail only as the ultimate sporting event, why did he not suffer the fate of a Gawain? Very possibly Guinevere was never out of his mind. But if there is any integrity to the *Quest* at all, it is unthinkable that he did not genuinely undergo a reorientation to the center and learn the attitude of *Gelassenheit*. Furthermore, Guinevere may very well have made Lancelot's Quest possible. It has to have been with her that he had his first lessons in *Gelassenheit*, his first lessons in following a Third. Probably most people who learn anything at all about following a Third have learned through relationship. This is surely how Rumi learned this lesson and became a mystic—through his friendship with Shamsuddin. In Lancelot, though, we have a unique opportunity. He transcended romantic love and entered the love of God; but he was not allowed to stay with God and therefore had to return to the mundane world and his flesh-and-blood mistress with all her jealousy and crankiness. Will his magic boat help him weather these emotional storms? Will he have any better success than Tannhaeuser in integrating the two sides?

Lancelot After the Quest

On his return from the Quest, Lancelot at first tries to behave coolly toward Guinevere, pleading the requirements of the Quest and the political danger of being caught. This enrages the queen, who banishes him from court. At the counsel of Bors, he stays nearby at a hermitage. Meanwhile at one of the queen's dinners, a knight eats a poisoned apple intended for Sir Gawain; although innocent, Guinevere is accused of the crime. At the last moment, Lancelot appears and defends her honor in combat. This restores him to his former place in her favor.

But not for long, as Lancelot soon insults Guinevere by wearing in a tournament the red sleeve of the Fair Maiden of Astolat. Generally, this would be a sign he had given his heart to the girl, but in this case he believed he was only flattering a maid who twice nursed him to health.[1] He intends only to disguise himself in the tournament, for no one would expect Guinevere's knight to wear another woman's token. When the queen hears the whole story, she forgives Lancelot but makes him promise that he will in the future always wear her golden sleeve on his helmet at jousts and tournaments. The Fair Maiden of Astolat starves herself to death on being refused Lancelot's love.

In a third post-Grail episode, Lancelot is shot in the

---

1. Many of these episodes have parallels in the Tristan cycle. An interesting parallel, here, is the name of the maiden, Elaine le Blank, Elaine the White. Tristan enters an unconsummated marriage with Isolde of the White Hands, while Isolde the Fair was called in twice to nurse him to health. Some of the more prominent parallels mentioned in this synopsis of the end of *Morte* are: bloodying the queen's bed with his wounds, an extended period of madness on being separated from the queen, saving the queen from execution by a daring knightly act, and living with the queen at Joyous Guard.

buttocks by a stray arrow from a huntress. He nevertheless does well at a joust.

After this the queen is abducted while out "Maying" with a group of knights and their ladies—many of her knights suffering severe wounds in her defense. She sends for Lancelot, whose horse is speared and killed; he arrives riding in a cart, as though for a hanging. To spend the night with her, he tears the bars off her window with his bare hands, injuring them so that he bleeds all over her sheets. In the morning the Queen is accused of sleeping with one of her wounded knights and condemned to be burned at the stake. Lancelot successfully defends her on a field outside of Camelot.

Next, a badly wounded Hungarian knight is brought to Camelot. He has been cursed so that his wounds fester and will not heal unless the "best knight in the world" search them. Lancelot heals him while calling on the Trinity. So far from being inflated by this show of power, Lancelot is humbled and weeps like a child.

In the sixth and final episode before the downfall of Camelot, Agravain and Mordred set a trap to catch Lancelot with the queen. Lancelot, naked and calling on Jesus to be his shield and armor, kills thirteen of his fourteen attackers. Mordred escapes to inform King Arthur, who again finds himself required to burn Guinevere at the stake. Again Lancelot saves her, this time inadvertently killing in the process Gawain's brothers, Gaheris and Gareth. He takes her to his castle, Joyous Guard, which he formerly gave to Tristan and Isolde when they fled King Mark. King Arthur would have taken the queen back and been reconciled with Lancelot, except for the strenuous objections of Gawain. Lancelot refuses single combat both with Gawain and with Arthur, and tries his best to avoid warfare. When it becomes inevitable, he does what he can to save the men of Arthur's party and even rehorses the king; "and then the tears brast out of [Arthur's] eyen, thinking on the great courtesy that was in Sir Launcelot more than in any other man" (Malory: bk. 1, 482).

Arthur finally accepts Guinevere back on order of the pope, but Gawain will accept no retribution for his brothers' deaths and requires Lancelot's departure from Britain.

At Gawain's urging, Arthur then assembles a formidable army and pursues Lancelot's company to France, where again Lancelot avoids the clash of arms as well as he can. Meanwhile Mordred, Arthur's illegitimate son who has been left in charge in England, declares himself king of the land and husband of Guinevere. Arthur brings his forces back across the channel to fight Mordred. In the battle Gawain is mortally struck on a wound he originally received from Lancelot. Seeing his death before him, he forgives Lancelot and calls for a reconciliation between the king and the queen's lover in order to restore the Round Table. But before this can happen, the two English armies wipe out one another. In the battle, Mordred and Arthur kill one another.

Guinevere enters a nunnery and Lancelot a hermitage, where he takes the robes of a monk and is eventually ordained to the priesthood. He dies groveling in prayers on the tomb of Arthur and Guinevere, while the bishop of the hermitage has a vision of the knight-lover-priest borne up to heaven by angels.

Relations between Lancelot and Guinevere are described as both hotter and cooler; she is confused at his change in attitude; and he takes as his advisor Bors, the only one of the three virgin[2] knights and protectors of the Grail who returned to Camelot. It would be reasonable to think that it will take her a while to appreciate the changes the Grail has wrought in him. She must be confused by his coolness and not realize that it has nothing to do with the depth or endurance of his love for her. This is, in fact, a very difficult paradox to understand. Generally it requires a relationship of some years or even decades duration before we stumble upon this kind of curiosity in our soul.

A man in his late thirties reported to me that the great love of his life ended badly some fifteen years before. He had been married to a

---

2. Bors "abused his virginity" only once and "atoned so fully by the purity of his life that the offense is wholly pardoned" (*Quest*, 170). In Gawain's dream, there are one hundred fifty bulls (the number of knights of the Round Table), and all but three are dappled with blots on their virginity. Two are pure white (Galahad and Perceval) and one bears traces of spots (Bors).

second woman for fourteen years; and although he loved his wife dearly, he regretted that she had had to live under the shadow of his great love the whole time. Now, after fifteen years and only intermittent communication with the first woman, he had an opportunity to spend a day with her. He describes it as an eye-opening experience. The two of them spent most of the day struggling with their defenses against each other. But about an hour before he had to leave to catch his plane, they finally began to deal with the primary issue. Suddenly the curtain fell and he saw her again through the lens of his anima, saw the spiritual light in her soul, saw how her shyness and self-hatred screened a lovely and radiant core. He saw in her eyes that they had not changed, that they loved one another as they always had. His fascination with her and the tenderness he felt for her were identical and undiminished by the fifteen years during which there had been continents between them. He was elated to learn that his belief about the eternality of their connection during the time of their separation was perfectly ratified by this one instant's eye-to-eye gaze. But he knew something else in this moment—a much more surprising and revolutionary fact. It dawned on him that he loved his wife *no less* than he had loved his great beloved.

There are two lessons in this story. The first is that this man and his old flame had indeed persisted in their love for one another. It had exactly the same character as it had had a decade and a half earlier. But it was *cooler* in the sense that it was no longer surrounded with the panics, doubts, and youthful ardor it used to have. The man felt he was looking into the soul of his beloved with great calmness. He said it was as though he were standing on a precipice. He could jump if he wished and be back in the ardor and tumult of earlier days. But there was no impulse to jump. He knew their love did not require that and that it was no longer appropriate. In this sense, the coolness of his great love for her is contrasted with the impetuous heat they had experienced during the two years of their earlier association. But he reports that he had unknowingly experienced another kind of heat in his love for his wife. This heat always lacked impetuosity. It was a slow heat that did not force itself on their attention. It grew hot so slowly, in fact, that it needed the contrasting coolness of his meeting with his earlier friend to reveal it.

I suspect the situation between Lancelot and Guinevere is something like this. Through the more intense experience with the Third he had had in following the Grail, and especially through his detachment from nonultimate concerns, he comes back to Guinevere a changed man. There is a coolness in his manner resulting from his lack of impetuous ardor. But behind this coolness is a steadier and a hotter glow, a subtler but more intense love. Lancelot apparently knows that it will take her a while to appreciate that the change in him has enhanced rather than diminished his love. He respects her confusion and withdraws by counsel of Bors, who proved himself on the Quest to be at least equal to Lancelot in sensitivity to the Third.

The queen and the knight are behaving, here, as worthy opponents. They remain conscious of their Self-level connection as they dodge and feint on the mundane level. If I am the partner who has gained a new psychological awareness, I must be clear that I cannot simply teach it to my beloved. She or he[3] needs to unfold into this new space through a process that is probably as painful and individual as mine was. When I take a superior stance, I make her feel inadequate, and she begins to suspect me of arrogance. On the other hand, when I approach her with the same loving delight in her uniqueness that I have always shown, she can afford to marvel at this new facet I show her and allow herself to be influenced by it.

Lancelot must withdraw for another reason as well: he cannot hurry the course of their relationship by his demands. We can never get ahead of the Third. However much our intuitions about the direction of the relationship prove correct, we cannot move in that direction before the relationship is ready for it. One of the most highly differentiated examples of instructions for following the "transcendent function" is the Chinese *I Ching*, the *Book of Changes*. Its most frequent counsel is that when the time and circumstances are not right, the individual must withdraw and wait or seek guidance or look within. Therefore when we have shown the new

---

3. It is unfortunate for our gender-specific grammar that the more advanced figure in this relationship is male. In real life the genders might well be reversed. Bear in mind, too, that the Third, when it has a gender, is usually feminine: the Holy Spirit, the Grail, the ubiquitous unknown lady on a white palfrey, and the Ladies of the Lake.

radiance of our soul to our beloved and resisted her habitual moves as no longer appropriate, usually our best course is to withdraw and wait for some indication from the Third before we make another move. In the puzzlement and resistance of our beloved, we meet our own failure to integrate the new psychological material.

After Lancelot's withdrawal, there are two deaths: a knight at the queen's table and a maiden who falls in love with Lancelot. This suggests that both parties had some painful adjustments to make and perhaps that Lancelot was not so much advanced as he may have thought. The poisoned apple at Guinevere's table suggests the apple of spiritual death in Eden. The fact that it was intended for Gawain underlines its reference to the "first Adam," as the Apostle Paul generally designates the mundane individual. If the queen's dinner party represents her psyche, with its several "complexes" or "part-personalities" assembled for communion and nourishment, the death of the unlucky knight points to her letting go of one of her mundane attitudes. Because it is linked with Gawain, she must have overcome a part of her soul, which clung so tightly to nonultimate desires that she could not recognize the Third. This Gawain-like part of her probably viewed the affair with Lancelot as a kind of "sporting event"—rather as Gawain understood the Quest. Meanwhile the Fair Maiden of Astolat falls in love with Lancelot and starves herself to death because his heart has already been claimed. This implies that within Lancelot, despite his success with the Grail, there still remain clinging, possessive motives.

These two deaths symbolize what needs to take place in order for a relationship to become both cooler and hotter. It is cooler insofar as they accept the naked sword and come to tolerate a certain distance between themselves. They give up their need to possess and control one another, symbolized by the young man and woman who died. The kind of coolness achieved by the sacrifice of nonultimate desires is nothing like the kind that comes in consequence of our losing our feelings for our beloved. Generally at the beginning of a relationship of romantic love, there is a great flurry of activity. A large number of dormant inclinations are aroused by a new sense of wholeness and the dawning of a new day. Many of these are disorganized and working at cross-purposes with one another. Many constitute nonultimate attachments, which give rise to anxieties and obsessions. A great deal of heat is created by what amounts to a kind of psychological friction. It is a heat that distracts us from the Third. The coolness Lancelot and Guinevere experience comes from the purification of their love for one another.

The two deaths symbolize that these friction-causing and distracting motives have been let go. If the young people who died represent ego-centered needs for possession and control, Lancelot and Guinevere must now have discovered that less stands in the way of their *fana*. It is paradoxical that we can only attain our heart's deepest longing to the extent that we give up striving for it. Only an attitude of *Gelassenheit* allows the unattainable to yield itself freely. This, too, is why Lancelot has to retire to a hermitage when Guinevere becomes outraged and confused at the changes in him; for only in meditation and the attenuation of ego can the Third take the lead.

Unfortunately the story has no more to say about the psychological state of Guinevere. We have to confine our study to the male partner, although I think what we discover here is equally applicable to the woman in an affair of romantic love.

The narrative now provides us four incidents whose significance seems to be to demonstrate the nature of the spiritual transformation that Lancelot has undergone in consequence of his Quest and his new mode of loving the queen. First is the peculiar episode of Lancelot's being shot by the huntress. This appears to be an adaptation of the story of Artemis and Orion. In the Greek story, the huntress and goddess of the moon shoots a giant by mistake; and when she learns she has killed him, she transforms him into a heavenly constellation. His earthly life is ended, but he gains glory and immortality in the sky. It is a symbol of transcending the mundane and an indication that Lancelot's attitude has become a good deal more comprehensive. He is more able now to see things in a holistic manner. Also, as the constellation of Orion is associated with the summer months, it implies Lancelot's transformation gives him access to the fullness of life.

In the next episode, Lancelot heals the Hungarian knight, showing the powers of a Galahad or Jesus. But he does not identify with this power; he sees himself only as a humble conduit for the working of the divine will. This is the most convincing symbol of Lancelot's connection with the Holy Spirit. We never possess and control the

Third, we can only follow it and cooperate with it or close our eyes and act possibly in opposition to it. When we are unaware of this subtle kind of cooperation we may be induced to identify our ego with the action of the Third and take credit for it ourselves. For when we see extraordinary results apparently following an unconscious act of ours, we may conclude we have powers we had not known. But *genuine* awareness of the nature of the Third can only produce humility.

Humility and self-sacrifice, too, are symbolized in his coming to the imprisoned queen riding in a cart, as though to his execution. In this case we may say that the world has worked against him. Instead of the seemingly glorious event of a healing, he is presented with the humiliating event of having his horse killed. It is a clumsy and embarrassing situation for a knight to be in, powerlessly and foolishly trying to walk in his armor. A proud man would find riding in a cart to be no solution at all. The fact that Lancelot accepts such humiliation proves not only his dedication to the queen, but his acceptance of the requirements of fate. Just as he does not take the glory of the cure as his own, so he does not take the humiliation as dispiriting.

He is willing to ride to his execution. In this again, he is like Jesus. He begins to identify outwardly with those young people who died in the early incidents, for his self-sacrifice now includes his ego and persona. We are often called upon to make this kind of sacrifice when following our relationship. Disputes arise, for example, and we are tempted to defend ourselves over what our partner claims we did or said a few minutes, weeks, or even years ago. It is a significant complaint, because our partner is pointing to a habit of ours. We feel ourselves humiliated by our partner's version of the incident, and so we justly want to defend ourselves and our reputation. But, in the context of worthy opposition, it is counterproductive. It leads us away from the here and now and away from the Self-Self connection that has to be the foundation of a valuable exchange. In trying to defend our ego and persona (our image in our own and others' eyes), we are led further from the Third. Lancelot accepts the humiliation in order to stay with the Third.

Malory makes another kind of claim about Lancelot, however, when he describes him as twice saving the queen from death by fire.

This is a regular refrain, almost like a Homeric epithet, throughout *Morte*. Malory honors Lancelot again and again for saving his queen from the fire. Symbolically, this means that he saved his anima from being destroyed in the fires of carnal passion. The social function served by burning the queen to death is to declare that she has violated her public trust by indulging her carnal appetites. Society sees their affair as aflame with lust, without dignity, and in violation of public values. Society cannot afford to recognize the significance of the Third, just as orthodox Muslims are uncomfortable with Avicenna's angels and Christians with the Holy Spirit.

Lancelot cannot let the queen be burnt, either as chivalrous knight or as lover. Because his gallantry is required by the rules of knightly sport as well as by the dictates of a heart that gazes at Guinevere through the lens of an anima, his heroic act reconciles both sides of his personality. In the sexual episodes, however, eros threatens to overbalance fealty. Although Arthur does not seem personally to resent his wife's affair, it could become a liability to his royal prestige. Therefore he cannot afford to acknowledge it publicly and pretends not to know about it. If it is brought publicly to his attention, his position requires him to crush it mercilessly. Every time Lancelot sleeps with the queen, therefore, he threatens the kinghood of the king.

If the Holy Spirit is conducting this drama, we must conclude that God is countenancing adultery and endangering the kingdom. Is this preposterous, or are these the kinds of exceptions Khidr exemplified by drilling a hole in a poor man's boat and killing a boy? Is the sexual union of these two souls of more value than the Round Table? A Holy Spirit which can countenance the queen's extramarital affair may well be able to countenance ours. Sometimes, indeed, such an affair may be good for the marriage of the married party and for the psychological well-being and professional advancement of the single partner—although rarely without involving a good deal of work between worthy opponents. Sometimes it leads to the development of new self-knowledge, a reassessment of one's values, and especially to a new acquaintance with one's feelings.

I say this not to encourage people to initiate affairs, but rather to provide a perspective for individuals who are already so involved. It would be reasonable to guess that the number of extramarital affairs actually inspired by the Third is fairly small, because it is much easier for us, like Gawain, to slip unconsciously into entanglements than conscientiously to follow the relationship like Lancelot. To follow the relationship in an unorthodox direction, therefore, requires a good deal of self-confidence and the courage to face our guilt feelings squarely. It is no solution to sweep them under the rug or to tell ourselves that we should not have them. The guilt we feel from hurting another individual or bucking public opinion needs to be used as a lever to pry open the full gamut of our needs and intentions.

It is natural for us to want to be relieved of our feelings of guilt and to have our burden lifted. It is normal, also, to want reassurance and direction to help us to "do right" in the eyes of our society or of authorities we trust. But to be relieved of them—if indeed we can be—means that we no longer have them as pointers to the tension wherein the Third resides. People sometimes come into analysis hoping to be scolded into giving up their affair. I never oblige them, for I do not know whether their affair is right or wrong. Generally, it is too complicated for easy answers. I can only help them to find out why they are having the affair and to learn from it. To do this, we have to tolerate our guilt enough to let it speak to us. We have to open ourselves in humility and pain to the thoughts and images and feelings associated with our guilt and sort out which feelings we have unconsciously taken over from our family and society and which are appropriate to our individual situation. In a case like this, the Third is speaking to us through our guilt; and we accomplish nothing by hiding from it.

Often our guilt prompts us to shut down, almost to pretend we are not enjoying the affair. When we react this way, we can be sure we are not following the Third. If we are going to be having an affair anyway, we owe it to ourselves, our lover, and our injured spouse, to learn something from the experience. We need to question our honesty if we cannot entertain *both* the possibility that the Holy Spirit is guiding this affair *and* the possibility that we are fooling ourselves. The transcendent function always emerges out of a tension between opposites.

The imagery of the sexual episodes in *Morte* is appropriately ambiguous. In one of them Lancelot injures his hands ripping out the bars on the queen's window and then bloodies her sheets, leaving her open to the accusation that she had made love with one of the knights who had been wounded in the fight with her abductors. The reader sees the absurdity of the accusation against the queen—even though she did in fact sleep with a bleeding knight. It was not one of those bleeding Gawains in the next room; it was Lancelot. The qualitative difference between these two sex partners is unmistakable. In the one case, the queen would be guilty of the lust and depravity of which she is accused. In the other case, we are not sure that the Holy Spirit is not guiding them. Lancelot's injuring his hands is also an ambiguous image. It is reminiscent of his bout with madness (Malory: bk. 2, 201–30), when he injures his hands breaking the chains that bind him. Shall we take this madness as a regression to base and animalistic instinctuality, sexual compulsiveness? Or may not be the divine madness of a man who is following a Third not recognized by his compatriots? In the earlier madness, Lancelot was not in the grip of his lust but brokenhearted to have been duped by the Ladies of the Lake into betraying Guinevere. Finally, too, he is cured by the Holy Grail. We know the Grail heals only its special servants and that the Grail required Lancelot's intercourse with Elaine in order to produce Galahad.

All of this supports the possibility that Lancelot may have been in the grip of a divine madness and that the Holy Spirit was behind his tryst with the queen. Similarly, in the second sexual incident, Lancelot—naked from his lovemaking with the queen—wades into hand-to-hand combat with fourteen knights, calling upon Jesus to be his shield. Does Jesus want him to kill thirteen knights? Is he fighting for his own honor or the king's? The fact that the treasonous pair Agravain and Mordred are behind the attack lends a certain honor to Lancelot. But it remains a puzzling and disturbing incident—especially since the queen's reputation is not saved.

Following the relationship is always fraught with ambiguity. An ethical code or moral consensus is too much oriented to typical situations to be of much help in the most subtle of interpersonal debates. We are left then to rely upon our feeling and intuition to find our way. But these, too, are of little use until we have developed them as we would cultivate any skill. As with drawing and bicycle riding, we only learn by trying and failing. Refining our technique is a very slow process, but we do have several guidelines to follow. One is the depth dimension of our relationship. We need to keep coming back to this again and again as a kind of touchstone against which we test the truth of our intuitions. Another guideline is the perspective of our partner. If we are in disagreement with our partner, at least one of us must be wrong about the direction the Third is leading us. When we find ourselves at odds with one another, we have several ways to proceed. One way is playfully to juggle alternative images of one another and of the relationship, as was described in chapter 8. Another is to square off as worthy opponents. A third is to seduce and be seduced, investigating alternatives as calls that are leading us on and leading us aside from our habitual paths and ego-centered goals. In all of these we are actively fostering our receptivity to the not-yet-known, enabling ourselves to be surprised by the truly new. It is the attitude of *Gelassenheit*. It is never found in advance and stored up for the right moment to be sprung on our partner. It is always a joint discovery, made by those who can stay in the moment with one another.

Perhaps the most difficult aspect of following the relationship is bearing the several tensions. It would be easy if we could be confident beyond a shadow of a doubt that we are following the will of God, that is, a path expressive of ultimate and transcendent truth. But Holy Grails rarely appear to us in the modern world. If they do, they are most likely to appear in the form of some kind of inner sense of fittingness—and rarely to individuals who are unable to carry the responsibility for their own decisions. In this regard, I think of two gray-haired former monks who consulted me. They had a great deal in common: both were from the same order, although from different monasteries and completely unknown to one another, and both had been married twice.

One was still—twenty-five years later—not reconciled with his departure from the monastery and very much afraid that he had let God down and committed a grave sin. He had left in his twelfth year only because his spiritual director had detected his unhappiness in the monastic life as well as his inability to consider the option of leaving. Consequently the superior had ordered him "under holy obedience" to request release from his vows. My client had felt himself relieved of a great responsibility and was sometimes able to believe that God's will was expressed through the orders of his superior. But he felt guilty that he was happy to be out of the monastery and had moments and days when he was sure he had "let God down." His first marriage and divorce were no less traumatic for him; and, although his second marriage seems to have been particularly felicitous, he felt triply guilty: for not being a monk, for not being married to his first wife, and for being married to a non-Catholic.

In his first session of analysis, I thought that he should not be working with me, because he wanted me to take charge as the spiritual director had done twenty-five years earlier. I felt I could not save him from his decisions, but also could not tell him this lest I reenact the relationship with the spiritual director. Therefore I was delighted when, after about three months of dream work, he announced his resolution to leave analysis because he knew he had to make his own decisions without looking to me for approval.

The other ex-monk had developed an entirely different attitude toward what amounts to almost identical decisions. While praying one day, in his sixth year in the monastery, it dawned on him that God's will for him was what he truly wanted to do himself, that God gave him the freedom to choose his own course. A week or two later he drew the further conclusion that this principle of free will applied also to his monastic vocation. In very short order he realized that he had joined the order out of a much narrower and more rigid conception of the divine will, and that deep in his heart he had never really wanted to be a monk. He therefore applied for release from his vows and left with a light heart. His first marriage ended in similar fashion. He and his wife encountered difficulties based on rather different approaches to life. They spent many months working through their issues with a marriage counselor and arrived at a mutual conclusion that they were better off living separately. In this case, too, the second marriage was much more successful than the first.

This man, although outwardly in the same situation as the first, is at peace with himself. He sees his first two life choices as honest mistakes that he learned to improve upon. He is confident that he has followed the will of God for himself as well as he has been able to discern it. From my perspective, both men have done the best they could with the outward course of their lives. But there is all the difference in the world between an individual who has a "feel" for the Third and one who is looking for authoritative confirmation of his decisions.

These ex-monks correspond very well to Gawain and Lancelot. Gawain follows the letter of the law enthusiastically, has no feel at all for the Third, and brings about the fall of Camelot by his vengeful insistence on propriety. Lancelot stumbles and makes many mistakes, but does manage to follow the Third. Even this does not save him from the tragedy, for he contributes to the destruction of the Round Table by allowing his erotic connection with the queen to embarrass the king.

14

The Fall of Camelot:
Love's Phoenix

Entering "ordinary time" after the Quest of the Holy Grail has been an instructive experience. As long as we stayed within the Quest itself, it appeared that following the relationship was a joyful—even glorious—experience in which the Holy Spirit simply took over and whisked us off to where we had to go. The example of Galahad suggested that really to know the Third was to travel in a mystic boat and avoid all frustration and difficulties. Although he spent a year in prison, he did not suffer; for the Grail attended him and fed him his heart's desire—both physical and spiritual food. Lancelot was by no means so well-favored as Galahad, yet once he had undergone a dual process of repentance, he, too, was carried along by a mystic boat. It might have seemed from this that all we have to do is repent and change our ways to enjoy conflict-free progress in our relationships.

But once Lancelot returned from the Quest and resumed his affair with Guinevere in ordinary time, we obtained quite a different impression about following the relationship. It was no longer so easy and no longer so clear. Now the mystic boat of *Gelassenheit* was much harder to distinguish from more ordinary means of progress. Lancelot's ambiguous adventures brought home to us the difficulty, pain, and uncertainty of following the Third. Apart from his curing the Hungarian knight, there was nothing like a magic boat. Yet we had to conclude that Lancelot must have been in an attitude of *Gelassenheit* at least intermittently, for his accomplishments left us no other conclusion. He had to suffer humiliation, disappointment, and, particularly, the loss of very comforting part-personalities. He had to detach himself from possessiveness, vanity, and apparently well-earned fame. He not only suffered several losses but got himself embroiled further and further in an intolerable situation. He got to the point where he had to oppose his king in order to save the life and reputation of his beloved queen. He became estranged from his best friends and relatives. There was no longer time to enjoy the queen, even though he had her apparently to himself at his own castle, Joyous Guard. His sufferings and those of the queen caused him to change its name to Dolorous Guard. Worst of all, his love affair with the queen led to the Round Table's destruction, as the knights divided into factions and began killing one another.

Through all of these events in ordinary time—whether glorious or dolorous—we have asked ourselves again and again whether the Holy Spirit of the Quest could possibly be guiding Lancelot in a love affair that was not only adulterous but endangering the very kingdom God had favored with the Holy Grail. If we follow the principle Jesus articulates in Matthew (7:15–20), we are to distinguish false prophets from true "by their fruits." What shall we say about this adulterous love affair, which ends in the fall of Camelot and the loss of the greatest Christian fellowship since Jesus and his Twelve Apostles? By the end King Arthur has had his heart broken by his nephews and best-loved knights and been killed by his own illegitimate son. Lancelot and Guinevere survive the whole tragedy and enter separate monasteries, completely relinquishing sexual expression of their love.

Let us begin our investigation of the fall of Camelot with the man who presided over the debacle. Arthur seems to have become little more than a figurehead in the final days of Camelot. He would very much like to ignore the affair between Lancelot and Guinevere and retain the courtly and military services of his best knight. He tells us a great deal about himself:

> "Wit you well my heart was never so heavy as it is now, and much more I am sorrier for my good knights' loss than for the loss of my fair queen: for queens I might have enow, but such a fellowship of good knights shall never be together in no company. And now I dare say," said King Arthur, "there was never Christian king held such a fellowship together; and alas that ever Sir Launcelot and I should be at debate. Ah Agravain, Agravain," said the king, "Jesu forgive it thy soul, for thine evil will that thou and thy brother Sir

Mordred hadst unto Sir Launcelot that caused all this sorrow."
(Malory: bk. 2, 473f.)

Arthur is clearly innocent of romantic love. We could never
imagine Lancelot accepting a replacement for Guinevere. That Arthur would be prepared to do so, proves he never glimpsed the core
of her personhood, never saw her through the lens of his anima,
never entangled his wound with hers, never dallied in Venusberg
with her. For Arthur she is just the queen. He is entirely identified
with the fellowship of the Round Table and the unification of Britain
that it represents. Once he has unified the country, the *Morte* loses
all interest in Arthur, and the narrative begins to follow the careers
of his several knights. Also Merlin disappears about the time of the
unification. Merlin was Arthur's spiritual navigator, a flesh-and-
blood personification of the Third—for which Arthur, personally,
never developed a "feel." The one man sitting at the Round Table,
decade after decade, who lived his life on the path of the Third was
Lancelot. Very likely Lancelot and Guinevere clung together because
they were the only people at court who had even dreamt of the
possibility of a Third. No one else spoke their language. Lancelot
was the one knight able to keep alive the spiritual tradition on which
Camelot had been founded. This is why the Round Table could only
last as long as the king and the queen's lover could behave with the
greatest admiration, respect, and affection for one another.

In fact they never lost that love for one another, but were forced
into battle by Gawain's need to avenge his brothers' deaths.[1] Arthur
cannot afford to resist Gawain's demands, because to fail to punish
Lancelot publicly would be to acknowledge and accept his own
cuckolding and thereby undermine his royal authority. Gawain
represents the practical side of the king: temporal duties, outward
appearances, and the drama of kingship. Arthur cannot hold his
people without these qualities championed by Gawain, and he

---

1. Lancelot was able to kill them so easily and unconsciously that he did not know
what he had done until much later. The reason for this is that, out of respect for
Lancelot, Gareth and Gaheris had agreed to the king's order to stand as guards at the
queen's execution only on condition that they do so unarmed and without armor. It
is understood that they would not have been killed, had they taken ordinary
precautions.

cannot hold his nation on its course without a feel for the Third, represented by Lancelot.

This is an issue of utmost concern to us. For Lancelot is trying his best to follow the Third, and not a few incidents have occurred that seem to supply evidence that the Holy Spirit does, indeed, favor his course. But the Third is supposed to *integrate* us, harmonize our conflicting instincts. The very notion of a transcendent function is that it appears when the more logical conscious mind has reached an impasse. The Third is supposed to transcend such impasses. But here it seems to effect a very destructive rift. This is alarming news, for the new rift is devastating to the Camelot that Arthur and Lancelot both love. Hence the great sorrow with which both he and Lancelot take up their swords.

It is with this kind of sorrow that worthy opponents take up the cudgels after perhaps twenty years of marriage. The love is not gone. In fact it has been deepened and transformed by all those nights sleeping side-by-side, all the financial and health crises through which we have clung together, the joys and sorrows of our children. When we can see clearly, our spouse's smallest gesture calls up layers of affection. We feel our heart leap with the transparent flame of our mutual joy as we pedaled bicycle paths of lake shores and river banks in our twenties, climbed European wooded trails in our thirties, and met one another with open-hearted surprise side-by-side at traffic lights in our forties. As we look into our partner's eyes, we glimpse her slipping shyly around a bend deep in the dark cave of her solitude—that labyrinthine and cavernous world, damp and pulsing with thrill and terror. It pulls at our wound, and we find that a flood of tears lies just behind the threshold of our tremulous wonder. Perhaps we allow ourselves to be distracted for a moment, letting our gaze wander over the cliff-face pitted with the room-sized shallow little caves in which we have cuddled and sported on and off for two or more decades.

Tender reminiscences distract us from the business at hand. Back to the cudgels. We must hold our Lancelot's "feel" for the transcendent depth and direction of our relationship very close to the center of our field of vision. But we cannot ignore Gawain whispering in our ear. There are practical matters crying out for attention. Frustrating patterns have been established despite our best intentions.

We are hurting one another without wanting to and almost without knowing it. We have become defensive over matters that appear trivial to one another, but we know that deeper matters lurk beneath the surface. We are afraid to confront them. We do not know what needs, what murk, what slime from the depths will clog the channels of our communications. We even fear that these touchy matters might conceal a powder keg. We almost do not dare to proceed ahead. In fact, that is why we have postponed this confrontation for so long. But Gawain's whisper in our ear tells us it cannot go on. We have to take one another on, and give up the politeness and distance that have allowed matters to encyst and to fester.

Like Arthur and Lancelot, we look for any excuse to postpone or avoid confrontation altogether. We go to battle reluctantly and sadly, for we do not want to hurt that tender, joyful companion whose touch and smell are so familiar that we notice them only when they are missing. We go to battle only because we know that our little circumlocutions and tacit silences are no longer just "considerate"; they have begun to conceal lies, perhaps whole complexes of lies. Very likely we have only the foggiest notion of what these lies might be. We have not made them up deliberately but rather backed into them unconsciously. We may even feel at times that they are the heart of truth. We cling to them, like Gawain to his sinfulness, and convince ourselves that these defenses and diversions are of ultimate importance.

This edifice has to be brought down. The best and most careful way of doing it is through the hand-to-hand combat of worthy opposition—and precisely while we are still able to bring our beloved into focus through the lens of our anima or animus. We go to battle with the greatest sadness and reluctance. For only by consciously bearing the tension between our tenderness and our anger, between our savor for what has been and our hope for what might yet be, can we attain the *Gelassenheit* that enables the Third to appear.

In the short run, the easy way out of such an impasse with our beloved is to cling to the tenderness and the sense of eternal, unchanging wonder that has always held us together. But there are Agravains and Mordreds in every union, and their whispers are going to get louder and their evidence more and more difficult to dismiss. When we cling, frightened, to one pole of the tension, the other always gathers strength, weight, and momentum. Eventually our frustration, rage, and lust for vengeance will overcome our sense of depth, wonder, and tenderness. We will give up our tenderness and identify completely with the other pole where our anger will make things a lot easier for us. Our fight will be not sad and reluctant, but rabid and bitter. Because we will have forgotten the archetypal roots of our union, there will be little to temper our aggression; and we are sure to overween, like Gawain beheading the lady. We will cover our wound with our rage and believe ourselves almost invulnerable as we wade into an emotional slaughter.

In the short run this is the easy way out. In the long run it spells disaster. Too many relationships founder on quarrels like this. Quarrels occur when we cannot bear the tensions between our conflicting emotions. The aftermath rage of divorce continues to hide our woundedness and distract us from the deep, tender feelings that we still have for our ex-spouse. We allow our rage to reconstruct our past—by revising and distorting our memories—and we dredge up all the insults and injuries and convince ourselves of what a dupe we have been. Why is it that we could not see earlier what is so clear to us now? It is clear because we have let go of the tension and lost all "feel for," and perhaps all memory of, the Third.

The attitude of a Lancelot is always difficult to maintain. We never lose our propensity to slip back into a more simplistic Gawain attitude. But even though Arthur and Lancelot fought with love, care, sadness, and reluctance, even though they never lost their respect for one another, their battle brought down Camelot. Since childhood, I have carried a ball of sadness in my heart for the fall of Camelot. What an ignominious end for the "greatest Christian fellowship": to have fallen into warring factions over honor, adultery, and vengeance! Still the battle was fought with love and reluctance, rather in the style of worthy opponents. If we apply this to human relationship, the fall of Camelot might refer to the end of the affair, or a divorce after decades of what seemed to be happy marriage. But it might also refer to the demise of a much loved *style* of relating: perhaps a couple that stops sleeping together but remains friends, or a couple that gives up a sentimental cottage-for-two image for a much less defined and uncertain way of life.

Tragic as it may be, Camelot's fall appears to have been foreordained. This is made clear at the coming of the Grail to the Round Table, for the *Quest* tells us that many "were more vexed than joyful at the news" (46). Both the King and Queen express their sorrow that the Round Table will lose all of its one hundred fifty knights. The immediate literal meaning of this sorrow is that there will be—at least for a time—no soldiers to defend Camelot and Britain and no jolly fellowship around the table in the great hall. But there is a more essential meaning than this, whether or not it was known by the king and the others who were vexed. The Grail is accepted by all without dispute as a higher goal than that of a safe and prosperous kingdom. The Grail issues a transcendent call to commit ourselves explicitly to the One, to be open in *Gelassenheit* to whatever direction the Holy Spirit leads. This cannot be done unless we "detach" ourselves from less-than-ultimate concerns.

The Round Table is less than ultimate, but it has been the center of these people's lives: a magnificent success story of reconciliation, peace, prosperity, dedication to high ideals, and universal joy. They have believed, and they are right, that they have been doing the work of God on earth. Now God wants something else of them. They do not have to repudiate or in any way undermine the Round Table; they just have to recognize that it has lower priority than the Grail. As Gawain shows us, this ideal is more easily paid lip-service to than lived. But Lancelot tries to live it. He learns to follow the Third, disciplines himself to *Gelassenheit*. *Le Morte d'Arthur* so celebrates his transformation that it is hard to believe Lancelot was not also following the Third in his relationship with Guinevere. He does not lose his chivalric love of Arthur and the Round Table, but he "detaches" from these things. His detractors will say that it is in his self-interest to detach. Perhaps so, but conniving is inconsistent with following a Third. Cynical motivation is utterly opposed to the attitude of *Gelassenheit*.

If the Grail teaches us anything, it is to reorder our priorities. When this happens, Camelot is sure to fall. The Camelots that have to fall in our relationships are generally our dearest plans. Surely our castles in the air will mostly fall, but I refer to the joint projects we have worked on so long and hard and with quite a bit of success. It is the house we built or remodeled. All those trips to the salvage company and antique shops. How our plans grew as we laughed over the coffee table in the evening. Those personal touches we came upon spontaneously, saturated as they were with what we two were going through at the time we found them. A whole way of life is wrapped up in that house. The way we managed to schedule half-hour dinners on those nights we both were working. How we would arrange our whole day around that half-hour, so that our days were saturated with one another even when we barely met. The very forks and saucepans were molded and colored and imbued with those dinners. Imbued with us the way we were, the way we thought we would always be. Imbued with a heartbeat and a certain soft shade of yellow light.

When we follow the relationship, these are the things we have to be detached enough to leave. We could not have become the lovers we are without having created—in our joint love and wrangling—this unique *Mitwelt*, its every object pregnant with our plans and memories. Our Camelot will always be dear to us, for we put our whole selves into it. We are aware of the eternal quality of our bond. But Camelot is not eternal. If a relationship is alive, it will lead us onward. We will be able to follow it, as long as we do not cling to the past. Every Round Table in our life will eventually be superseded.

In the penultimate snapshot Malory provides us of the lovers, they are in separate monasteries. Like Eliduc and Guilliadun from chapter 2, Lancelot and Guinevere follow their relationship to a very large and institutional naked sword. This makes sense to our contemporary mentality only as a penance: because they see in the fall of Camelot what their adultery has wrought, they don sackcloth and ashes. They are sorry, indeed, that Camelot has fallen; but the narrative as a whole tells us that the Holy Spirit led them. They may feel at odds with the people at court and the citizens of Britain, that their mutual affection brought a golden age to its end; but I do not believe they feel at odds with God. Rather in the style of Shiva and Parvati, they continue their meditation on the One but now in solitude rather than in physical union. This is not a punishment, self-inflicted or otherwise, but the next stage of their love affair. The Third has led them to a unity of even greater transparency. Whereas formerly they had needed to gaze into one another's eyes and feel the tremulous interpenetration of souls with their bodies, the fall of

Camelot has been their "dark night." The Holy Spirit is weaning them from her maternal breasts so that they can enjoy a far more sublime and satisfying union. Formerly they united with God in one another, now they unite with one another in God.

Perhaps the clearest example of such a transformation in love making is that of Teresa of Ávila. In her earlier years she enjoyed a spiritual and somewhat bodily lovemaking with her confessors. From a literal point of view, this appears grossly sinful. But in the context of her whole life, it is clear that the Holy Spirit was leading her; for these human affairs were explicitly about the love of God. They nourished her mystical longings while employing the faculties she already knew how to employ. By this means, she was led to more and more subtle and sublime experiences of love. Gradually she moved from one chamber to the next of her Interior Castle.

If the Holy Spirit can lead Teresa to such spectacular sainthood by way of years of earnest romantic love despite her perpetual vow of chastity and that of the priests she befriended, may Lancelot and Guinevere not also be on the right track? Here again we see the Third acting like Khidr when he drove holes in the boat of poor and virtuous fisher folk. It seemed inconsistent with our expectations for an angel of God, but there were reasons we had not guessed. This is the way it is, too, with the dark night. We work hard at our prayers and meditations and seem to be making important progress; and then suddenly everything comes to a halt. The God who seemed "nearer than our jugular vein" (Quran 50:16) seems remote and unreachable. We languish in a desert of apathy. Did the Holy Spirit lead us here? Is this the way the Third rewards our sincere spiritual efforts? John of the Cross tells us that this may very likely be the case, for the dark night is a necessary disappointment and discipline that enables us to enjoy God in a far more satisfying manner—"both hotter and cooler."

We have found that the structure of romantic love is identical with that of the love of God. Therefore, if erotic love also has its dark night, we might begin our exploration of the last days of Camelot with the question of whether the ideal Christian kingdom did not *have* to suffer disaster. Literally, we could say that Camelot had to fall in order that Britain might enter "ordinary time." Symbolically, we might speculate that every relationship creates its own Camelot over time and that each Camelot is splendid in proportion to the quality of the lovers' relationship. But success in building a Camelot is not rewarded by its becoming eternal. The reward comes, rather, after the dark night of the soul; after something of seemingly highest importance is destroyed; after our hearts are broken.

We will consider this possibility that Camelot had to fall, first by looking at the end of an affair and then by looking at a relationship that survives the crisis unbroken.

In the beginning there is a good deal of fumbling and physical exploration, as we gradually get to know one another's souls through our bodies. We laugh at conventional assumptions of physical attractiveness, as we find an extraordinarily satisfying beauty in one another's middle-aged, out-of-shape bodies. I find her body is the perfect expression of her soul. I do not want her to gain or lose weight. Thus, when she tells me she dreams of my soft, white belly, I believe her, even though I am generally ashamed of it. There comes a time, however, when our meetings nourish our union more in nonphysical ways. For example, there are those moments in which a golden rainbow arches between our breasts and we feel a quasi-physical sensation as it cascades through us. Perhaps we find one another standing across a crowded room from one another. The moment our eyes meet, we feel our bodies drop like curtains, and our souls join.

When our relationship so leads us away from the physical into a more and more spiritual direction, it may be preparing us for a parting. It is teaching us that we do not need to be in the same room with one another to enjoy a sublime union. Our bodily intercourse has fed something that develops a life of its own independent of the body. Thus when we have those sad, reluctant conversations about how the spirit is beginning to lead us in different directions, we know that there is a sense in which we will never be parted. We know we can always take it up again, if life somehow draws us back together. Majnun has become Layla. The years of our common quest have transformed us, bound us inextricably, and yet somehow given us a greater freedom. We know that if we live at opposite ends of the earth we will still be together.

This proves true, as well, in our subsequent relationships. We have less patience for the kinds of connection that used to satisfy us. And at the same time, we have an eye for potentials we formerly over-looked. It is not just that I have an eye now for matronly figures. I certainly have that. More important, I have an eye now for geysers of yellow light in a woman's aura and that shadowy black core in her heart that resonates so movingly with my wound. My Guinevere lives on in my subsequent relationships because she has so widened and deepened my knowledge of my own soul. I have all that to bring now to new relationships. And not only to new relationships, to every undertaking in my life. Like Lancelot in his last years, my notion of prayer has deepened and become more satisfying and effective. My enthusiasm for my professional activities has, in the words of Malory, grown both cooler and hotter. In this sense I have "become" my Guinevere, and I bring both of our souls to everything I do. She is always near me.

In this case the fall of Camelot is our physical parting. It is an occasion of great sadness, of course; but there is also a transcendent joy in our reluctant and lingering adieux. We know that what we have achieved can never be lost. We have taught each other one of the greatest secrets of human life, and our lives will never be the same again.

While the fall of Camelot may symbolize the end of an affair or a divorce, it may also be experienced by a couple whose marriage or affair continues. When we have discovered these mysteries by which our love gradually becomes spiritualized so that we require less bodily contact or even physical presence, the Third does not neces-sarily lead us in separate directions. Fortunately, there are also occasions in which we are allowed to stay together and enjoy our deeper, more spiritual union as companions. In this case the fall of Camelot represents all the favorite fantasies we have long entertained and even accomplished. We give this up with the same sadness and reluctance as another couple might resolve to go its separate ways. As we look back on the years of innocent hope and joy and hard work that built our Camelot, we cannot close our eyes to our fighting and misunderstanding and disappointed expectations. Through it all we have been intermittently—and now perhaps more continuously and deeply—aware of our Self-level connection. Indeed, we know this now in a different way than ever before.

Now we see how our Camelot fantasies were a necessary but

distracting vision and how our wrangling—sometimes more than our cuddling—defined for us the tender heart of our union. There may have been long periods of time in the last decades when we related more like brother and sister than like lovers. It was as though we had the same blood flowing through our veins as we worked on our complementary projects and saw one another from the outside only. We took our unity for granted. We never looked for it—much less used it as a touchstone or discovered it as an autonomous entity we might follow. We forgot how much we had to say to one another in our early days and how much we bowled one another over with our divergent perspectives. We got to the point where we thought we knew one another. No doubt what we knew about one another was important and useful and assisted the building up of Camelot. We even came to accept for ourselves these two-dimensional images we took in exchange for one another.

There were certainly moments when we glimpsed one another again with our original eyes of innocence: an angel gleaming in gold from across a smoke-filled room; a whirlwind with shy, dancing eyes and an entire sun bursting from her chest. We were too innocent and too sure of ourselves to notice that these visions were but the sheen on our wounds. The angel was out of place in a world of space and time and too frightened to acquire the necessary experience. The whirlwind's darling swagger was terrified of coming to rest and harbored a horror of the very naivete the angel seemed to cultivate.

This is the way it generally is with couples. We share the same wound but we try not to notice it. Unconsciously we conspire to avoid all reference to it. A major function of our Camelot is to deny the very existence of our wound, to prove by our strength and success that we are whole. We need to believe that our *Mitwelt* is built on solid rock. We cannot tolerate the bridge of fog that really supports Camelot.

While all this is going on, our wounds fester. We begin to feel dissatisfied, although we try not to admit it. We cannot work as hard on the expansion of Camelot. We may even begin to dream about other designs and look for new adventures. We are not following the Third anymore. We become more aware of one another's faults—and rightly so, for these bring us back to the central matter of the wounds. But we are not looking at one another through the lens of our anima and animus. We are carping at superficial matters while we feel our partner is kicking us in our sorest wound. We just will not let ourselves realize that she or he is feeling the very same pain from our carping as we from her or his kicking.

In this very typical kind of breakdown, the Holy Spirit is shouting at us through our pain. When we forget to keep in touch with our Self-level connection, we do not know that our pain is mutual. When we are newly in love and barely know one another, we are aghast at all the evidence for mystical participation: reading one another's minds, knowing the exact moment to call, preparing one another identical valentines. But when we think we know one another, all this stops. We neglect the Self-level and forget how much in harmony we really are. In the beginning we felt the same ecstasy and marveled over it to one another, thereby reinforcing our sense of oneness. Now again we feel a mutual emotion; but this time it is painful; and we recoil from one another, feeling puzzled and resentful. We feel isolated and alone with our pain, not knowing that our pain is what binds us. It is the spirit of the relationship right now. It is the Third. We have to follow our pain.

Not realizing any of this consciously, we blame one another for our misery. We carp and we kick back, aiming without knowing it at one another's wound. Painful as it may be, there is an advantage in this; for we are learning the shape of our wound. Although we are in an aggressive, intolerant mood, our common pain is right there for us to see. It is just as plain as our common esctasy was a few years ago. Above all, it is a common emotion that binds us together and makes us one.

Camelot begins to fall the moment we realize that our partner is feeling just as misunderstood as we are. This is the crucial insight. It is the moment we recover the elusive Third, and with it our anchor in our Self-level bond. When we pay attention to the pain itself and give up simply trying to ward it off, we begin to notice our joint woundedness. If, as our fighting continues, we do not entirely lose sight of our wound, pretty soon our attention shifts and we can see that the one who is flailing away at us and so much in pain is really the same beloved whirlwind with a swagger we have not glimpsed, perhaps, in months or years. At this moment the fray is all about us, and we stand in the center, the same darling god and goddess we always were.

It is not easy to hold onto a bit of *Gelassenheit* when we are in pain and feel attacked by our beloved. But if we can, a marvelous transformation of our struggle takes place. Our quarrel becomes worthy opposition the moment we appreciate that we are mystically participating in the same pain. Worthy opposition becomes love-play when we can again appreciate and enjoy our beloved's protean transformations. When we get to this point, we can hardly continue to regret the fall of Camelot. Our love has risen phoenix-like from its ashes.

Bibliography

Publication dates that appear in the form "1920/58" provide both the date of the first version of the work (1920) and the latest revision (1958). References to the *Collected Works* of C. G. Jung (Princeton University Press; translated by R. F. C. Hull) are indicated by *CW* followed by the volume number.

Abelard and Heloise. *The Letters of Abelard and Heloise*. Translated by B. Radice. New York: Penguin, 1974.

Allende, I. *The House of the Spirits*. Translated by M. Bogin. New York: A. A. Knopf, 1985.

Andersen, H. C. *A Treasury of Hans Christian Andersen*. Translated by E. C. Haugaard. Garden City, N.Y.: Nelson Doubleday, 1974.

Arasteh, A. R. *Growth to Selfhood, the Sufi Contribution*. London: Routledge & Kegan Paul, 1980.

Augustine. *Selected Writings*. Translated by M. T. Clark. New York: Paulist Press, 1984.

Balint, M. *The Basic Fault: Therapeutic Aspects of Regression*. New York: Brunner/Mazel, 1968.

Basham, A. L. *The Wonder That Was India: A Survey of the Indian Sub-Continent Before the Coming of the Muslims*. New York: Grove Press, 1954.

Bedier, J. *The Romance of Tristan and Iseult*. Translated by H. Belloc; completed by P. Rosenfeld. New York: Vintage, 1965.

Benet, W. R. *Benet's Reader's Encyclopedia*. New York: Harper and Row, 1987.

Benfey, C. "Lady in the Dark." *New York Review of Books* 34:5 (March 26, 1987): 46–49.

Berg, A. *Lulu*, opera in three acts. Translated by A. Jacobs. Vienna: Universal Edition, 1977.

Bergman, I. *The Devil's Eye: A Rondo Capricioso*. Svensk Filmindustri, 1960.

Bernstein, A. *Three Blue Suits*. Athens: Ohio University Press, 1933/88.

———*The Journey Down*. Athens: Ohio University Press, 1938/87.

Bibliography

Beroul. *The Romance of Tristan and the Tale of Tristan's Madness.* Translated by A. S. Fedrick. New York: Penguin, 1970.

Bonewits, P. E. I. *Real Magic: An Introductory Treatise on the Basic Principles of Yellow Magic.* Berkeley, Cal.: Creative Arts Book Company, 1971/79.

Bridger, D., with S. Wolk. *The New Jewish Encyclopedia.* New York: Behrman House, 1962.

Brontë, E. *Wuthering Heights.* New York: New American Library, Signet Classic, 1959.

Buber, M. *Hasidism and Modern Man.* Edited and translated by M. Friedman. New York: Harper Torchbooks, 1958.

——*The Origin and Meaning of Hasidism.* Edited and translated by M. Friedman. New York: Harper Torchbooks 1960.

Byron, G. G. *Don Juan.* New York: Modern Library, 1949.

Campbell, J. *The Masks of God: Occidental Mythology.* New York: Viking, 1964.

——*The Mythic Image.* Assisted by M. J. Abadie. Princeton, N.J.: Princeton University Press, 1974.

Carotenuto, A. *A Secret Symmetry: Sabina Spielrein between Jung and Freud.* Translated by A. Pomerans, J. Shepley, and K. Winston. New York: Pantheon, 1982.

Casanova, G. *The Life and Memoirs of Casanova.* Translated by A. Machen; selected and edited by G. D. Gribble. New York: Da Capo Press, 1929.

Castaneda, C. *A Separate Reality: Further Conversations with don Juan.* New York: Simon & Schuster, 1971.

——*Journey to Ixtlan: The Lessons of don Juan.* New York: Simon and Schuster, 1972.

——*The Power of Silence: Further Lessons of don Juan.* New York: Simon and Schuster, 1987.

Castillejo, I. C. de. *Knowing Woman: A Feminine Psychology.* New York: Harper Colophon, 1973.

Chittick, W. C. *The Sufi Path of Love: The Spiritual Teachings of Rumi.* Albany: State University of New York, 1983.

Cloud of Unknowing, The. Edited by J. Walsh. New York: Paulist, 1981.

Coleridge, S. T. *Samuel Taylor Coleridge.* Edited by H. J. Jackson. New York: Oxford University Press, 1985.

Conze, E. *Buddhism: Its Essence and Development.* New York: Harper Torchbooks, 1951.

Corbin, H. *Creative Imagination in the Sufism of Ibn' Arabi.* Translated by R. Manheim. Princeton, N.J.: Princeton University Press, 1969.

Crowley, A. *Magick in Theory and Practice.* New York: Castle Books, [n.d.].

Donald, D. H. *Look Homeward: A Life of Thomas Wolfe.* New York: Fawcett Columbine, 1987.

Dostoyevsky, F. *The Brothers Karamazov*. Translated by D. Magarshack. Hardmondsworth, Middlesex: Penguin, 1958.

———*The Insulted and Injured*. Translated by C. Garnett. New York: Grove Press, 1962.

Dupre, L. "The Mystical Experience of the Self and Its Philosophical Significance." In Woods (1980): 449–66.

Duras, M. *The Ravishing of Lol Stein*. Translated by R. Seaver. New York: Pantheon, 1966.

———*The Lover*. Translated by B. Bray. New York: Pantheon, 1985.

Eckhart, M. *Meister Eckhart: The Essential Sermons, Commentaries, Treatises, and Defense*. Translated and introduced by E. Colledge and B. McGinn. New York: Paulist, 1981.

Edwards, P. (Ed.). *The Encyclopedia of Philosophy* in 8 vols. New York: Macmillan & The Free Press, 1967.

Eibl-Eibesfeld, I. *Love and Hate: The Natural History of Behavior Patterns*. Translated by G. Strachan. New York: Schocken, 1978.

Eliade, M. *Shamanism, Archaic Techniques of Ecstasy*. Translated by W. R. Trask. New York: Pantheon, 1951/64.

———*Yoga, Immortality and Freedom*. Translated by W. R. Trask. Princeton, N.J.: Princeton University Press, 1954/69.

Ellenberger, H. F. *The Discovery of the Unconscious: The History and Evolution of Dynamic Psychiatry*. New York: Basic Books, 1970.

Eschenbach, W. von. *Parzival*. Translated by H. M. Mustard and C. E. Passage. New York: Vintage, 1961.

Flaubert, G. *Madame Bovary*. Translator not identified. New York: Grosset & Dunlap, [n.d.].

Fox, D. A. *The Vagrant Lotus: An Introduction to Buddhist Philosophy*. Philadelphia: Westminster, 1973.

García Márquez, G. *Love in the Time of Cholera*. Translated by E. Grossman. New York: A. A. Knopf, 1988.

Gibb, H. A. R. *Mohammedanism: An Historical Survey*. 2nd. ed. New York: Oxford University Press, 1953.

Goldberg, A. (Ed.). *The Psychology of the Self: A Casebook*. New York: International Universities Press, 1978.

Gray, W. G. *Magical Ritual Methods*. Cheltenham, Glos., England: Helios, 1971.

Grimm. *Die Maerchen der Brueder Grimm: Kinder und Hausmaerchen*. Munich: Wilhelm Goldmann, 1857.

———*The Complete Grimm's Fairy Tales*. Translated by M. Hunt and revised by J. Stern. New York: Pantheon, 1972.

Happold, F. C. *Mysticism: A Study and an Anthology*. Harmondsworth, Middlesex: Penguin, 1970.

Hardy, T. *Jude the Obscure*. New York: New American Library, 1961.

———*Tess of the D'Urbervilles*. New York: New American Library, 1964.

———*The Life and Death of the Mayor of Casterbridge: A Story of a Man of Character*. New York: New American Library, 1980.

———*The Return of the Native*. New York: Bantam, 1981.

———*Far from the Madding Crowd*. New York: New American Library, Signet Classic, 1984.

Haule, J. R. "Archetypes and Integration: Exploring the Janetian Roots of Analytical Psychology." *Journal of Analytical Psychology 28* (1983): 253–67.

———"From Somnambulism to the Archetypes: The French Roots of Jung's Split with Freud." *Psychoanalytic Review* 71:4 (1984): 635–59.

Heidegger, M. *Discourse on Thinking*. Translated by J. M. Anderson and E. H. Freund. New York: Harper and Row, 1968.

Hillman, J. *Archetypal Psychology: A Brief Account*. Dallas: Spring Publications, 1983.

———*Anima: An Anatomy of a Personified Notion*. Dallas: Spring Publications, 1985.

Hobson, R. F. "The Archetypes of the Collective Unconscious." M. Fordham, *et al.* (eds.). *Analytical Psychology: A Modern Science*. London: Academic Press: 1980: 66–75.

———*Forms of Feeling: The Heart of Psychotherapy*. London & New York: Tavistock Publications, 1985.

I Ching or Book of Changes, The. Translated into German by R. Wilhelm, rendered into English by C. F. Baynes. Princeton, N.J.: Princeton University Press, 1950/67.

Ignatius Loyola. *The Autobiography of St. Ignatius Loyola with Related Documents*. Edited by J. C. Olin; translated by J. F. O'Callaghan. New York: Harper Torchbooks, 1974.

Izutsu, T. *Sufism and Taoism: A Comparative Study of Key Philosophical Concepts*. Berkeley: University of California Press, 1983.

Janet, P. *Les obsessions et la psychasthenie*, in two volumes; volume 2 in collaboration with F. Raymond (1903). Reprinted, New York: Arno, 1976.

———*Psychological Healing: A Historical and Clinical Study*, in two volumes. Translated by E. and E. Paul (1919). Reprinted, New York: Arno, 1976.

John of the Cross. *The Collected Works*. Translated by K. Kavanaugh and O. Rodriguez. Washington, D.C.: Institute of Carmelite Studies, 1979.

———*The Dark Night*. In *Collected Works*, 293–389.

———*The Spiritual Canticle*. In *Collected Works*, 391–565.

Bibliography

Johnson, R. A. *We: Understanding the Psychology of Romantic Love*. San Francisco: Harper & Row, 1983.

Jung, C. G. *Symbols of Transformation: An Analysis of the Prelude to a Case of Schizophrenia*. (1912/52). *CW* 5.

———"On the Psychology of the Unconscious." (1917/43). *CW* 7, 3–125.

———"Instinct and the Unconscious." (1919/48). *CW* 8, 129–38.

———"The Relations Between the Ego and the Unconscious." (1928/35). *CW* 7, 123–241.

———"On Psychic Energy." (1928/48). *CW* 8, 3–66.

———"Archetypes of the Collective Unconscious." (1934/54). *CW* 9, pt. 1, 3–41.

———*Dream Analysis: Notes of the Seminar Given in 1928–1930*. (1938/84). Edited by W. McGuire. Princeton, N.J.: Princeton University Press.

———"Conscious, Unconscious, and Individuation." (1939). *CW* 9, pt. 1, 275–89.

———"Concerning Rebirth." (1939/50). *CW* 9, pt. 1, 111–34.

———*Psychology and Alchemy*. (1944/52). *CW* 12.

———"On the Nature of Dreams." (1945/48). *CW* 8, 281–97.

———*The Psychology of the Transference*. (1946). *CW* 16, 163–323.

———"On the Nature of the Psyche." (1946/54). *CW* 8, 159–234.

———"Synchronicity: An Acausal Connecting Principle." (1952/55). *CW* 8, 417–531.

———*Mysterium Conjunctionis*. (1955/56). *CW* 14.

———"Schizophrenia." (1958). *CW* 3, 256–71.

———*Memories, Dreams, Reflections*. Recorded and edited by A. Jaffe. Translated by R. and C. Winston. New York: Pantheon, 1961.

———*Letters*, in two volumes. Selected and edited by G. Adler and A. Jaffe. Translated by R. F. C. Hull. Princeton, N.J.: Princeton University Press, 1975.

Jung, E. and M.-L. von Franz. *The Grail Legend*, 2nd ed. Translated by A. Dykes. Boston: Sigo, 1986.

Klein, C. *Aline*. New York: Harper and Row, 1979.

Kohut, H. *The Restoration of the Self*. New York: International Universities Press, 1977.

———*How Does Analysis Cure?* Edited by A. Goldberg with P. Stepansky. Chicago: University of Chicago Press, 1984.

Kundera, M. *The Joke*. Translated by M. H. Heim. New York: Penguin, 1982.

Laclos, C. de. *Les liaisons dangereuses*. Translated by P. W. K. Stone. Harmondsworth, Middlesex: Penguin, 1961.

Larousse. *Larousse Encyclopedia of Mythology*. London: Paul Hamlyn, 1959.

Lawrence, D. H. *Women in Love*. Harmondsworth, Middlesex: Penguin, 1982.

———*Mr. Noon*. Edited by L. Vasey. New York: Penguin, 1985a.

———*Sons and Lovers*. New York: Signet Classic, 1985b.

Leach, M. and J. Fried (Eds.). *Funk & Wagnalls Standard Dictionary of Folklore, Mythology and Legend*. San Francisco: Harper and Row, 1984.

Lévi-Strauss, C. *Structural Anthropology*. Translated by C. Jacobson and B. G. Schoepf. New York: Anchor, 1967.

Levy-Bruhl, L. *Primitive Mentality*. Translated by L. A. Claire. Boston: Beacon Press, 1966.

Lincoln, V. *Teresa: A Woman, A Biography of Teresa of Ávila*. Edited by E. Rivers and A. T. de Nicolas. Albany: State University of New York Press, 1984.

Lorde, A. *Zami: A New Spelling of My Name*. Trumansberg, N.Y.: Crossing Press, 1982.

McBrien, R. P. *Catholicism: Study Edition*. Minneapolis: Winston Press, 1981.

McKenzie, J. L. *Dictionary of the Bible*. New York: Macmillan, 1965.

Malory, T. *Le Morte d'Arthur*, in two vols. Edited by J. Cowen. New York: Penguin, 1969.

Marie de France. *The Lais of Marie de France*. Translated by G. S. Burgess and K. Busby. New York: Penguin, 1986.

Molière, J. B. P. *Don Juan, or, The Stone Guest*. In *Tartuffe and Other Plays by Molière*. Translated by D. M. Frame. New York: New American Library, 1967.

Moustakas, C. E. *Loneliness*. Englewood Cliffs, N.J.: Prentice-Hall, 1961.

———*The Touch of Loneliness*. Englewood Cliffs, N.J.: Prentice-Hall, 1975.

Mozart, W. A. *Don Giovanni*. Libretto, L. da Ponte. Translated by L. Salter. [no city] Germany: Deutsche Grammophon Gesellschaft #2711006, [n.d.].

Nasr, S. H. *Sufi Essays*. Albany: State University of New York Press, 1972.

Neruda, P. *The Captain's Verses*. Translated by D. D. Walsh. New York: New Directions, 1972.

Nicholson, R. A. *Studies in Islamic Mysticism*. Cambridge: Cambridge University Press, 1921.

———*The Mystics of Islam*. Boston: Routledge and Kegan Paul, 1963.

Nikhilananda. *The Upanishads (Abridged Edition)*. New York: Harper Torchbooks, 1963.

Niwano, N. *Buddhism for Today: A Modern Interpretation of the Threefold Lotus Sutra*. Translated by K. Miyasaka. New York & Tokyo: Weatherhill/Kosei, 1976.

Nizami. *Die sieben Geschichten der sieben Prinzessinen*. Translated by R. Gelpke. Zurich: Manesse, 1959.

———*The Story of Layla and Majnun*. Translated and edited by R. Gelpke with E. Mattin and G. Hill. Boulder, Colo.: Shambhala, 1966.

O'Flaherty, W. D. *Siva: The Erotic Ascetic*. New York: Oxford University Press, 1973.

Opera Libretto Library, The. New York: Crown Publishers and Avenel Books, 1980.

Otto, R. *The Idea of the Holy: An Inquiry into the Non-Rational Factor in the Idea of the Divine and Its Relation to the Rational*. Translated by J. W. Harvey. New York: Oxford University Press, 1958.

Ozak, M. *Love Is the Wine: Talks of a Sufi Master in America*. Edited by R. Frager. Putney, Vt.: Threshold, 1987.

Person, E. S. *Dreams of Love and Fateful Encounters: The Power of Romantic Passion*. New York: W. W. Norton, 1988.

Peters, F. E. *Greek Philosophical Terms: A Historical Lexicon*. New York: New York University Press, 1967.

Quest of the Holy Grail, The. Translated by P. M. Matarasso. New York: Penguin, 1969.

Rabi'ah al-'Adwaiyah. *Doorkeeper of the Heart: Versions of Rabi'ah*. Translated by C. Upton. Putney, Vt.: Threshold Books, 1988.

Remarque, E. M. *Arch of Triumph*. Translated by W. Sorrell and D. Lindley. New York: D. Appleton Century, 1945.

Rhein, J. von. Untitled review of Peter Sellars's production of *Tannhaeuser*. In *Opera News* 53:12 (March 4, 1989): 37f.

Rice. C. *The Persian Sufis*. London: G. Allen & Unwin, Ltd, 1964.

Rinpoche, K. *The Dharma That Benefits All Beings Impartially Like the Light of the Sun and the Moon*. Translated by J. Gyatso. Edited by The Kagyu Thubten Choling Translation Committee. Albany: State University of New York Press, 1986.

Rougemont, D. de. *Love in the Western World*. Translated by M. Belgion. Princeton, N.J.: Princeton University Press, 1956/72.

———"Love," in P. P. Wiener (Ed.), *Dictionary of the History of Ideas*. New York: Charles Scribner's Sons, 1973.

Rumi, J. *Night and Sleep: Versions*. Translated by C. Barks and R. Bly. Cambridge, Mass.: Yellow Moon Press, 1981.

———*Open Secret: Versions of Rumi*. Translated by J. Moyne and C. Barks. Putney, Vt.: Threshold Books, 1984.

———*Unseen Rain: Quatrains of Rumi*. Translated by J. Moyne and C. Barks. Putney, Vt.: Threshold Books, 1986.

———*We Are Three: New Rumi Poems*. Translated by C. Barks. Athens, Ga.: Maypop Books, 1987.

————*This Longing: Poetry, Teaching Stories, and Selected Letters*. Versions by C. Barks and J. Moyne. Putney, Vt.: Threshold Books, 1988.

Schimmel, A. *Mystical Dimensions of Islam*. Chapel Hill: University of North Carolina Press, 1975.

————*As Through a Veil: Mystical Poetry in Islam*. New York: Columbia University Press, 1982.

Scholem, G. *Major Trends in Jewish Mysticism*. New York: Schocken, 1941.

————*The Messianic Idea in Judaism and Other Essays on Jewish Spirituality*. New York: Schocken, 1971.

Searles, H. "Oedipal Love in the Countertransference." *Collected Papers on Schizophrenia and Related Subjects*. New York: International Universities Press, 1965.

Shaw, G. B. *Man and Superman: A Comedy and a Philosophy*. Harmondsworth, Middlesex: Penguin, 1946.

Shostak, M. *Nisa: The Life and Words of a !Kung Woman*. Cambridge, Mass.: Harvard University Press, 1981.

Silesius, A. *Angelus Silesius: The Cherubinic Wanderer*. Translated and foreward by M. Shrady. New York: Paulist, 1986.

Smith, M. *Rabi'a the Mystic and Her Fellow-Saints in Islam*. Cambridge: Cambridge University Press, 1984.

Stein, R. *Incest and Human Love: The Betrayal of the Soul in Psychotherapy*, 2nd ed. Dallas: Spring Publications, 1973/84.

Strassburg, G. von. *Tristan*. Translated by A. T. Hatto. Hammondsworth, Middlesex: Penguin, 1960.

Stutman, S. (Ed.). *My Other Loneliness: Letters of Thomas Wolfe and Aline Bernstein*. Chapel Hill: University of North Carolina Press, 1983.

Tanizaki, J. *Naomi*. Translated by A. H. Chambers. New York: Knopf, 1985.

Teresa of Ávila. *The Interior Castle*. Translated by K. Kavanaugh and O. Rodriguez. New York: Paulist, 1979.

Tillich, P. *Systematic Theology*, in 3 vols. Chicago: University of Chicago Press, 1963.

Time-Life Editors. *The Lore of Love*. Alexandria, Va.: Time-Life Books, [n.d.(a)].

Time-Life Editors. *Tales of Terror*. Alexandria, Va.: Time-Life Books, [n.d.(b)].

Todi, J. da. *The Lauds*. Translated by S. and E. Hughes. New York: Paulist Press, 1982.

Tolstoy, L. *Anna Karenina*. Translated by R. Edmunds. New York: Viking Penguin, 1978.

Trungpa, C. *Cutting Through Spiritual Materialism*. Edited by J. Baker and M. Casper. Boston & London: Shambhala, 1973.

Twain, M. *A Connecticut Yankee at King Arthur's Court*. New York: Penguin, 1971.

Vatsyayana. *Kama Sutra: The Hindu Ritual of Love*. New York: Castle Books, 1965.

Verdi, G. *La Traviata*. (An F. Zeffirelli Film). Universal City, Cal.: M. C. A. Home Video, 1982.

Vergil, M. P. *The Aeneid*. Translated by P. Dickinson. New York: New American Library, 1961.

Wagner, R. *Tristan und Isolde*. London Records #A4506. Libretto not paginated; translator not identified, [n.d.].

———*Tannhaeuser*. Hollywood, Cal.: Paramount Home Video, 1986.

Welwood, J. (Ed.). *Awakening the Heart: East/West Approaches to Psychotherapy and the Healing Relationship*. Boston: Shambhala, 1985a.

———(Ed.). *Challenge of the Heart: Love, Sex, and Intimacy in Changing Times*. Boston: Shambhala, 1985b.

Wharton, E. *The Age of Innocence*. New York: Macmillan/Collier, 1968.

Wilde, O. *Salome: A Tragedy in One Act*. Translator not identified. New York: Williams, Belasco & Meyers, 1930.

Wilson, P. L. and N. Pourjavady (Translators and commentators). *The Drunken Universe: An Anthology of Persian Sufi Poetry*. Grand Rapids, Mich.: Phanes Press, 1987.

Wolfe, T. *Of Time and the River: A Legend of Man's Hunger in His Youth*. New York: Charles Scribner's Sons, 1971.

———*The Web and the Rock*. New York: Harper and Row, 1973(a).

———*You Can't Go Home Again*. New York: Harper and Row, 1973(b).

Woods, R. (Ed.). *Understanding Mysticism*. Garden City, N.Y.: Image/ Doubleday, 1980.

Zaunert, P. (Ed.). *Deutsche Maerchen seit Grimm*. Duesseldorf: Eugen Diederichs, 1964.

Zimmer, H. *Myths and Symbols in Indian Art and Civilization*. Edited by J. Campbell. Princeton, N.J.: Princeton University Press, 1946.

Credits

Index